Theravāda Meditation

THERAVĀDA MEDITATION:

The Buddhist Transformation of Yoga

Winston L. King

The Pennsylvania State University Press
University Park and London

The author gratefully acknowledges the permission of George Allen & Unwin to quote from Marie B. Byles's *Journey into Burmese Silence*, and that of the Pāli Text Society to quote various copyrighted materials. Sincere thanks are extended to Mahasi Sayadaw, U Win Pe, the *Guardian*, Daw Khin Myo Chit, and the International Meditation Centre, all of Rangoon; the Buddhist Publication Society of Kandy; and the Word of the Buddha Publishing Committee of Colombo for their permission to use various uncopyrighted materials published by them.

Library of Congress Cataloging in Publication Data

King, Winston Lee, 1907–
    Theravāda meditation.

Includes bibliography and index
    1. Meditation (Buddhism)   I. Title.
BQ5612.K56   294.3′4′43   79-25856
ISBN 0-271-00254-9

Contents

Preface

That the basic world view (weltanschauung) embodied in a developed religious tradition strongly influences, or even determines, its prescribed salvational methodology, seems to be an unexceptionable general statement. But in the case of a given tradition the determining factors and determined techniques must be clearly specified.

Such is the attempt in this volume. The given tradition is the Theravāda Buddhist; and the prescribed technique of salvation is meditation. The thesis maintained here is that the orthodox Theravāda world view determines the motivations, practice, and resulting experiences of the orthodox meditational discipline. Perhaps even aboriginally, the yogic experience of a timeless, utterly detached, transic peace was an important ingredient and determinant of the Buddhist conception of Nibbāna: that is, it is an experience-produced doctrine. But it is also true that the pre-Buddhist yogic techniques had their contextualizing world view too, one which was not totally unlike the Buddhist world perspective developed later; and, further, the developed Buddhist meditational tradition with which we deal here, portrayed in the Pāli Canon, the *Vimuttimagga*, and the *Visudhimagga*, *did* operate with the basic Buddhist weltanschauung as its all-pervasive given.

The Pāli Canon world view is sharply defined in terms of the polar opposites of *saṃsāra* and *Nibbāna*. Saṃsāra is thus described:

> Monks, everything is burning. . . . The eye . . . the ear . . . the nose . . . the body . . . the mind . . . the feeling which raises through impingement on the mind, be it pleasant or painful or neither painful nor pleasant, that too is burning. With what is it burning? I say it is burning with the fire of passion, with the fire of hatred, with the fire of stupidity; it is burning because of birth, ageing, dying, because of grief, sorrow, suffering, lamentation and despair.[1]

And the other pole, Nibbāna, is described thus: "He focuses his mind on the deathless element, thinking: 'This is the real, this is the excellent, that is to say the tranquillising of all the activities, dispassion, stopping, nibbāna.' " And a description of the way to it follows immediately: "If he is steadfast therein, he achieves destruction of the cankers . . . one who attains nibbāna . . . not liable to return."[2]

Briefly, this is the geography of that terrain on which salvation must be achieved in Theravāda Buddhism. And the mode of that achievement is determined by the polarized terrain. A methodology has been designed to put out the fires of saṃsāric craving (destruction of the cankers) and to introduce the deathless element, Nibbāna, in which only eternal coolness and calm are to be found. It is a technique by which the Nibbānic pole neutralizes and finally eliminates the saṃsāric in its entirety.

This quenching of saṃsāra's fevers is a functional description of Theravāda meditation. This meditative practice, then, is an operational model, a dynamic embodiment of the Theravāda world view. In this model the existential experience of both the saṃsāric pole (of the impermanence, emptiness, and suffering of all existence) and the Nibbānic pole (of deathless peace, of awareness of the unconditioned absolute) are deliberately intensified. This is the purpose of *vipassanā* (insight) meditation. The meditator in his or her awareness and lived quality of life becomes, so to speak, an incarnation of the Theravāda world view, which touches and transforms everything experienced.

But, because Buddhism derives from Indian (Brāhmaṇical-yogic) spirituality and meditation methodology, an alien, or non-Buddhist, element exists in the orthodox Theravāda meditational structure. This is the Brāhmaṇical-yogic technique of inducing transic states which, in the form of its *jhānas* and formless-base meditations, are integral to the Buddhist meditational structure. The Brāhmaṇical-yogic technique had become an intrinsic part of that structure by the time many of the Pāli Canon passages were written, to say nothing of the later time of the writing of the *Visudhimagga*, ca. A.D. 500.

What then is the relation of this yogic methodological inheritance, with its latent but intrinsic Brāhmaṇical presuppositions and values, to the Buddhist world view embodied in vipassanā meditation? This relationship of rejection-acceptance, use-transcendence, and of fundamental qualification of the yogic inheritance by its Buddhist contextual setting and employment, is perhaps the central feature of the total meditational structure. It seems to me also to be a basic functional dynamic, a creative tension within the theory and practice of meditation that explains its distinctive character. In this book, I am concerned with unraveling and clarifying this inner pattern of interactive relationship.

Thanks are to be given to the many persons with whom I have discussed these matters during the years, both in Burma and in the United States; to Buddhaghosa for his massive work, *The Path of Purification* (*Visudhimagga*); to my wife with whom I have endlessly discussed the substance of these pages, and to whom I have read them all for criticism; to Mrs. Myrle Phelan, who has expertly typed them all; and to the copyediting staff of The Pennsylvania State University Press.

Thanks of a very special sort are to be given to the Buddhist Association of the United States, Professor Charles Prebish, and Garma C. C. Chang, without whose generous support and encouragement this book would not have been published.

1

Yogic Factors in
Gotama Buddha's Enlightenment

Gotama, called the Buddha or Enlightened One by his disciples, was declaredly a Brāhmaṇical nonconformist. Such is the central Pāli Canon tradition and we have no reason to doubt it, though the degree of nonconformism and its precise nature may have changed in its centuries-later telling in the canon. Gotama Buddha is portrayed as being at odds with the developing Brāhmaṇical tradition, both in its Vedic-ritual and Upanishadic-modified forms. For example, he demotes the Brāhmaṇical gods to attendant godlings, is antagonistic to all ritual, especially sacrificial ritual, and he undercuts the Brahmin's caste pretensions. This is too strong and consistent to attribute to later Buddhist tradition alone.

On the whole Gotama Buddha was in greater accord with the burgeoning Upanishadic influence of his time, for this too was critical of ritualistic Vedism and its elaborate sacramentalism. But Upanishadic Brāhmaṇism was a modification of ritual Brāhmaṇism, not its rejection; and its philosophical-mystical qualities left the ritual structures largely intact for those who wished to use them. In addition, its increasingly definite doctrine of an Absolute Reality (*Brahman*) and its defining of final salvation as union with Brahman represent a view to which Buddhism was unalterably opposed even in the earlier forms of that doctrine, which Gotama perhaps encountered. Nevertheless, this opposition must not be magnified out of proportion, for genuine though it was, it did not at first represent that open warfare between Buddhism and Brāhmaṇism that developed later. The followers of this new teacher were no doubt viewed as radicals, but as generally within the wide fold of Brāhmaṇical tolerance. Even the Pāli sources, whose authors were eager to maximize the differences between Buddhist and Brāhmaṇical *dharmas* (i.e., social-cosmic orders), portray the Buddha in friendly conversations and discussion with Brahmins. These sources often show him in intellectual disagreement with Brahmins, but not in a context of mutual enmity. Nor does extant literature from the Brāhmaṇical side contain active anti-Buddhist sentiments until much later, when the developing Buddhist fellowship seemed to threaten.[1] And it is also important to note that for some centuries, at least until after the reign of Asoka (274–232 B.C.), the Buddhist community was firmly within the Indian (Brāhmaṇical) orbit of thought and within discussional range of Brāhmaṇical-Upanishadic teachers. The Pāli Canon was presumably written in India before Theravāda Buddhism became a fully separatist tradition cut off not only from Brāhmaṇical influences but also from those of developing Indian Mahāyāna Buddhism as well.

Here, however, I am not concerned with the broad and complex reaches of agreement and disagreement between Brāhmaṇical-Hindu and Buddhist streams of development but more narrowly with the interrelation of their respective meditational practices, both of which were nurtured by Indian religious inspiration. However, the precise relation of Upanishadic Brāhmaṇism to what later became the Yogic system of meditation and was combined with the Sāṃkhya philosophic school is too uncertain to be investigated in any detail here. As a *method* yoga was, of course, infinitely adaptable. It could be, and was, attached to the Upanishadic search for the Supreme Self (Brahman) as well as to the Sāṃkhyan search for pure individual selfhood (*kaivalya*). Either case entails implicit presuppositions that would be unacceptable to developing Buddhism; yet as method some elements could be and were adapted by Buddhism as *its* technique of higher (enlightening) knowledge.

This methodological interaction, even interpenetration, of Brāhmaṇism and Buddhism is neither surprising nor impossible in view of their common ancestry. Indeed, the final Theravāda meditational structure seems to be an intriguing, and sometimes confusing, mixture of Brāhmaṇical *and* Buddhist traits. In general, the position taken here is that the Theravāda meditational structure is a compound of some yogic techniques (accommodated in Brāhmaṇism to Upanishadic goals) with Buddhist values and viewpoints. To understand the nature of this complex pattern it is necessary to begin by comparing briefly the Buddhist and Brāhmaṇical-Upanishadic expositions of their respective salvational structures and dynamics. Then we shall be ready to observe their interaction in the Pāli Canon account of Gotama's enlightenment.

The Spiritual Universes of Brāhmaṇism and Buddhism

Though Upanishadic Brāhmaṇism and early Buddhism differed radically at important points in their basic philosophical and religious positions, structurally and functionally there were also important likenesses. Buddhism, as a "heretical" product of Brāhmaṇical culture, is to be expected to inherit from its "orthodox" parent as well as its "nonorthodox" one, Gotama. Two dynamic-structural features that Buddhism inherited directly from Brāhmaṇism, which were crucial in determining the nature of the Buddhist process of salvation, can be distinguished.

First is the central conviction that the universe of time-space experience is not ultimately real or fundamentally satisfactory. Therefore it must be radically transcended in order to achieve salvation. The second and corollary area of agreement is that a special methodology, meditation, is the best, and for Buddhism the only, means of achieving true salvational transcendence.

Salvation as Transcendence

The general course of the Brāhmaṇical development of its "other-worldliness" is well known. Early Vedic religion consisted largely of rituals directed toward a double benefit: procurement of the best possible earthly life and the gaining of eternal life in the heavens of the gods after death. These two goals were not seen as basically incompatible, though there was tension between their aims and accomplishment. That is, the loyal service to the gods by sacrifice, though suitably diversified for earthly and heavenly purposes, was one fabric. The gods, when properly sacrificed to, could be persuaded to bless their devotees *both* here and hereafter. In the end this ritualistic approach to salvation was elaborated into an immense and all-pervasive structure, the mainstream of the orthodox Brahmin piety of the Buddha's time.

Out of this ritualism, by means of the philosophical development that flowered in the Upanishads, arose a conception of the universe as causal, that permeated both the Brāhmaṇical and Buddhist structures. It took the form of the doctrine of *karma* (Pāli, *kamma*). Karma, first conceived of as the power and efficacy of the ritual deed that could, if properly performed, compel even the gods to the appropriate action, came to be viewed as the law of the universe, particularly in the realm of human actions. Every voluntary deed inexorably had its result-reward, good or bad, continuing in the life-stream of the doer. Often as not it was in some future life—for the natural companion and embodiment of karma was reincarnation for every living individual, worlds without end.

The milieu in which karma exerted its force—the space-time world of human experience—was known as saṃsāra, a veritable "sea of change." Its main characteristics were multiplicity and flux, with the social-cosmic orders of dharma and the personal-moral orders of karma providing some uniformity and dependability. Brāhmaṇism generally accepted and accommodated itself to the idea of saṃsāra. The ritual structures, intimately interwoven with social and cultural life, imparted meaning and pleasure to the pattern of existence, changing and uncertain though it might be. These rituals also provided some control over saṃsāra's flux. Thus the Brāhmaṇical tradition in general, though qualified in its Upanishadic expressions, did not represent a philosophy of truly radical disillusion.

But there were limits to this acceptance and a haunting sense of the relativism of even the most successful ritual-social ordering of experience. As Paul Younger states it:

> Man's "acceptance" of *saṃsāra*, however, never leads to the conclusion that this is the ultimate reality. . . . In spite of man's "acceptance" of *saṃsāra* he finds that in the final analysis the endless round of births is an experience of pain (*duḥka*). As a result, *saṃsāra* is eventually seen as a burden which must be thrown off, a poison which must be extracted, or a dangerous river which must be crossed in order to reach the higher Reality beyond.[2]

Thus although the Brāhmaṇical tradition recognized the *relative* worth of *artha* (pursuit of material welfare), *kāma* (enjoyment of esthetic values, especially in the forms of emotion, feeling, and passionate love), and particularly *dharma* (the all-embracing obligation of social duty), it also envisaged *mokṣa*, or release from all time-space goods, enjoyments, and obligations. This conception of the desirability, need, and existence of an absolute release from *all* saṃsāric existence—whether that existence be in hells, on the earth, or in the heavens with the gods—developed (in the Upanishads) as a counterpoise to the excessive ritualism of Brāhmaṇical orthodoxy. The Upanishads and their goal of mokṣa have been described thus:

> Their aim is practical rather than speculative. They give us knowledge as a means to spiritual freedom. . . . The goal is not a heavenly state of bliss or rebirth in a better world. Negatively, it is freedom from the objective cosmic law of *karma*; positively it is identity with the Supreme. Until we are released from the law of *karma* and reach *mokṣa* or deliverance, we will be in *saṃsāra* or the time process.[3]

Early Buddhism inherited this basic world-structuring concept of the changing, relativistic space-time order and the corollary need for an absolute escape from the power of its impermanence. The main difference was that early Buddhism, if we may believe the Pāli Canon version, emphasized relativism even more than the Upanishads and further developed the doctrine of kamma (Skt. *karma*). Karma was a genuine factor in the Upanishadic world view, and mokṣa was an escape from its power but karma's burden does not seem to oppress the Upanishadic authors. But the conviction of the utter bondage imposed by kamma finds a place on almost every page of the Pāli scriptures. Kamma inexorably controls the fate of human beings, binding them to saṃsāra, rebirths without end. (Rebirth is the Buddhist adaptation of Brāhmaṇical reincarnation.) It rules peoples' destinies at all levels, in their rebirths as ghosts, beasts, as tormented spirits in the hells, as humans, or as godlings (*devas*). That this chain is of their own past making does not weaken its iron-clad grasp of their present.

So too, early Buddhism on every possible occasion stressed the doctrine of a fluxing and pain-filled saṃsāra—much more so than Upanishadic Brāhmaṇism. In its classic phrasing, all existence is indelibly branded with the three signs of impermanence, suffering, and emptiness of any true reality. Early Buddhism was not fundamentally concerned with or interested in any of the four relative goods of Brāhmaṇism, except the last, mokṣa. Artha was seen as a grasping of the wind, kāma as ultimately painful and enslaving, and dharma as of secondary importance. Mokṣa alone was of prime consequence—to which early Buddhism gave the name of Nibbāna, a going out of and from existence into an utter beyondness.

Meditation as the Means of Salvation

That same Upanishadic thought-stream, in which the world of time and space and its rituals and gods are seen as lacking in fully satisfactory ultimacy, turned its attention, of necessity, to the means of control over, and final release from, the saṃsāric order. A scriptural warrant for such a means can be found in the Upanishads. The *Chāndogya Upanishad*, one of the earliest, which certainly predated Gotama Buddha, contains an instructive parable. It is said that the gods and demons alike, and at the same time, heard the good news of the existence of a Reality, the knowledge of which would release them from all the relativities and anxieties inherent in saṃsāric existence:

> "The Self," which is free from evil, ageless, deathless, sorrowless, hungerless, thirstless, whose desire is the Real, whose conception is the Real —He should be searched out, Him should one desire to understand. He obtains all worlds and all desires who has found out and who understands that Self.[4]

Hearing that Prajāpati, the supergod (a kind of proto-Brahman), could teach them this knowledge of the Absolute Self, gods and demons each sent a representative to him. The demon stayed for only one lesson and came away with an enslaving half-truth. It took Indra more than 100 years as a disciple (in four successive stages) to learn the final truth. But, significantly, his learning process proceeded progressively *inward*: from outer form, to mental self, to dreaming self, to ecstatic superconceptual awareness.

It is true that in the *Chāndogya* the full Advaitin doctrine of the Brahman as the Absolute Reality, whose identity with the inmost self of man (*ātman*) is the absolute and saving truth, is not explicitly present. Advaitinism has imposed this doctrine imperiously upon the total Upanishadic tradition, even where it was not found originally. In any case, its partial warrant is there, as well as an incipient meditational route to the saving realization of the Absolute. It may be that yogic techniques sprang from another source and were later conjoined with Upanishadic theology. Yoga is not identical with the Upanishadic teaching and at some points may be opposed to it. However, yoga could be used in conjunction with the Upanishadic Absolute as a method of detaching the attention from the multiplicity of space-time existents in order that it might realize that oneness of experience and Reality at the core of each person's being. It provided a technique for the saving gospel of the unity of individual ātman and universal Brahman, the One without a second. By the time of the writing of the *Maitri Upanishad*, meditation is specifically mentioned as one means for apprehending Brahman: "Therefore, by knowledge (*vidyā*), austerity (*tapas*), and by meditation (*cinta*) Brahman is apprehended."[5]

In the case of Buddhism, it is central that Gotama became the Buddha, the Enlightened One, who was capable of leading others to enlightenment (Nibbāna or mokṣa attainment) by means of his own attainment. Buddhism does not reject the general Upanishadic-Brāhmaṇical tradition that seeks release by the higher knowledge given through meditation; it wholeheartedly embraces it. The only difference involved is *which* meditative means should be used to attain the true release from saṃsāra; the wrong method would maintain saṃsāric bondage, not destroy it. The interesting, ambivalent situation is that the Pāli tradition portrays Gotama as searching through the contemporary methods for attaining mokṣa, both accepting and rejecting them.

This then seems to be the logical point at which to begin a more detailed analysis of Buddhist meditation vis-à-vis the Brāhmaṇical-yogic tradition.

Gotama's Acceptance-Rejection of Contemporary Spiritual Techniques

The relation of the Gotama-inspired modes of mokṣa- (Nibbāna-) seeking, which ultimately became the orthodox Buddhist meditational techniques, and the traditional proto-yogic (hereinafter yogic) methods of his time, is difficult to unravel. Our only "direct" source is the Pāli scriptural Canon, written some centuries after the events narrated therein. Hence we know of those contemporary methods encountered by Gotama in his search only through a later, stylized, and doctrinaire Buddhist account. Indeed, the names of two meditation teachers, Āḷāra and Uddaka (to be discussed later), whose methods Gotama mastered in his attempts to achieve his own enlightenment, are found nowhere outside two places in the Buddhist Canon and in Aśvaghosha's later *Buddhacarita*. Were they then fabricated names and accounts from a later age used in building up the Buddhist tradition?

Without being able to answer these and related questions definitely, I can say, however, that the Pāli materials are not therefore worthless for our purposes. Even if we know nothing more of Gotama's teachers than the canonical account gives us, that account does at least contain the orthodox Theravāda statement of the right Buddhist meditational method as well as of the rejected methods. They are the *only* relatively early accounts of Gotama's enlightenment in existence, so they must serve us in our study of its nature whether or no. Further, Buddhaghosa (ca. A.D. 500) conceived himself to be faithfully expositing this canonical technique of enlightenment in his work, *The Path of Purification*, Theravāda meditation's official manual ever since its writing. In short, our materials, however defective historically, do present us with the understanding which Theravādins have had of their own meditational process for nearly 2000 years, as well as their view of the rejected Brāhmaṇical-yogic modes.

Gotama's Rejection of Asceticism

Gotama rejected asceticism, not only in the general interest of establishing a broad Middle Way of salvation, but also in order to alter the meditational process. The *Majjhima-Nikāya* (i.e., *Middle Length Sayings*) contains the most extensive early accounts of that rejection. One account describes three exercises that Gotama successively tried and finally discarded as profitless [*MLS*, I, pp. 297–301 (I.242–46)]. The first consisted of clenching the teeth, pressing the tongue against the palate, and "restraining and dominating my mind by mind." The second consisted of a nonbreathing exercise in which he stopped "breathing in and breathing out through the mouth and through the nose." This was repeated over and over, presumably at longer intervals each time. Both types of meditation resulted in excruciating pain. The clenched-teeth variety produced terrible sweating, the nonbreathing such sensations as loud roarings in the head, sharp pains in head and stomach, a sense of constriction in the head, and intense bodily heat. The observing spirits disputed at the end of these meditations whether he was dead or not. Gotama's concluding evaluation, repeated for each of these in turn, is interesting:

> Although, Aggivessana, unsluggish energy came to be stirred up in me, unmuddled mindfulness set up, yet my body was turbulent, not calmed, because I was harassed in striving against that very pain. But yet, Aggivessana, that painful feeling, arising in me, persisted without impinging on my mind. [*MLS*, I, p. 299 (I.244)]

The mixed result should be noted: clear mindfulness *was* maintained, but against great odds such as fighting against the pain produced by the technique itself. Thus "unmuddled mindfulness" was maintained *in spite of* the method, not by means of it. And further, all these exercises led to bodily turbulence and agitation, which in the Buddha's (later) enlightened eyes was an evil result.

The third method tried by Gotama was a starvation diet. He contemplated going without all food, but the devas threatened to feed him sustaining essences through the skin to keep him alive. Hence he resolved to eat barely enough to sustain life. The result:

> All my limbs became like joints of withered creepers . . . my protruding backbone became like a string of balls . . . my gaunt ribs became like the crazy rafters of a tumble-down shed . . . the pupils of my eyes appeared lying low and deep . . . my scalp became shrivelled and shrunk as a bitter white gourd cut before it is ripe.

Still further, his complexion became dark, his hair rotted away in his skin and fell out, and he fainted on numerous occasions [*MLS*, I, pp. 300–301 (I.245–46)].

In another and variant account which, however, ends with this same description of his final condition, the Buddha details a long, miscellaneous set of ascetic practices—including the extremes of accepting only absolutely undefiled food (Brāhmaṇical fastidiousness) and of living in meager garments, filth, and even eating animal excrement [*MLS*, I, pp. 103–7 (I.77–79)]. Both versions of his asceticism portray the Buddha as insisting that no one has ever, or will ever, be able to equal the intensity of his suffering. "I became an ascetic, the foremost ascetic; I became loathly, the foremost loathly one. . . . I became aloof, the foremost aloof one." And again: "Some recluses and brahmans in the past have experienced . . . and some recluses and brahmans in the future will experience feelings that are acute, painful, sharp, severe; but this is paramount, nor is there worse than this" [*MLS*, I, p. 103 (I.77) and p. 301 (I.246)]. The implication is that he pushed the contemporary (Brāhmaṇical in a loose sense) ascetic and meditational methods to their absolute limits. And the verdict is negative: "But I, by this severe austerity, do not reach states of further-men, the excellent knowledge and vision befitting the ariyans. *Could there be another way to awakening?*" [*MLS*, I, p. 301 (I.246); italics added].

In what follows we learn what Gotama substitutes for these rejected austerity methods. Harking back to a boyhood experience, he remembers a different meditative procedure, one with results beneficial to the body and with no diminution of mental clarity. Decisively rejecting asceticism as not productive of the enlightenment he seeks, he takes substantial nourishment and in its strength sets out on the new-old way, in whose first stage he reproduces that boyhood experience, and then goes on beyond it:

> But when I, Aggivessana, had taken some material nourishment, having picked up strength, aloof from pleasures of the senses, aloof from unskilled states of mind, I entered and abided in the first meditation which is accompanied by initial thought and discursive thought, is born of aloofness, and is rapturous and joyful. . . .
>
> By allaying initial thought and discursive thought, with the mind tranquillised and fixed on one point, I entered on and abided in the second meditation which is devoid of initial and discursive thought, is born of concentration, is rapturous and joyful. . . .
>
> By the fading out of rapture I dwelt in equanimity, attentive and clearly conscious, and I experienced in my person that joy of which the ariyans say: "Joyful lives he who has equanimity and is mindful," and I entered on and abided in the third meditation . . . .
>
> By getting rid of joy and by getting rid of anguish, by the going down of former pleasures and sorrows, I entered into and abided in the fourth meditation which has neither anguish nor joy and which is entirely purified by equanimity and mindfulness. [*MLS*, I, p. 302 (I.247)]

These, the well-known four *jhānas* (absorptions, trances), are basic to the Theravāda meditational structure, and will be considered in detail later. Following each of them is a statement about their effects which corresponds to the post-nonbreathing meditation statements: "But yet, Aggivessana, the pleasurable feeling, arising in me, persisted without impinging on my mind." That is to say, just as he had been able to achieve unmuddled mindfulness in spite of the pain and bodily turbulence of the ascetic meditations, using this type of body-calming meditation—perhaps because of it—he is also able to achieve one-pointed concentration of mind. The "pleasurable"—higher-pleasurable, not sensual—state of mind does not touch or disturb his mental concentration. Herein lies the Buddhist rejection of the whole ascetic tradition that seems to have persisted in Indian religiosity since Vedic times.

With the mind now in workable order "quite purified, quite clarified, without blemish, without defilement, grown soft and workable, fixed, immovable" as a result of the newly adopted method, Gotama now proceeds directly to enlightenment. The preenlightenment stages of the memory of former births, of the deva-eye vision of karma working in the destinies of living beings, and the ability to communicate with beings in all levels of existence need not detain us here. The crown of the process arrives when he turns the powers of this new clear-mindedness on to the true nature of existence, i.e., his perception of the Four Noble Truths: "I understood it as it really is: This is anguish, this is the arising of anguish, this is the stopping of anguish, this is the course leading to the stopping of anguish" [*MLS*, I, p. 301 (I.246)]. Understanding now that all existence on any level and for any length of time is impermanent, painful, and unreal, he is freed from any desire for continued existence in any form whatsoever: "Knowing this, seeing thus, my mind was freed from the canker of sense-pleasures, . . . from the canker of becoming . . . from the canker of ignorance." And the result is freedom (mokṣa, Nibbāna) from being reborn as "such and such": "In freedom the knowledge came to be: I am freed; and I comprehended: Destroyed is birth, brought to a close is Brahma-faring, done is what was to be done, there is no more of being such and such" [*MLS*, I, p. 29 (I.23)].

Before dealing with Gotama's encounters with Āḷāra and Uddaka, we need to examine briefly the significance of his rejection of asceticism and its related meditational methods. The primary reason for this rejection seems to be practical: the ascetic methods divide the meditator's available resources; they set the effort at concentration of mind against the distracting pain and debilitating physical weakness produced by, perhaps even sought as desirable by, the method itself. Thus the bodily condition works against rather than for a full concentration of all the psychosomatic powers upon a break-through awareness. And it is implied that deliberate intensification of pain is not necessary for the *enlightening* awareness of the intrinsic pain and impermanence of the human condition.[6] This can be achieved by visual and imaginative devices, as we shall see later, which feed directly into the mental-emotional comprehension of saṃsāra, rather than by the attention-weakening, mind-destroying burden of self-induced pain.

It is also implied that quiet, subdued bodily states are more consonant with the clarity of enlightenment than are turbulent bodily states, which war against the total concentration of attention, and when stirred up in one form also stimulate the emotional, passionate nature. Such seems to be the practical wisdom embodied in this consideration. As we shall see, bodily quietness and calm are integral to the jhānas.

Clear and understandable as all this seems to be from a Buddhist point of view, there is a serious ambiguity in the texts themselves. In the passage earlier noted in the *Middle Length Sayings*, p. 297 (I.242), the clenched-teeth, tongue-touching-palate type of meditation was rejected because it left the body turbulent and pitted mental attention against bodily pain. But in another passage in the same work the identically described method is praised as a means of *attaining* one-pointedness of mind:

> While, with his teeth clenched, his tongue pressed against his palate, he is by mind subduing, restraining and dominating the mind, those evil and unskilled thoughts associated with desire and associated with aversion and associated with confusion, are got rid of, they come to an end. By getting rid of these, the mind subjectively steadies, calms, is one-pointed, concentrated. [*MLS*, I, p. 156 (I.121)]

There is no possible way in which to harmonize these two statements. And the contradiction seems to fit in with the viewpoint taken here: the Pāli Canon tradition both accepts and rejects yogic-Brāhmaṇical methods, and in its canonized, traditional form it somewhat inconsistently embodies several stages of interaction between Buddhist and yogic views. Thus Gotama's initial rejection of Brāhmaṇical-yogic methods is portrayed as sharp and decisive. This accords with the developed Buddhist self-view of its teaching and discipline as an entity distinct from its general Indian religious heritage —a view that dominated the writing of the Canon. Yet, as noted, in the early periods the separation was not actually that sharp, and there was considerable interaction of traditions, particularly of meditational methods.

Another similiar inconsistency, the real force of which will become apparent later, involves the jhānic pattern adopted by Gotama after his rejection of the ascetical meditations. The jhānic pattern is later conjoined to, and forms the initial stage of the further meditational process of reaching the attainments of Āḷāra and Uddaka. These attainments, first rejected by Gotama-the-seeker, are accepted by Gotama-the-Buddha as integral to the meditative system he enjoins upon his own disciples.

Gotama's Encounters with Āḷāra and Uddaka

The following, in abbreviated form, is the Pāli Canon's account of Gotama's encounter with Āḷāra:

> I spoke thus to Āḷāra the Kālāma; "To what extent do you, reverend Kālāma, having realized super-knowledge for yourself, entering thereon, proclaim this *dhamma*?" When this had been said, monks, Āḷāra the Kālāma proclaimed the plane of no-thing. Then it occurred to me, monks: ... Suppose now that I should strive for the realization of that *dhamma* which Āḷāra the Kālāma proclaims ... ? So I, monks, very soon, very quickly, having realized super-knowledge for myself, entering on that *dhamma*, abided therein. [*MLS*, I, p. 208 (I.164)]

Gotama then informs Āḷāra of his attainment and is invited by him to be a colleague. But Gotama refuses and goes on to be a disciple of one Uddaka, the son of Rāma, who, he finds out on inquiry, has attained a state called "neither-perception-nor-non-perception." Given only the difference in level of attainment, the Āḷāra scene is repeated, word for word. Gotama achieves

Uddaka's attainment in short order, is invited to be his colleague, and refuses in words identical to those with which he had refused Āḷāra:

> "This *dhamma* does not conduce to disregard nor to dispassion nor to stopping nor to tranquility nor to super-knowledge nor to awakening nor to nibbāna, but only as far as reaching the plane of neither-perception-nor-non-perception." So I, monks, not getting enough from this *dhamma*, disregarded and turned away from this *dhamma*. [*MLS*, I, pp. 209–10 (I.165–66)]

Shortly after this rejection of Uddaka's attainment as the answer to his searching, Gotama—who later describes himself at this juncture as "a quester for whatever is good, searching for the incomparable, matchless path to peace" [*MLS*, I, pp. 209–10 (I.165–66)]—found the site of the Bo-tree in Uruvelā and settled into his final successful meditation, which has already been sketched.

What is the significance of this complicated and ambiguous account? Clearly in the above canonical form it climaxes Gotama's seeking among, and rejection of, all available Brāhmaṇical-yogic techniques for the achievement of what *he* considers to be enlightenment. It is intended to portray the final cutting of the umbilical cord between Gotama and contemporary religious resources within the Brāhmaṇical-Upanishadic tradition and of his setting out on his own independent enlightenment-bringing way, the Middle Way of Buddhism.

But many difficulties prevent the acceptance of this simplistic account. For example, as noted before, neither Āḷāra nor Uddaka is mentioned in any extant source outside the Pāli Canon's *Majjhima-Nikāya* and the Canon-based statements found in Aśvaghosha's *Buddhacarita*, perhaps a product of the second century A.D. Nor do Aśvaghosha's statements about their teaching correspond clearly to any known Brāhmaṇical philosophical school, though some parts of Aśvaghosha's historically dubious account do have a Sāṃkhyan flavor.[7] But these external difficulties are minor in comparison to those internal to the canonical materials. First, the terms of Gotama's rejection of Āḷāra's and Uddaka's attainments invite analysis. His basic indictment is that they do not "conduce to nibbāna." And all the other terms used to indicate this basic failure—nonconducing to "disregard, dispassion, stopping, tranquility, super-knowledge, awakening"—are also Nibbānic synonyms or surrogates. Thus, whatever their values, the tested and mastered methods do not produce Nibbānic ultimacy: a complete detachment from saṃsāra now, or the final going-out of and from saṃsāra itself. And the context, as we might expect, suggests that Āḷāra's and Uddaka's methods represented the final heights of Brāhmaṇical-yogic attainment—here rejected as insufficient, perhaps even wrong. To become enlightened Gotama must go beyond them or use other means.

This rejection of contemporary meditational practice parallels the Buddha's postenlightenment rejection of the theoretical questions posed by a disciple named Māluṅkyāputta—answers to whose questions were being given by contemporary Brāhmaṇical teachers. The Buddha tells his disciple that his questioning about the infinity or finitude of the universe, the state of those who have entered final Nibbāna, and the like, "is not connected with the goal, is not fundamental to the Brahma-faring, and does not conduce to turning away from, nor to dispassion, stopping, calming, super-knowledge, awakening nor to nibbāna" [*MLS*, II, p. 101 (I.431)]. The main point of these rejections is clear: whether practical or theoretical, contemporary Brāhmaṇism was on all counts insufficient for attaining true mokṣa. To be sure, no reference is made to the attainment of unity with Brahman, the True Self. Possibly the presumed encounters took place before this unity theme, already present in the Upanishads, had been fully articulated in thought and in yogic practice. The nearest the Pāli Canon comes to referring to ultimate, suprapersonal Brahman is in the personalized creator-god form of Brahmā. Nevertheless, it appears that even from the beginning the Buddhist viewpoint was antithetical to any salvation that even hinted at attaining a heavenly presence or union with some ultimate Reality, or gaining some perfect soul-state.

But there is a greater difficulty, only mentioned earlier: the same Ālāra-Uddaka states of attainment that are rejected in the passages quoted above for not going far enough or in the right direction for gaining Nibbāna are, in other passages of the *Middle Length Sayings*, integrally incorporated into a succession of meditational attainments which culminate in the attainment of cessation (*nirodha-samāpatti*). And this attainment is described in the Canon and by Buddhaghosa as the *fullest and most extended realization of Nibbāna possible to human beings in this life.*

A canonical delineation of this ultimate attainment occurs in the Buddha's questions to his disciple Anuruddhas and his companion meditators about their meditative progress. They are obviously experts, being able "for as long as we like . . . to enter into and abide in the first meditation . . . second meditation . . . third meditation . . . fourth meditation." "Meditations," of course, are jhānas, as also are "abidings." But the progression does not stop here; the Buddha asks another didactic question: "Did you, Anuruddhas, by passing quite beyond this abiding . . . reach another state . . . an abiding in comfort?" Anuruddhas replies: "How could this *not* be, Lord. Here we, Lord, for as long as we like, by passing quite beyond all perception of material shapes, by the going down of perception of sensory reactions, by not attending to the perception of variety, thinking, 'Ether is unending,' *entering on the plane of infinite ether, abide in it*" [*MLS*, I, pp. 259–61 (I. 207–9); italics added]. Then Anuruddhas relates the further attainment of a trance based on infinity of consciousness, and then in order the two trances already made familiar to us in the attainments of Ālāra and Uddaka, namely those of nothingness and of neither-perception-nor-nonperception.

But he reports that there is still one further attainment superior to these, "the stopping of perception and feeling" [*MLS*, I, pp. 259–61 (I.207–9)], that is, nirodha-samāpatti. Beyond this is there any further "abiding in comfort" (that is, trance-state)? asks the Buddha. Anuruddhas flatly replies: "But we, Lord, do not behold another abiding in comfort that is higher or more excellent than this abiding in comfort" [*MLS*, I, p. 261 (I.209)]. And the Buddha gives his assent to Anuruddhas' statement in almost identical words: There *is* no abiding that is "higher or more excellent than this abiding in comfort."

One other treatment of the same theme is worth noting. In conversation with a certain Udāyin the Buddha comments on the series of eight meditative states (the four jhānas and the four succeeding "immaterial states"), vigorously asserting, after describing each of them: "This is not enough! I say, 'Get rid of it.' I say, 'Transcend it.'" ("Transcending" each state means progressing on to the next higher.) But, again, as before, with the attainment of cessation the formula differs:

> As to this, Udāyin, a monk, by wholly transcending the plane of neither-perception-nor-non-perception, enters and abides in the stopping of perception and feeling. This is its transcending. It is for this that I, Udāyin, speak even of the getting rid of the plane of neither-perception-nor-non-perception. Now do you, Udāyin, *see any fetter, minute or massive* of which I have not spoken to you?
> No, revered sir. [*MLS*, II, p. 128 (I.455–56); italics added]

Thus in this highest of all states, reached by a progression up through the traditional four jhānas and the four successive immaterial meditations (two of which were rejected by Gotama as non-Nibbānic), every fetter binding one to saṃsāra—including *all* of the preceding meditational states!—is now wholly transcended.

To this I must add one more statement about the attainment of cessation, a ne plus ultra assertion made by Buddhaghosa nearly 1000 years after the Buddha's death: "*Why do they attain it?* Being wearied by the occurrence and dissolution of formations, they attain it thinking: Let us dwell in bliss by being without consciousness here and now and reaching the cessation that is nibbāna."[8]

Summary and Transition

Such then are the ambiguous data in the Pāli Canon for determining the relationship between the Brāhmaṇical-yogic and the Buddhist meditational methods. In general the relationship can be described in the terms already used, that of the Buddhist rejection-acceptance of Brāhmaṇical yoga.

So far as the historical relations are concerned, E. J. Thomas may be quoted with approval:

> All that we know of the Yoga system is later than Buddhism, and no direct comparison can be made about the origins, but we find it assumed in Buddhist works that the practice of concentration was not orig-

inal in Buddhism. What was claimed as original was the true method —right concentration. A more important cause of the resemblance between Buddhist practice and Yoga is the fact that they developed side by side. Not only would there be comparison and imitation, but a member of one sect might pass over to the other and take his methods with him.[9]

Generally, the methods of yoga in its Brāhmaṇical or orthodox context and those "same" methods in their Buddhist context undoubtedly share many features. But they also differ, at least in their use; for yoga directed toward an implicitly Vedāntic union with Brahman or toward a Sāṃkhyan attainment of pure isolated selfhood would not be identical with the "same" yogic means directed toward the attainment of nonsubstantialist Nibbāna by a nonself! And so too it may be said that yogic methodology contains in its very structure Brāhmaṇical-yogic implications and presuppositions, for example, the hope of attaining oneness with some supraindividual entity.

If the jhānic-formless-state series be taken to represent Buddhism's yogic heritage, and if the nonself, Nibbānic thrust—in which all existence is seen as empty of true reality, impermanent, and full of suffering—be taken as the new Buddhist component, the question arises: how do the yogic elements function within the Buddhist meditational structure, as they can and do according to the Canon and Buddhaghosa? And, further, what is the relation of the jhānic states, routinely portrayed as Gotama's method of achieving enlightenment, and the four formless meditations, which elsewhere in the Canon are added on to the jhānas as their logical extensions, finally resulting in the attainment of cessation? These two problems will be sketched here in anticipation of their detailed discussion and hoped-for solution in the subsequent chapters.

Relation of the Jhānas and the Formless Meditations

How can it be that the states *rejected* by the *seeking* Gotama are later joined by him (or the early tradition) to those meditational states (jhānas) by which he had attained enlightenment, as their further continuous progression leading to the peerless this-life experience of Nibbāna (the attainment of cessation)? When Gotama, as the Buddha, later says that Āḷāra's no-thingness and Uddaka's neither-perception-nor-nonperception attainments were not a sufficient *dhamma*, what did he mean? Was he referring to their inability to achieve cessation? Or was he stating the need for the use of the vipassanic critique of *all* experiences, that is, insight into their still fettered saṃsāric character?

The canonical statements are not clear, though many statements are made about the jhānas and the four formless meditations. Those passages concerning Gotama's own enlightenment, related by him subsequently, mention neither the formless meditations nor the attainment of cessation. The crowning and enlightening experience is the realization of the utter emptiness, painfulness, and impermanence of existence. That alone brings enlightenment, *is* enlightenment, and it follows after the mastery of the four jhānas.[10] There is also another, less numerous set of passages that describe or allude to the formless meditations apart from the four jhānas, whose attainment supposedly makes possible the attainment of the formless meditations, and also apart from nirodha-samāpatti, whose attainment the formless meditations make possible.[11] Finally, a third set of passages portrays the joining of the four jhānic attainments and the four formless meditations in a continuous series of states climaxing in nirodha-samāpatti.[12]

In the present state of Pāli scholarship there is no decisive way to determine the "authenticity" of these three sets of passages. It may never be possible to thus distinguish them, so tightly were they interwoven at the time the scriptures were written down. And by the time of Buddhaghosa, the joining of the jhānas and formless meditations had become fully orthodox.

Some years ago Friedrich Heiler proposed a solution to the problem which, despite some needed qualifications, is generally the best in my opinion. Heiler proposed that the formless meditations represent a later "Yogic superimposition" upon the "four original" Buddhist jhānas. He also speaks in general of a Buddhist "content" given to Yogic structures and forms.[13] What "original" means in this case may be dubious. How "originally" Buddhist were the four jhānas? Their absolutely de novo character seems suspect; they are more probably yogic adaptations, possibly with new features or uses. So too the word "superimposition" seems a little strong, and superficial in connotation; it must be confessed that at least by the time of Buddhaghosa the two structures were melded into each other smoothly. The meditation upon the infinity of space (ether), for example, follows naturally from the gradual expansion and etherealization of the limited earth *kasina*, and so on up to and including nirodha-samāpatti.

However, the melding of two distinct elements, as evident in our texts, suggests a "reyoganization" of earlier forms, supporting Heiler's general hypothesis. Whether this resulted from the continuing interaction of Buddhist and yogic traditions, as may well have been the case, or whether two variant *Buddhist* traditions were later joined into one, may be forever impossible to determine. But there is little doubt of some joining; and the presumption seems to be that the four jhānas were more original to the structure than the formless meditations.

The Vipassanic-Jhānic Tension

Heiler suggests a Buddhist content was given to yogic structures and forms, but this scarcely applies to the relation of jhānic states and the formless meditations, for they are both yogic. And even if we apply his terms to the relation between the jhānic-formless-state series and the vipassanā discipline, the "contextualization and permeation of yogic techniques by the Buddhist weltanschauung and its implications," seems preferable to "content-form" terminology. In any case, this contextualizing is exemplified in the relationship of the discipline of vipassanā to that of the jhānas in the final Theravāda meditational pattern. Therein acceptance and rejection are mixed together, and even the final result of the blending in the ultimate attainment of cessation (nirodha-samāpatti) remains ambiguously jhānic-vipassanic, and both this-worldly and other-worldly.

This tension and ambivalence are as follows: the jhānic and immaterial meditation series are called "peaceful abidings," that is, peaceful states of consciousness; they become ever more subtle and of greater transic depth until they climax in the attainment of the cessation of all (ordinary) consciousness. Their essence is samādhic. And they are congenial with the general thrust of later systematic yogic methods aimed at achieving either a unity of pure, supra-personal consciousness in the Sāmkhya-Yogic mode or union with the Absolute Brahman in the Vedāntic style. On the other side stands vipassanā, insight into the empty, impermanent, pain-filled nature of all existence, *including the jhānic and formless meditational states*. As we shall observe in detail later, these "peaceful abidings" are reviewed one by one immediately after their experiencing and pronounced to belong to samsāra *not* to Nibbāna. They may be seen as pseudo-Nibbānas, tempting the meditator to remain in them indefinitely and to return to them whenever possible; or equally, they may be seen as the progressively subtlized but still tainted forms of selfhood—*attā* rather than *anattā*.

We must remember that vipassanā sets Buddhism apart from all other methods (especially Brāhmanical); it alone brings the meditator to full and final release (Nibbāna) in the Buddhist view. Vipassanā is the methodological embodiment of the Buddhist (Theravāda) world view. It contains the heart of the Four Noble Truths of the intrinsic painfulness or unsatisfactoriness of all conditioned existence, the denial of any substantial self, the denial of any Absolute such as Brahman with whom unity is to be realized, and a resolute determination to refuse any less-than-ultimate release found in subtle self-bolstering meditative states, however peaceful their abidings. Vipassanā is absolutely essential to Nibbānic attainment, but the peaceful abidings (jhānas and formless meditations) are not. Although this is not clearly formulated in the Pāli Canon, the later tradition (see Buddhaghosa) recognizes as authentic those bare-insight workers or "dry-visioned saints" who, with no reference to jhānic attainments, let alone the higher formless meditations, achieve arahantship.

In the end, then, the Buddhist world view predominates in the Theravāda meditative structure and practice. Whatever else it may be or do, Buddhist (Theravāda) meditation is viewed as futile unless it brings enlightenment, an illuminative awareness of existence seen through the lens of the Four Noble Truths. Whatever use may be made of yogic (jhānic) attainments, they must be subservient to this end. Only when the negativity of this world view is fully existentialized can the positive apprehension of Nibbāna itself be achieved by means of Path realization and fruition experiences— experiences not available to mere jhānic adepts.

The final anomaly, however, is that in nirodha-samāpatti, the direct vipassanic apprehension of Nibbāna itself *and* the transic attainments up to the state of neither-perception-nor-nonperception must *both* be achieved before this highest of all earthly states can be entered into. That is, nirodha-samāpatti is the true child of the full union of (Buddhist) insight and (yogic) peaceful abidings. In the words of Buddhaghosa:

> (ii) *Who attains it?* (iii) *Who does not attain it?* No ordinary men, no Stream Enterers or Once-returners, and no Non-returners and Arahants who are bare-insight workers, attain to it. But both Non-returners and those with the cankers destroyed [Arahants] *who are obtainers of the eight attainments* [jhānas, formless meditations] *obtain it.* [*PP*, XIII.18; last italics added]

2

Conditions, Preparations, and Lower Levels of Meditation

The basic models for Theravāda meditation are found in the Pāli Canon and in Buddhaghosa's *Path of Purification*. The Pāli Canon, as we have seen, contains an ambiguous portrayal of the development and meaning of the classical meditational pattern as the supreme way to enlightenment. This may well be, as suggested, the result of the varied interactions of the early Buddhist and (Brāhmaṇical) yogic traditions. But any further speculation on the historical features of that interaction is beside the point, because for many centuries the original yogic elements have been integral to Theravāda practice.

Our further consideration of Theravāda meditation will depend on Buddhaghosa's massive manual of meditational theory and practice, with some assistance from the less well-known *Vimuttimagga* or *The Path of Freedom*, which was perhaps the forerunner of *The Path of Purification*.[1] Together they represent how the Theravāda community of monks developed the meditational tradition during a thousand-year period. These works are the fruit of long theorizing and practice on the basis of scriptures and important commentaries, worked into a consistent whole, and institutionalized. These volumes provide something the Pāli Canon lacks: the specifics of actual practice and a substantial rationale for them in a fully systematic form. But rather than speculate here on the developments that occurred in the meditational tradition during this thousand years or on what additions were made to the scriptural version, I will accept the version of the two manuals as it now stands.

The texts of the manuals will be considered authoritative on the subject of orthodox theory and practice, and the historical question of the original interrelation of yogic and Buddhist elements will not be reexamined, but the *functional* relation between these elements within the orthodox structure is the core of the following discussion. Their creative tension and ambivalence explain the dynamics of Theravāda meditation. For the purpose of further analysis, then, the Buddhist doctrines and doctrinal emphases, onto which yogic techniques were originally grafted, must be examined in greater detail than heretofore.

Basic Assumptions of Theravāda Meditation

Any consideration of the actual methodology of Theravāda meditation must begin with the reminder that we cannot understand a method of religious salvation without comprehension of the world view it involves. Salvational methodologies never exist in a vacuum. They necessarily *embody* the world view of their own religious tradition. As ways to achieve salvation they presuppose a world and an existential situation that need to be changed or escaped from, and propose an appropriate solution—a mode of salvation.

This is especially true of Theravāda. Its salvational schema emerges directly from its world view; its meditational structure articulates that view. The methodology of meditation is a way of seeing the space-time realm as it truly is, says Theravāda; and once truly seen, reality, both mundane and supramundane, will exert its saving power upon the seer. The important thing is to see clearly without preconceptions and misapprehensions, to see with freedom from emotional factors.

The basic character of the Theravāda weltanschauung was summarily described in the first chapter as the perception of all existence in the space-time world (including heavens, hells, and human, animal, and ghostly existences) as intrinsically impermanent (*anicca*), empty of self or reality (*anattā*), and full of pain (*dukkha*). Our source for a more detailed examination of this saṃsāric world is the Pāli Canon statement, a classic expression of the Theravāda weltanschauung that Buddhaghosa took for granted.

The impermanence (anicca) of all things is a basic conviction of Theravāda Buddhism. There is nothing in space-time experience that "endures" for more than a relatively short time, given the eternities, past and future, that Buddhism (in the Upanishadic mode) envisages. Buddhist Stcherbatsky's "point-instant" theory of existence was developed directly from this conviction. According to this theory, physical or mental reality is an infinitesimally split-second affair, a linear-temporal series of here-now submoments in which the sense-perceived phenomena of our experience flash into and out of existence. Physical reality is just these flashes, a becoming rather than a being. But whether we think of these point-instants, or a "long" hundred-year human life, or a very "long" deva existence (billions of human years), in the final analysis, existence is fleeting. And it applies to cosmic as well as personal existence: worlds too come and go, endlessly and perpetually, inexorably destroyed by fire, wind, and water [*PP*, XII.28–65]. Nothing known to our senses or experience is dependable or permanent, as the Buddha declared to Rahula:

> What do you think about this, Rahula? Is the eye . . . are material shapes . . . is visual consciousness . . . is impact on the eye permanent or impermanent? Is the ear . . . the nose . . . the tongue . . . the body . . . the mind . . . are mental states . . . is mental consciousness . . . is impact on the mind permanent or impermanent?
> Impermanent, revered sir. [*MLS*, III, p. 329 (III.278–79)]

Hence it is appropriately termed saṃsāra, a veritable "sea of change."

Nothing is permanent because everything is empty of reality (anattā). Here the Buddhist view of the universe contradicts the Upanishadic. Although the Upanishadic authors generally agreed that existence was perpetual flux, they posited two absolutely permanent entities, ātman and Brahman—which in the end were One—in the light of whose absolute permanence, impermanence could be regarded as an illusion. This substratum of permanence was flatly and fully rejected by Buddhism from the beginning. It could find permanent substance nowhere in empirical experience and was unwilling to posit any absolute permanence to shore up the perpetual flux of time-space existence and experience. It denied substantiality to both physical and mental orders of being, particularly negating the latter. The supposedly unchanging ātman that perceived change because it was changeless was considered by Buddhists to be imaginary. It could not be found in the careful analysis of subjective experience, and the supposed existence of an immutable self was, as the Buddhists saw it, the heart of human bondage to karmic continuity, that is, to endless rebirths. And since this selfhood seemed most obvious and most cherished in its bodily manifestation, the early Buddhist attack upon selfhood was often an attack upon body-mind individuality. In the famous chariot analogy, from a near canonical source, the illusion of selfhood is described in these terms:

> "Then if you came, Sire, in a carriage, explain to me what it is. Is it the pole that is the chariot?"
> "I did not say that."
> "Is it the axle that is the chariot?"
> "Certainly not."
> "Is it the wheels, or the framework, or the ropes, or the yoke, or the spokes of the wheels, or the goad, that are the chariot?"
> And to all these he still answered no.
> "Then is it all these parts of it that are the chariot?"
> "No, Sir."
> "But is there anything outside them that is the chariot?"
> And he still answered no.

The questioner, Monk Nagasena, goes on to aver that "Chariot is a mere empty sound," because an analysis of it yields no genuine item or substance that can be called "chariot" in any real or experienceable sense. A "chariot" is "a generally understood term, the designation in common use,"[2] a mere practical linguistic convenience and nothing more. So too, Nagasena concludes, individual selfhood is at best only a "generally understood term, the designation in common use."

Not content, for practical existential reasons, to merely demolish the body analytically, the early Buddhists often attacked it in emotional terms. Thus:

Body full of blood and matter

And of plenteous other carrion,
So by human skill and wit is
Rendered fair like painted casket,
That the bitter suffering from it
Shows as sweetly satisfying,
Bound to what we hold beloved,
As a razor-blade, that's hidden
'Neath thick crust of honey-syrup
Undiscerned (by the greedy).[3]

Finally, existence in this world is intrinsically unsatisfactory, even painful (*dukkha*), because it is impermanent and empty. In the conclusion of the passage quoted above in which Rahula answers the Buddha's question about eye, material shapes, visual consciousness, and so forth, by saying that they are all impermanent (anicca), there is one further question: "But is what is impermanent, anguish or happiness?/Anguish, revered sir" [*MLS*, III, p. 329 (III.279)]. *All* experience involves suffering, according to the Theravāda view:

> It is both now, good Gotama, that contact with fire is painful, exceedingly hot and afflicting, and also before that contact with that fire was painful, exceedingly hot and afflicting. Yet, good Gotama, this leper, a man with his limbs all ravaged and festering, being eaten by vermin, tearing his open sores with his nails, his sense-organs injured, might, from the painful contact with the fire, *receive a change of sensation and think it pleasant*. [*MLS*, II, p. 186 (I.507); italics added]

And in response to this answer to his previous question about whether fire is *always* painful, the Buddha goes on to compare the condition of ordinary human beings who are still attached to "pleasures of the senses" to the leper of the above analogy. "From painful contact with sense-pleasures themselves, [they] receive a change of sensation and think it pleasant." That is, "pleasure" in the ordinary sense is nothing but a new and *different* pain, which seems delightful only because it provides some novelty. Obviously this leads to an infinite and infinitely frustrating pursuit of ever-new pain-pleasures; such is the intrinsic nature of human existence!

One final quotation will round out the picture of the Theravāda world view, which determines its mode of release. Not only is human sense pleasure intrinsically painful, like fire, but human existence *as such* is on fire, or "burning," so to speak. All the factors of human sensibility—eye, ear, nose, body-sensing—are burning with all the ills that are the intrinsic lot of humankind, life after life: "With what is it [i.e. any one of the above sensibilities] burning? I say it is burning with the fire of passion, with the fire of hatred, with the fire of stupidity; it is burning because of birth, ageing, dying, because of grief, sorrow, suffering, lamentation and despair."[4] Such a "life" is more properly "life-death."

The Theravāda view then is that sentient existence at all levels is desperate for remedy, for genuine mokṣa. That should be the supreme goal of human endeavor, for only human beings are capable of realizing the true nature of existence. (And who knows whether one's next birth will *be* in the human sphere?) But given that all existence, even human and deva, is instinct with impermanence and emptiness and pain, true mokṣa will be both radical and negative sounding in its opposition to "life." Its name is Nibbāna.

The Buddhist Mokṣa: Nibbāna

The root meaning of Nibbāna is negative—to "go out." The metaphor at its base is the going out of a flame, which is either blown out by wind or breath, or which dies because its fuel supply is exhausted. The discipline of meditation that eventuates in Nibbānic enlightenment is impliedly a deliberate quenching of the flame of saṃsāric existence by repressive measures, or perhaps more appropriately, by depriving it of psychic sustenance. Deprival of psychic sustenance must be specified because no mere suicidal destruction of physical life would end the rebirth process—quite the contrary![5] In either case the name of the supreme goal of meditation expresses the essence of the Theravāda world view: saṃsāra (rebirth-redeath) exists, so to speak, only for the "purpose" of its escaping; escape is the paramount motive, fundamentally it is the only motive for meditation. Nibbāna in its final attainment after death is saṃsāra's absolute antithesis, its utterly transcendent escape and denial.

What then *is* Nibbāna? This has been endlessly discussed both within and without the Buddhist world, and here we can only touch on a few relevant points.[6] The minimal definition of Nibbāna is absence of greed, hatred, and delusion; and perhaps for Buddhism as a whole this is the best definition, because it does not necessarily specify any particular location inside or outside time and space. However, for the Pāli Canon, greed, hatred, and delusion are the primary moving forces of all sentient existence.[7] Hence Nibbāna's final import is total saṃsāric escape.

The Buddha's own statements about Nibbāna tend to be carefully agnostic. To speak of where (what state) an enlightened one goes out into upon his death is as meaningless as to ask where or in what direction the flame has gone when it goes out [*MLS*, II, p. 166 (I.487)]. When he is questioned by a disciple whether after death the Buddha (and enlightened arahants by implication) will *cease* to exist, *will* exist, will *both* exist and *not* exist, or will *neither* exist nor *not* exist, he flatly refuses all these designations. "Exist" here would seem to mean some type of continuing individualized awareness; and it seems that the Buddha might have adopted the neither-nor answer— certainly some later Buddhists have done so. Yet even this specification is rejected out of hand as not of religious profit (*MLS*, II, *Sutta* 63, *passim*).

This shunting aside of all such speculative questions as "not tending to edification" is an answer in itself. Clearly the truth and reality of repeated rebirth in saṃsāra and the companion truth of the necessity of escape there-from are taken for granted. They are the basis for shunting aside such questions in favor of getting on with that spiritual discipline that alone can lead to release from the bondage of saṃsāra. Philosophical-ontological truth is here directly converted into practical existential procedure.

The question of the nature of Nibbāna has persisted in the Buddhist community, however, and the practical agnostic flavor of this "answer" of the Buddha has been qualified. To what extent and in what directions that modification has taken place is too tangled a question to deal with extensively here. But on general religious and historical grounds the opinion may be hazarded that early in the career of Buddhism, the agnostic negativism of such replies as the above was modified. In addition, it must be kept in mind that the Buddhist negativity concerning the final goal (Nibbāna) was intended as a methodological and psychological device rather than an ontological statement; later on in the growth of the tradition and its conflict with other traditions, such statements were ontologized into "descriptions" of the Supreme Reality.[8]

Similarly, with respect to anticipation of Nibbāna by the early Buddhists, there are the deliverance verses, the postenlightenment statements of monks and nuns in the *Psalms of the Brethren* and of the *Sisters* (*Theragāthā* and *Therīgāthā*). In her introduction to the *Sisters* volume, Mrs. C. A. F. Rhys Davids says that despite a *possible* sense of a future ineffable bliss awaiting them,

> their verses do not seem to betray anything that can be construed as a consciousness that hidden glories, more wonderful than the brief span of "cool" and "calm" they now know as Arahants, are awaiting them.

> They have won up out of the Maelstrom of Saṃsāra, they have "crossed over," they have won to something ineffable, that *now is*, but is not to be described in terms of space or after-time; and resting, they sing.[9]

But even if this is the case, tradition did not stop here. As Rhys Davids points out, there are in the Pāli Canon many emotionally positive, even ontological, statements about Nibbāna:[10]

> The harbour of refuge, the cool cave, the island amidst the floods, the place of bliss, emancipation, liberation, safety, the supreme, the transcendental, the uncreated, the tranquil, the home of ease, the calm, the end of suffering, the medicine for all evil, the unshaken, the ambrosia, the immaterial, the imperishable, the abiding, the further shore, the undying, the bliss of effort, the supreme joy, the ineffable, the detachment, the holy city.

To this it must be added that the predominant opinion in contemporary Theravāda Buddhism is that Nibbāna is not, and never has been, viewed as total extinction. That would be the annihilationist view specifically rejected by the Buddha himself. And aside from the question of its ontological *or* purely experiential nature, but closely related to its quality as experience, Nibbānic awareness, or better, the essence of Nibbāna, may be attained *in the midst of saṃsāra*, here and now; it is not solely an after death matter.

There are two technical terms used to define "this-life" and "after-life" Nibbāna, respectively: the full extinction of defilements (*kilesa-parinibbāna*) and the full extinction of the groups of existents or *khandhas* (*khandha-parinibbāna*). The Buddha after his enlightenment lived for forty-five years in the state of the full extinction of defilements. His entering into the second-level Nibbāna, sometimes inaccurately called pari- or full-Nibbāna, was merely the death of the body-mind groups that composed Gotama the man. Nibbāna, even full-Nibbāna, had been entered forty-five years previously and he had been living "in" it all that time. The same is true of the arahant, or enlightened disciple. In essence the only distinction between the two levels is that upon the cessation of the khandhas (physical death), there will be no more rebirth, no more Gotama, no more arahant. They have gone out of saṃsāra, finally and fully released from time-space existence.

Now if one can still be "in" the world even after having "gone out" of it, that is, entered into Nibbāna, this implies a certain positive and concrete quality in Nibbāna. And such *is* the general quality ascribed to those Nibbānic persons, the Buddha and his enlightened disciples. It is obviously not merely a withdrawn-into-trance or withdrawn-into-asceticism life or quality of spirit, but a calm, cool serenity of mind and heart in the midst of space-time life. Perhaps the term blissful can be applied to it, provided bliss be kept separate from the emotional or transic ecstacy. Thus *The Path of Freedom* makes a distinction between the joy found on some of the lower jhānic levels and the higher bliss:

> What are the differences between joy and bliss? Buoyancy is joy, ease of mind is bliss. Tranquility of mind is bliss. Concentration of mind is joy. Joy is coarse; bliss is fine.... Where there is joy there is bliss, but where there is bliss there may or may not be joy.[11]

And it is further said that "The bliss of non-defilement is according to the Buddha's teaching '*highest Nibbāna*'" (p. 90). However, at a higher-level jhāna, even bliss is superseded by equanimity or tranquility of mind, which might be called the psychologically dominant quality of the enlightened consciousness. But again, even bliss has higher levels. Destroyed on one level, it appears in sublimated form in the highest meditational state possible to human beings, that of cessation (nirodha-samāpatti). We read in *The Path of Purification*, to requote:

> *Why do they attain it?* For the purpose of abiding in bliss here and now. ... Being wearied by the occurrence and dissolution of formations, they attain it thinking "Let us dwell in bliss by being without consciousness here and now and reaching the cessation that is nibbāna." [XXIII.30]

And one commentary defines "bliss" as being "without suffering" rather than being ecstatic vision. The quality of nirodha obviously conforms to this in general.

Context of Nibbāna Seeking

Even after having thus recognized the "positive" factors in Nibbāna, it is nevertheless true that its essentially negative nature—such as final escape from saṃsāra—leads to a qualified withdrawal from saṃsāra while still present in it. That is, the process of gaining Nibbāna through meditation must almost of practical necessity be carried on in a congenial situation, namely the monkhood. Such at least has been the Theravāda tradition in the past; only the full-time monk can seek Nibbāna directly or with any prospect of success.

The reasons for this are primarily practical, not religiously sacramental, though the tradition that an arahant cannot live as a layman for more than seven days after his enlightenment seems to be a move toward sacramentalizing the monkhood.[12] They are essentially the same reasons for founding monasticism throughout the world in various religious traditions: the "layman" is one who chooses to concern himself with occupation and family and cannot therefore give full attention or sufficient time to religious practices —particularly to prolonged and intensive meditation. On the other hand, the monk has only minimal responsibility in this area, such as begging his food, mending his own clothes, and the simple housekeeping of the monastery. He thus has seclusion without major social responsibilities.

And of particular importance for the Buddhist meditator is the difficulty of controlling the sense life in the secular world. For basic to the Buddhist viewpoint is the danger of sense pleasures to the higher life of the Nibbānic quest. For example, in the Pāli Canon, we read that sense pleasures, though superficially attractive, are in actuality like a meatless bone thrown to a hungry dog, a lump of flesh over which the carrion vultures fight, a blazing grass torch in the hand on a windy day, a pit of glowing embers, a fruitless dream, borrowed wealth sought by avaricious creditors, grasping at ripe fruits while in the branches of a tree that is being cut down, and so forth [*MLS*, II, pp. 28ff. (I.346ff.)]. In such a world as this—to say nothing specifically about the special dangerousness of the attractive female form—the monk-meditator must go always and everywhere with controlled senses: he must literally "guard the doors of the sense-organs." And how shall he do this?

> As to this, Mahānāma, an ariyan disciple, having seen a material shape with the eye is not entranced by the general appearance, is not entranced by the detail. For if he dwell with the organ of sight uncontrolled, covetousness and dejection, evil unskilled states of mind might predominate. So he fares along controlling it, he guards the organ of sight; he achieves control over the organ of sight .... [And so with all the senses, including the mind.].... It is thus, Mahānāma, that an

ariyan disciple is one who guards the doors of the sense-organs. [*MLS*, II, pp. 21ff. (I.335–56)]

An arahant could no doubt properly guard the doors of the sense organs in the midst of any circumstances, but where except in the monastic life could the not-yet-arrived seeker of enlightenment find conditions favorable to and designedly supportive of his quest of going-outness? Certainly not in the layman's worldly life; and not even in the deva-worlds (heavens) where he may be reborn for his generosity to monks, for that matter!

The *Saṅgha* or monkhood can then be defined as a fellowship of Nibbāna-seekers, deliberately constituted to ensure the maximum of favorable conditions for the quest of enlightenment: minimal effort for livelihood, such as begging for alms food only; a simplified way of life requiring only eight personal possessions, which are on loan as it were—three robes, begging bowl, needle, thread, water strainer, medicine; elimination of all worldly attractions and distractions; a supportive community of fellowseekers and attained teachers; a carefully ordered daily regimen to provide opportunity for Nibbāna seeking and the transmission of the Dhamma, that is, the Nibbāna seeker's discipline, to succeeding generations of Nibbāna seekers. The fact that the Buddhist Saṅgha was so carefully organized in its way of life—in some contrast to the rather desultory arrangements between Brāhmaṇical teachers and disciples in contemporary India—indicates how seriously the Buddhists took this quest. Thus in the most precise sense of the word one can say that only the Nibbāna seekers, the monks alone for all practical purposes, were genuine Buddhists or enlightenment seekers.[13]

One more contextual aspect of meditation is to be observed before proceeding to the closer description of the actual techniques of meditation. One might call it the major strategy of meditation, the point on which meditational method centers its main thrust and most intense energies in order to achieve its final goal of Nibbānic release. This key point is the destruction of the ordinary sense of selfhood or individuality.

That the teaching of anattā (no-self) is central to Theravāda Buddhism has already been noted. But what needs particular emphasis is its absolute centrality in the whole process of meditation, because in the Buddhist view the attachment to self, that is, to distinctive individuality, is the central, the strongest, and the most subtle of all the bonds that tie each human being to his or her own career of perpetual birth-death. It is the core of all that enslaves people, the cause of all their miseries. The ability to destroy this fundamental self-attachment within oneself means to be on the path to enlightenment, from which there is no backsliding.[14]

How then shall this destruction of the self-sense be accomplished, how shall the anattā doctrine be effectively appropriated? Two levels of appropriation may be distinguished. First, intellectual conviction of the truth of anattā: this is endlessly reiterated in the Pāli Canon; and the purpose of that reiteration seems to be reinforcement by reassertion as well as offering intellectual proof that anattā is the only logically demonstrable analysis of the human being that can be based on careful empirical observation.

But intellectual conviction of the truth of anattā, no matter how seemingly complete, is not sufficient to cut the cords of existential attachment to self-hood. There may continue to be an emotional attachment that keeps alive in subtle forms the hope and desire for renewed becoming in some form or other, such as the eon-long existences in the "fine-material," that is, in the almost disembodied levels of existence opened up (according to Thera-vāda) by some of the higher meditational trances. There is still further a cellular, bodily attachment to the next moment of life, even with the know-ledge that existence is suffering. Perhaps this is another way of saying that even one who "knows" this is not in actuality fully convinced of the truth of anattā. In any case, the main thrust of the meditational techniques is toward the total destruction of belief in and attachment to self, in what-ever form, at the existential, personal level.

Thus we must be prepared to see in every device used in meditation an-other tool for the destruction of the sense of integral selfhood. Meditation seeks to weaken, undercut, seize upon, and dismember every manifestation of individualized self (and Theravāda Buddhists reject other meanings of self out of hand). One must learn by first-hand experience and introspection to see that what goes on within oneself is merely a set of impersonal elements and to view them as impersonally as though they occurred in "someone" to whom "I" am personally indifferent. In the words of a modern Theravāda writer, in keeping with the spirit of the Pāli Canon,

> As to the ultimate purpose of Satipaṭṭhāna (attention to breath), Mindfulness on Postures will bring an initial awareness of the imper-sonal nature of the body, and will be conducive towards *an inner aliena-tion from it.* In the course of the practice, one will come to view the postures just as one unconcernedly views the automatic movements of a life-sized puppet. The play of the puppet's limbs will evoke a feeling of complete estrangement, and even a slight amusement like that of an onlooker at a marionette show.... By looking at the postures with such a detached objectivity, the *habitual identification* with the body will begin to dissolve.[15]

What must be remembered in reading this passage is that it is one's own body that is being observed, for the gut-level realization of one's own im-personal nature is the nub of the whole matter. And after training in this fully existential process of seeing one's bodily self "as it really is"—an im-personal set of limbs—then the meditator turns the same analysis "inward" upon thought and emotion. So by first-hand experience comes the realiza-tion that even one's inmost mental-emotional "self" is likewise a set of factors in constant flux.

The Ethical Foundations and Fruits of Meditation

In the traditional Theravāda formulation of the way to Nibbāna, three stages are recognized: *sīla* (morality), *samādhi* (concentration of mind) and *paññā* (insight that achieves Nibbāna). Since some of the side effects and psychic accompaniments of meditation are given considerable space in the canonical and postcanonical treatments of meditation, it is important to keep in mind that morality is a taken-for-granted prerequisite, component, and fruit of meditation.

Morality is fundamental for two reasons. First, it is often explicitly stated, and always assumed, that only a morally sincere and good person can undertake meditation with success. The steadiness of intent and deep purposiveness required for meditation cannot be found in one unable to keep even the basic Five Precepts to avoid killing, stealing, lying, unchastity, and intoxicants, or who lacks the positive moral qualities of generosity, loving-kindness, compassion, and joy in the joy of others.

An excellent example of this intimate interweaving of the ethical and the meditative is found in the following description by the Buddha of his own conditioning for the first jhānic attainment on the eve of his enlightenment:

> Possessed of this ariyan body of moral habit [earlier described as temperateness in habits] and possessed of this ariyan control over the sense organs and possessed of this ariyan mindfulness and clear consciousness, I chose a remote lodging in a forest. . . . Returning from alms-gathering after the meal, I sat down cross-legged, holding the back erect, having made mindfulness rise up in front of me. By getting rid of covetousness for the world, I dwelt with a mind devoid of coveting. . . . By getting rid of the taint of ill-will, I dwelt benevolent in mind; and compassionate for the welfare of all creatures and beings, I purified the mind of the taint of ill-will. By getting rid of sloth and torpor, I dwelt devoid of sloth and torpor; perceiving the light, mindful and clearly conscious, I purified the mind of sloth and torpor. By getting rid of restlessness and worry, I dwelt calmly. . . . By getting rid of doubt . . . I purified the mind of doubt.
>
> By getting rid of these five hindrances . . . I entered on and abided in the first meditation. [*MLS*, III, pp. 87ff. (I.35–6)]

The magical and psychic powers that accompany meditative achievement probably have always been a part of the Buddhist schema, though conceivably their role and importance may have been progressively expanded as the Buddha-figure was increasingly supernormalized and lay influence began to be felt within Buddhism itself. The central emphasis has never been on meditation as a device for achieving magical powers, which are considered by Buddhists to be the inevitable accompaniments of increasing mind control and moral perfection. Their casual, self-serving manifestation, as well as their direct pursuit, has always been condemned in the mainstream teaching.

The second reason that morality is fundamental is that meditation is not only supported *by* moral character and practice but is supportive and perfective *of* that same practice and character. The use of the four divine abidings in the meditational process illustrates this. One bases his meditation upon one of these qualities and universalizes it. Let us take loving-kindness (*mettā*):

> The extension of the object takes place either in access or in absorption [i.e., jhāna]. Here is the order of it. Just as a skilled plowman first delimits an area and then does his plowing, so first a single dwelling should be delimited and loving-kindness developed towards all beings there in the way beginning "In this dwelling may all beings be free from enmity." When his mind has become malleable and wieldly with respect to that, he can then delimit two dwellings. Next he can successfully delimit two, three, four, five, six, seven, eight, nine, ten, one street, half the village, the whole village, the district, the kingdom, one direction and so on up to one world-sphere, or even beyond that. [IX.103]

Buddhaghosa goes on to say that compassion and the other abidings also are to be thus universalized.

So also, a point of some consequence for our later discussion, he connects this directly with specific achievement states in the formalized meditational progression. He tells us that these attitudes (abidings) cannot be fully universalized except in one who has attained at least the first jhāna (IX.44). Thus again it is assumed that technical proficiency in the meditative techniques, and moral development, are mutually creative and supportive.

Further, Nibbāna, as the primary goal of meditation, is basically defined as the absence of greed, hatred, and delusion—whether in this life or in final afterdeath Nibbāna. Thus the meditative process can legitimately be understood as fundamentally directed toward the moral perfection of the meditator. Only those who have achieved the meditative heights of perfect detachment and clarity of view can be said to embody the full inwardness of morality in their every thought, word, and deed, that is, to be perfected saints perfectly fulfilling the moral precepts. Here, for example, the "avoidance of killing" has become internalized in the saint as absolute nonenmity of action. The saint continues to live in the ordinary world and interact with other beings but is perhaps more restricted and withdrawn.[16] It must be added that in the Buddhist view, space-time individuality—except for enlightened last-existence saints and Buddhas—is possible only if some degree of greed-hatred-delusion still remains. They are the driving hub of the Wheel of Life (see note 7). To destroy them completely is to end existence or to go out of it into Nibbāna.

The Role of the Teacher

The yogic seated posture and general modes of concentration of attention are the rule in Buddhist meditation, and so is the teacher. The so-called *pacceka* ("silent," "private," or "small") Buddha seems to be the only teacherless attainer of Nibbāna recognized in Theravāda Buddhism. What this figure represents, appearing more as a classificatory type than as an actually existing individual, is difficult to determine. The primitive, and to some extent ideal, Buddhist archetype of the meditator is the solitary forest dweller. Was the pacceka Buddha the absolutized stereotype of this ideal when it began to disappear and the vast majority of meditators became monks in the community of monks? Or is it purely an intellectualized category to explain how one may attain enlightenment even in Buddhaless world epochs? In any case, this private Buddha is defined as one who needs no teacher, possibly not even the Buddha of his own world epoch, to reach enlightenment; but he is limited (as contrasted to the universal Buddhas) by being unable to teach the enlightening Dhamma. As "silent" he is a nonteacher.

For all the rest, including those who finally become arahants or enlightened meditators, a teacher is taken for granted. Of course, each teacher in turn has had a teacher all the way back to the original disciples. This represents an oral tradition, so to speak, that must be assumed in the Theravāda tradition, even though theoretically it is not made as much of as in the "secret transmission" from master to disciple of Tibetan and Zen Buddhism. Yet the distinction between knowledge of the scriptures, or what might be called "knowledge about" meditation and enlightenment, and that "knowledge of" which comes only through actual practice of meditation (under a teacher) must be taken for granted as standard in Theravāda throughout its history, even though the actual vitality of the meditative practice undoubtedly waxed and waned considerably during the centuries.

The guru-like teacher, called a "good friend" in Buddhism, is presumed to be able to lead the pupil successfully only as far as he himself has gone in the attainment of the higher states of realization. Hence the Buddha was —and is, through his words—the incomparably best teacher. But the Buddha is long since gone from saṃsāra, and those who know from their own personal realization *something* of the enlightenment experience he achieved, of which he speaks in the scriptures, must now lead others. In this sense the arahant would be the best teacher, though teaching is not his basic responsibility. But one must be satisfied with those available who have attained something more than oneself. And there is the conceivable, though unlikely, possibility that the seeking meditator who gets started on the right road might go beyond his teacher, since the Buddha has set forth the way in his teachings and since the real "work" must be done by the meditator himself, be there teacher or not. Buddhaghosa put the matter thus:

> So if someone with cankers destroyed is available, that is good. If not, then one should take it from a non-returner, a once-returner, a stream

enterer, an ordinary man who has obtained jhāna, one who knows three Pitakas ... two Pitakas ... one Pitaka, in descending order [according as available]. [III.64]

More practically speaking, the instructor in meditation is presumed to be in frequent contact with the pupil, frequent enough to know the pupil's progress, make suggestions about next steps, counsel about difficulties, and both encourage and humble as seems necessary. Buddhaghosa tells us of an instance in which a young monk went to a senior elder saying that his meditation on a certain subject (loving-kindness) was not producing results. After inquiry, the elder, apparently acting as teacher in this instance, told him he was directing his loving-kindness meditation wrongly to his dead teacher. Upon turning it toward a living person, he meditated successfully (IX.7).

In addition, the master assigns to the meditator the meditative subject that seems best suited to the disciple's needs and state of development (see Table 1). Further, and not unimportantly, the teacher who takes over a meditator for direction, by the disciple's desire and the teacher's agreement, is presumed to take over responsibility for his progress and assume protection of his pupil against all evil forces that may be aroused by his efforts. And so long as the disciple remains with him he must yield implicit obedience to this teacher alone—though he can usually change teachers if he so desires or if the teacher releases him.[17]

The Subjects of Meditation

Meditation, when considered as intensive concentration of mind, must of course have some subject (or object) of attention, at least in the beginning. And the proper subject, that is, one properly suited to the meditator and properly used, is of utmost importance. In the Theravāda tradition there are forty subjects of meditation (see Table 1), classified according to types of persons—or perhaps also to the stage or mood a person is in at a particular time—and in terms of the levels of meditative achievement to which each subject can lead when properly meditated upon.

The basic function of the meditation subject is obvious: it serves as a focus for the achievement of that one-pointedness of mind that must be developed for progress toward all of the higher states and finally for the achievement of Nibbāna. It is a device for achieving samādhi, in which ordinary attention, which jumps from subject to subject like a monkey in a tree, to use a favorite Buddhist figure of speech, is progressively restricted in its ranging about and brought under control of the one-directional will to attainment. Thus simple physical objects or single aspects of physical objects are good meditation subjects.

The precise choice of a subject makes no real difference; the quality and nature of the meditation are more important. But, as already suggested, some subjects are definitely better suited to certain personality types than

TABLE 1

MEDITATION SUBJECTS

Type of Person (to whom suited)	Subject and Themes	Absorptions (Jhānas) Attainable by Respective Type of Meditation
	I	
Devotional	Buddha, Dhamma, Saṅgha, Sīla, Benevolence, Devas	Neighborhood concentration
Intellectual	Calmness or Peace, Death	Neighborhood concentration
Passionate or sensual	Body Constituents	Neighborhood concentration
	II	
Intellectual	Repulsiveness of Food, Analysis of Four Material Elements	Neighborhood concentration
	III	
Passionate or sensual	Corpse or Cemetery Meditations	First Absorption
	IV	
Angry (choleric or irritable)	Illimitables (Mettā, Karuṇā, Muditā, and Upekkhā)	First Four Absorptions
Dull and unstable	Respiration	
	V	
	Kasinas	
All types	1. Earth, air, fire, water	All Absorptions
All types	2. Hole or gap, and light	All Absorptions
Angry type	3. White, yellow, red, blue	All Absorptions
	VI	
All types after they reach Fifth Absorption level	Formless (arūpa) objects, Infinity of Space, Infinity of Consciousness, Nothingness, Neither Perception nor Nonperception	Four highest (formless) Absorptions

others, and they are also designed to be used flexibly, as Table 1 suggests, to overcome specific, even if temporary, weaknesses or hindrances in the meditator's attitude. Thus the so-called cemetery meditations (on successive stages of the disintegration of the human body after death) are not necessarily useful for all people at all times, but they are especially adapted to destroying passion and sensuality.

There is another limitation as well—the limitation of the subject of meditation itself. A given subject may be used on different levels, that is, as the subject base for successive attainments. Thus, and rather surprisingly, the kasinas (single-colored uniform-textured triangular, square, or circular shapes) can be used to achieve any or all of the jhānas and on the level of the fourth serve as a negative base (to be "surmounted") for the unlimited-space meditation. Similarly, breath is "promoted" from among the *other* body components, which conduce only to the first jhāna, to reach up all the way to the fourth jhāna and then, in the words of Buddhaghosa, the meditator can "by making that same jhāna the basis for comprehension of formations (with insight) . . . reach arahantship" (VIII.155).[18] Yet there *are* specific and absolute limitations in the heights to which given subjects can lead a meditator; these are clearly and specifically set forth at several places in our manuals. (See right-hand column in Table 1.)

How then shall the subjects of meditation be classified or related to the levels of attainment? The order suggested by their attainment potential could be followed, but because of the ambiguities involved in flexibly using the subjects at different levels, this is not wholly satisfactory. *The Path of Purification* itself does not follow this order; in fact, the order in which the subjects are there presented is confusing when viewed in this light. Therefore, the order chosen here will be somewhat arbitrary, based partly on attainment potential and partly on Buddhaghosa's pattern, and constructed for ease of understanding and transition to the discussion of modern meditation practices.

First to be considered will be those preliminary low-level subjects— "thematic recollections"—in which one's mood is set favorably toward the meditative process but that produce no recognized level of higher awareness. Second will be the jhānic progression through the four levels, as recorded in our accounts of the Buddha's own enlightenment, and on up through the four formless meditations to the highest of all, the trance of cessation (nirodha-samāpatti) already referred to. Following Buddhaghosa, this progression will be mainly illustrated by the techniques of the use of the kasina as object. These techniques will be interpreted as essentially the yogic component of Buddhist meditation.

The third section will be concerned with the remaining subjects of meditation that do not seem to be an integral part of the yogic-jhānic order, even though they are rated on that scale and are sometimes developed as jhānic-type subjects. They seem to be the essentially Buddhist subjects, in contradistinction to the yogic-jhānic subject order, and they represent the Buddhist context and adaptation of that order. Their discussion leads inevitably to the fourth section, vipassanā meditation, the Buddhist quintessence of the total meditational discipline.

Preliminary Conditioning

Buddhaghosa begins his great compendium of meditation theory and practice by quoting the following words, which he attributes to the Buddha:

> When a wise man, established well in Virtue,
> Develops Consciousness and Understanding,
> Then as a bhikkhu ardent and sagacious
> He succeeds in disentangling this tangle. [I.1]

And well he might, for these words encapsulate the essence of the path leading to total "purification" that, says the author, "should be understood as nibbāna, which being utterly devoid of all stains, is utterly pure" (I.5). Nibbānic purity, in the Buddhist view, is always in three overlapping and mutually supportive modes or levels: ethical, psychological, and experiential. In the traditional Theravāda formulation they are sīla, samādhi, and paññā, here translated or interpreted as Virtue, Consciousness, and Understanding. The meditator begins with ethical practices; that is, all "higher" states of meditative awareness can be achieved *only* in a meditator who is morally stable and ethically sincere in his efforts to attain these higher states. The final perfection of purity is fully as ethical as psychological and experiential, for it is the arahant (purified one) alone who can keep the moral precepts fully and live the perfect ethical life, as noted above.

The second "stage" involves attaining the skills of the one-pointed concentration of the attention requisite for the final level of insight (understanding) attainment. A considerable part of *The Path of Purification* and *The Path of Freedom* is a descriptive analysis of the enabling techniques, with a view to their successive and successful attainment in practice.

But there is a third, and especially Buddhist, type of effort aimed at seeing everything in the light of the Buddhist view that embodied existence is impermanent, impersonal, and unsatisfactory. The experiential realization of this view, when it is so fully and integrally realized that it becomes the meditator's existential awareness of his own personal being, here and now, is called "understanding." Perfecting this understanding also perfects the enlightening Nibbānic insight. As already observed, even the states of awareness achieved by the samādhic techniques must themselves be experienced as impermanent, impersonal, and unsatisfactory.

Moral Virtues

It would be beside the point here to discuss the Buddhist ethic at length.[19] The meditator who is ethically prepared in attitude and action for meditation is described thus in the canon:

When he has thus become a recluse he lives self-restrained by that restraint that should be binding on a recluse. Uprightness is his delight, and he sees danger in the least of those things he should avoid. He adopts and trains himself in the precepts. He encompasses himself with good deeds in act and word. Pure are his means of livelihood, good is his conduct, guarded the door of his senses. Mindful and self-possessed he is altogether happy.

And the meditator preparing to meditate is described as follows:

Putting away the hankering after the world, he remains with a heart that hankers not, and purifies his mind of lusts. Putting away the corruption of the wish to injure, he remains with a heart free from ill-temper, and purifies his mind of malevolence. Putting away torpor of heart and mind, keeping his ideas alight, mindful and self-possessed, he purifies his mind of weakness and of sloth. Putting away flurry and worry, he remains free from fretfulness, and with heart serene within, he purifies himself of irritability and vexation of spirit. Putting away wavering, he remains as one passed beyond perplexity; and no longer in suspense as to what is good, he purifies his mind of doubt.[20]

The precepts referred to are the basic five: to avoid killing, stealing, lying, sensuality, and intoxicants. They are intrinsic to the monk's way of life outwardly and here become internalized as motive and attitude. This virtue, says Buddhaghosa, serves "as foundation for profitable states," that is, the higher meditational awareness, and is a "consciousness-concomitant" (I.32.17).[21]

And there is a consolation prize for those who do no more than cultivate virtue, or who, having cultivated virtue as a base for meditation, do not achieve the higher levels of meditative awareness: upon death they will be born in the deva-worlds and return finally to the human world in pleasant circumstances.

Ascetic Practices

It may seem surprising, in view of the Buddha's reputed rejection of Brāhmanical asceticism as unprofitable for Nibbāna-questing, to find Buddhaghosa recommending it. However, the "ascetism" found here is mild, and in no real sense a technical method designed to produce certain states of consciousness as were the breath-holding and starvation-diet practices attempted by Gotama in his preenlightenment years. The quality and role of the Buddhist "ascetic practices" in the meditational life are described as follows in *The Path of Purification*:

Now while a meditator is engaged in the pursuit of virtue, he should set about undertaking the ascetic practices in order to perfect those special qualities of fewness of wishes, contentment, etc., by which the virtue of the kind already described is cleansed. For when his virtue is thus washed clean of stains by the waters of such special qualities as fewness of wishes, contentment, effacement, seclusion, dispersal, energy, and modest needs, it will become quite purified; and his vows will succeed as well. And so, when his whole behaviour has been purified by the special quality of blameless virtue and vows and he has become established in the (first) three of the ancient Noble One's Heritages, he may become worthy to attain to the fourth called "delight in development." [II.1]

Buddhaghosa goes on to treat in detail the levels and fine distinctions in the practice of his asceticism. Two examples, however, will be sufficient for our purposes here. About forest-dwelling he notes:

This too has three *grades*. Herein, one who is strict must always meet the dawn in the forest. The medium one is allowed to live in a village for the four months of rains. And the mild one, for the winter months too. [II.54]

There were also grades among those who had taken the more strenuous vow of never lying down again. We read:

The sitter can get up in any one of the three watches of the night and walk up and down; for lying down is the only posture not allowed. ... This has three *grades* too. Herein one who is strict is not allowed a backrest or clothband or binding strap (to prevent falling while asleep). The medium one is allowed any one of these three. The mild one is allowed a backrest, a binding strap, a cushion, "five limb" and a "seven limb." [II.74]

The "limbs" turn out to be four-legged chairs with back, and with back and arms, respectively.

Obviously what we have here is not some new superascetical pattern of life but basically the spare, self-denying monk's life of "fewness of wishes" (and possibilities for their fulfillment) and implied "contentment" therewith. Buddhaghosa apparently views the monastic way of life as the normative context of meditation. But within that general context the "full-time" meditator—for not all monks were such—had a special vocation that might call for particularly supportive practices such as those just mentioned. And *The Path of Purification* leads us to believe that these specialized practices were regularized by prescriptive definition, but that the individual might himself (or his meditation director?) choose whether he wished to be strict, medium, or mild in his practice.

In any case, this "asceticism" was not truly outside the general monastic pattern nor was it indulged in for its own sake, but solely as instrumental to the meditational goals.

Settling In

The place for meditation must be carefully chosen, even in a monastery. With respect to the kasina meditation, to be discussed later, Buddhaghosa describes some eighteen faults that a given location may have for meditational use: "These are largeness, newness, delapidatedness, a nearby road, a pond, (edible) leaves, flowers, fruits, farmhouses, a nearby city, nearby timber trees, nearby arable fields, presence of incompatible persons, nearness to the frontier of a kingdom, unsuitability, lack of good friends" (IV.2). Possible distractions and interruptions for the solitary would-be meditator are the common failings of the first seventeen—including "unsuitability," which means "risk of encountering visible data, etc., of the opposite sex as objects or to haunting by non-human beings" (IV.17). And the last means to be without a master.

Once a proper place has been selected the actual meditation itself must be settled into, both physically and mentally. We are told with reference to the kasina meditation that the meditator should sweep out the place, take a bath, seat himself on a "well-covered chair with legs a span and four fingers high." Then the mind and emotions must be prepared for the dull-difficult discipline ahead by devices that were probably standard ways of beginning all meditation, especially for the novice:

> So after seating himself in the way stated, he should review the dangers in sense desires in the way beginning "Sense desires give little enjoyment ... " and arouse longing for the escape from sense desires, for the renunciation that is the means to the surmounting of all suffering. He should next arouse joy of happiness by recollecting the special qualities of the Buddha, the Dhamma, and the Sangha; then awe by thinking "Now this is the way of renunciation entered upon by all the Buddhas, Pacceka Buddhas and Noble Disciples"; and then eagerness by thinking "In this way I shall surely come to know the taste of the bliss of seclusion." [IV.27][22]

The Lower-Level Meditations

This brings us to the matter of the *subjects* of meditative concentration. As noted previously, some subjects are inappropriate for achieving the higher levels of awareness, particularly the jhānic and formless or immaterial states. Some permit attainment only of what is termed "neighborhood" or "access" concentration.

These two terms indicate that this level of concentration is near to the jhānic type, or, as with an access road, leads on to the higher and deeper states. It is a relatively shallow one-pointed concentration of attention. The surroundings are quiet, even solitary; the meditator quietly sits with eyes closed or only partially opened and has withdrawn attention as far within as possible. Abstracted from sense stimuli and with thoughts concentrated on a chosen theme, the meditator at this level is no doubt unaware of most of what is around him. Though he is in a deep musing or study, the senses are not cut off entirely from external stimuli nor is attention totally devoid of ordinary content. The meditator could be easily interrupted by a sudden noise, light, or even a strong physical sensation. Hence this type of meditation never reaches that deep inner isolation of consciousness, completely cut off from outer stimuli, that takes place in the jhānas, sometimes called "absorptions."

The Eight Thematic Recollections   Of the ten items that yield only access concentration, eight come from the so-called recollections or items to be brought to mind as meditation subjects. They are: Buddha, Dhamma (teaching), Sangha (brotherhood of monks), virtue, benevolence, devas or deities, death, and peace.

We may take the meditation on the Buddha, which *The Path of Purification* develops at length (VII.2–67), as an example of the meditational use of all eight recollections. The Buddha is to be meditated on as one who is fully enlightened, endowed with clear vision and virtuous conduct, sublimely gone to enlightenment, as knower of worlds, incomparable leader of men, teacher of gods and men, and blessed. This traditional Theravāda ascriptive-devotional salutation to the Buddha is now used item by item and in elaborate detail as a meditative theme. One may doubt that the meditator would actually "meditate" on the subject to the doctrinal extent set forth by Buddhaghosa; yet any of the items could be reflectively and lovingly dwelt upon for some minutes. It is not entirely unlike the layman's meditative method set forth by Loyola in *The Spiritual Exercises* though specifically without its visualizations and seemingly without the initial use of a Buddha image, as in some Chinese Pure Land techniques, to induce samādhi.

At the end of his long discussion of the use of this recollection Buddhaghosa sums up its purpose:

> When a bhikkhu is devoted to this recollection of the Buddha, he is respectful and deferential towards the Master. He attains fullness of faith, mindfulness, understanding and merit. He has much happiness and gladness. He conquers fear and dread. He is able to endure pain. He comes to feel as if he were living in the Master's presence.... When he encounters an opportunity for transgression, he has an awareness of conscience and shame as vivid as though he were face to face with the Master. And if he penetrates no higher, he is at least headed for a higher destiny. [VII.67]

Two Analytic-Reductive Meditations   These two are termed "perception of repulsiveness of food" and "definition of the four elements." They are analytic because of a systematic development of the respective themes. And they are reductive because they break down the processes and entities considered into elements that can be seen by the meditator as saṃsāric; that is, as impermanent, impersonal, and painful. The psychological goal is to produce disgust and indifference, thus pointing on to the vipassanā or insight meditations.

To define the four elements we are thus instructed:

So firstly, one of quick understanding who wants to develop this meditation subject should go into solitary retreat. Then he should advert to
his own entire material body and discern the elements in brief in this
way "In this body what is stiffenedness or harshness is the earth element, what is cohesion or fluidity is the water element, what is matur-
ing (or ripening) or heat is the fire element, what is distension or movement is the air element" and he should advert and give attention to it
and review it again and again as "earth element, water element," that
is to say, as mere elements, not a being, and soulless.

As he makes effort in this way it is not long before concentration
arises in him, which is reinforced by understanding that illuminates
classification of the elements. [XI.41]

The elements into which the person resolves himself are, obviously, the
ancient four of earth (hardness), fire (heat), water (liquidity), and air (vola-
tility). Thus a person realizes his "oneness," that is, qualitative bodily same-
ness, with the physical universe.

The "perception of repulsiveness in nutriments" is specifically designed
to induce an emotional disgust toward the process of nourishing the body
that can be analyzed into the four elements. The state of food at various
stages of mastication, digestion, and excretion is described in fulsome and
gruesome detail. A few items will suffice. When eating (with fingers) the
sweat from the eater's hand makes crisp food soggy. Once in his mouth
the food is turned over and over "like a dog's dinner in a dog's trough"
and becomes smeared with mouth-filth and thick spittle. When ready to
swallow it is "as utterly nauseating as dog's vomit." When swallowed the
food descends into "a place like a cesspit unwashed for a hundred years,"
shrouded in darkness, bubbling and oozing like a garbage "pit at the gate
of an outcaste village." What is left over from the body's use comes out as
urine and excrement. And the meditator on this subject should think of his
searching for food as a jackal's going to the burial field, the road as one
of stumps and thorns, and his garments as covering an abcess and skeleton
(XI.1–26). When the meditator meditates on food and eating in this way,
repeatedly, then "the hindrances are suppressed, and his mind is concentrated
in access concentration, . . . his mind retreats, retracts and recoils from craving for flavours. He nourishes himself with nutriment without vanity and
only for the purpose of crossing over suffering, as one who seeks to cross
over the desert [by eating] his own dead child's flesh" (XI.26).

It should be reasonably clear why such meditational subjects can bring
the meditator only to access concentration. One reason is that the meditator
approaches these subjects intellectually. As noted above, they are thought
about rather than being directly experienced. This sometimes inheres in the
nature of the subject, such as Buddha, Dhamma, benevolence, peace, and
so on. Perhaps this is true even of the repulsiveness theme just discussed.
The thought content may be visceralized by its induced emotional contextualizing; but even with this one-pointed thought-feeling and attention given

to the subject, it is still thought-felt about and remains a semiconcept.

Buddhaghosa's comments on the four elements as a meditation subject apply here as well: that subject cannot produce anything more than access concentration, "because it has states with individual essences as its object" (X.41). That is, the object (subject) of higher meditative attainments must be capable of a deindividualization and complete abstraction, or at least move in that direction. The fully thematic-conceptual items *cannot* be so treated; they are multiple concepts. The physical object, a sensation, and perhaps some mental constructs, *can* be so treated by a special nonideational fixation of attention to the total exclusion of all other content, intellectual or emotional, and the progressive refinement (dematerialization) of that content until it achieves its logical perfection in the trance of total cessation of thought and perception (nirodha-samāpatti). This result, of course, is no mere increase of pious feelings; it is a deep trancelike state of mind. And this is the basic quality of the jhānic series of meditational states to which we now turn.

3

The Jhānic and Formless States

The jhānas and formless (immaterial) states have been spoken of several times before incidentally. Here I will recapitulate and develop their meaning, relationship, and attainment in some detail.[1] Jhāna is the Pāli word for the Sanskrit *dhyāna* or meditative concentration, which was later translated into Chinese as *Ch'an* and into Japanese as *Zen*. It therefore refers specifically to those meditative states most radically separated from ordinary consciousness by their deep inward abstraction from outer stimuli.

As noted before, the viewpoint adopted here is that the jhānic series of meditative attainments represents the Indian yogic heritage taken over and adapted by Buddhism. And further, even if, as appears possible, the formless states were added to the original four jhānas in the process of the "reyoganization" of later Buddhism, the process joined like to like. The series is continuous in quality and method through all eight stages even into the ninth stage of cessation of thought and perception, though this last is a special case of combined Buddhist-yogic essences that requires separate treatment. Indeed, "jhānic" as a characterizing adjective applies equally well to the four jhānas *and* to the four immaterial states. "*Jhāna*" *is a mode of meditative concentration not a content*, whereas the immaterial states represent a *content*, that is, a focal subject of meditational attention. Hence "jhānic" as indicating the methodology can appropriately be applied to the total succession of eight stages, though ordinarily it will signify only the traditional first four meditative states.

With this introduction the often repeated formulation of the four jhānic states may be quoted:

> So I, brahman, aloof from the pleasures of the senses, aloof from unskilled states of mind, entered into the first meditation which is accompanied by initial thought and discursive thought, is born of aloofness and is rapturous and joyful. By allaying initial and discursive thought, with the mind subjectively tranquillised and fixed on one point, I entered into and abided in the second meditation which is devoid of initial and discursive thought, is born of concentration, and is rapturous and joyful. By the fading out of rapture, I dwelt with equanimity, attentive and clearly conscious: and I experienced in my person that joy of which the ariyans say: "Joyful lives he who has equanimity and is mindful,"

and I entered into and abided in the third meditation. By getting rid of joy, by getting rid of anguish, by the going down of my former pleasures and sorrows, I entered into the fourth meditation *which has neither anguish nor joy and is entirely purified by equanimity and mindfulness.*[2] [*MLS*, I, pp. 27–28 (I.21–22); italics added]

Another passage, after repeating this formula, speaks of the monk who "passes beyond" perception of material shapes and whose consciousness is characterized by "the going down of perception of sensory reactions, by not attending to perceptions of variety." He thinks "Ether (space) is unending" and so enters the first formless meditation after leaving the fourth jhāna—and so on, up through the successive meditations with infinity of consciousness, no-thingness, and neither-perception-nor-nonperception as their base, on into the cessation of *all* "perception and feeling" [*MLS*, II, p. 17 (I.352)].

The main experiential development embodied in this series of states is reasonably clear: a progressive winding down of emotional fervor and a steady eroding of material, external, and even distinguishable components or contents of consciousness. Thus "initial and sustained thought," that is, overtly conceptual thought, is eliminated at the second jhānic level; then progressively "rapture" and "joy" as the fourth jhāna is attained, and notably "anguish" also. Indeed, the whole former (ordinary) pleasure-sorrow gamut of feeling is destroyed. The fourth jhāna involves only consciousness "purified by equanimity and mindfulness." And obviously there can be no reintroduction of these eliminated emotional elements in the increasingly rarefied climate of the formless states. The "bliss" of cessation of perception and feeling will be examined later.

The subtilizing of the subject of meditation will be clarified in the following discussion of the kasina method of attaining the jhānic and formless states. Here it may be noted that these states can be developed by a variety of meditational subjects. They are essentially levels of abstractive consciousness into which the mind may be projected in several ways; or, they represent a progressively abstractive awareness that may be given to almost any physical entity until its materiality, that is, its specific form and substance-sense, are transcended in consciousness. To do this the mind is trained to "thin out" its awareness of an object of attention until that object seems less and less distinct, solid, and particularized, until it becomes an objective nonentity. And it goes almost without saying that as an object of consciousness fades out, the "self" that is thus conscious also tends to collapse as a separable entity or center of awareness.

In passing, the yogic character of the jhānic progression should be noted again. Patañjali's yogic system was developed long after the appearance of Buddhism. But its pattern of beginning with moralistic elements, progressing on to concentrative exercises, thence to the emptying of sense content in the forms of its "out-thereness," its materiality, its separation from the mental states of the meditator, and finally its apprehension of indistinctness-as-such as the central datum of consciousness, has many similarities to the process now being examined. And given the common yogic heritage, the similarities cannot be accidental. But, embedded in their Buddhist (vipas-sanic) context, the jhānic-yogic states are bound to yield a theoretical and experiential result different from the Hindu Yoga systems.

There is one final preliminary remark: the successive levels of awareness are clearly distinct to the experiencer, no matter how indistinguishable they appear to the outsider. And, being aware of these differences, the meditator can proceed on to the next higher level when he has thoroughly mastered the one below.[3] An attained state can be entered, maintained, and left at will. Thus, either using the same subject of meditation as a springboard into a different apprehension of it, or taking a new subject, as with the form-less meditations, the meditator is said to "allay," "surmount," or "abandon" the former subject, and then to project awareness on to the new level.

The Kasina Method of Jhānic Development

The kasina has already been minimally defined as a color, element, or single-colored uniform-textured shape. That definition can now be expanded. A kasina is primarily an embodiment of physical materiality. As such, it is contemplated in terms of its constituent elements (earth, air, fire, water) and some of their qualities or forms. Earth is best seen as a physical shape (triangular, square, or circular) of such limited size that it can be gazed at steadily as a whole without movement of the head or undue eyestrain. Thus the size might vary from a saucer to a small clearing in the forest. Sometimes the kasina may be conceived of as the *hardness* or *rigidity* in one's body. Air as a kasina may be movement in the tops of sugarcane, trees, ends of the hair, or even as it touches one's skin. Fire as a kasina may be the *heat-light* in a lamp flame, furnace, pottery kiln, or forest fire. The water kasina may be meditated upon as *liquidity* in a bowl or in its natural form in pools, lakes, or the ocean. Natural forms are more likely to be profitable, Buddhaghosa tells us, among those "who have had practice in previous lives" (V.2).[4] The color kasinas frequently arise from the sight of a single color in a flower, piece of cloth, gem, or in the case of white, with silver or tin dishes or even the moon. And finally, any patch of light (over and above the four material elements) such as sunlight or moonlight coming through tree leaves, the roof or the wall of a hut, can be used.

Two comments on the meaning of the word kasina suggest the significance of this meditation. *The Path of Freedom* defines a kasina thus: "Pervasiveness—this is called *kasina*" (p. 72). More technically a kasina is

> perhaps related to Skr. *kṛtsna* "all, complete, whole" . . . the name for
> a purely external device to produce and develop concentration of mind
> and attain the 4 Absorptions (jhānas). . . . While still persevering in the

concentration on the object, one finally will reach a state of mind where all sense-activity is suspended, where there is no more seeing and hearing, no more perception of bodily impression and feeling, i.e., the state of the 1st mental Absorption (jhāna).[5]

Two or three implications are immediately evident: the kasina device is primarily to be attended to or sensed, not thought about, and locks the mind into one narrow mode of awareness like a vise. Correlative to this, there is essentially no content in the kasina-type attention; or perhaps better, only a single-datum or single-flavored impression. Blue is apprehended not as the concept blue in contrast to red, but as a sense datum only; and so on with the rest. If anything is hypnotic in Buddhist meditation, it is in this type of attention. And finally, as indicated by "wholeness" and "pervasiveness," these signs and the awareness state later built on the exclusive and intense concentration of attention upon them, are to be expanded until they become the total field of attention. The "perception" of materiality through the kasinas is progressively subtilized, delimited, and deindividualized, until it leads at last to the fourth jhāna, which is the jumping-off point into the formless states. The subtle but limited kasina then becomes "infinity of space" like the yogic perception of indistinctness. But whether infinity of space does in fact experientially equate with the yogic apprehension of indistinctness as a datum of consciousness is difficult to determine. In the Buddhist process movement is toward *cessation* of perception and feeling; the yogic movement is toward the awareness of indistinctness (Basic Substance) present in everything and toward unity with it. In the end, the two seem to differ.[6]

The kasina meditations, then, with their capacity for locking *out* sense data and conceptual thinking, while at the same time locking *in* the attention on a one-dimensional, universalizable object, and their inevitable upward push toward the increasingly formless dematerialized states of subject-object awareness, are the paradigm of meditational technique in its highest classical Indian form. They are the ancestor of all the later Buddhist mind-killing, concept-destroying devices, even in Zen. And their central importance for the meditative life is confirmed by the accounts of the Buddha's own enlightenment, which portray him as using the jhānic progression and teaching it as the *normal* way for everyone to achieve enlightenment, though, as we shall see, there is a *non*-jhānic method as well.

Buddhaghosa provides a detailed description of the actual use of the kasina for meditational practice and uses the earth kasina as his prime example. A meditator uses a "prepared" instead of "natural" earth kasina, such as a field, by selecting a place in the monastery where he will not be disturbed and sets up the kasina at a "two and a half times elbow to finger-tip" distance or "about the length of a plough-pole or a fathom" (IV.26)[7] from where he will sit in meditative posture. At this distance the meditator will not have to squint (and become drowsy) or open his eyes in a wide, straining position; nor will the slight irregularities in the clay surface be visible, thus avoiding particularizing, discriminative thought possibilities in the object of attention. *The Path of Purification* says that the circular kasina is best in general—perhaps because more easily expanded to infinity? The kasina itself may be of many forms and materials, but Buddhaghosa recommends that

> a portable one should be made by tying rags or leather or matting on to four sticks and smearing thereon a disk of the size already mentioned [saucer to bushel size] using clay picked clean of grass, roots, gravel, and sand, and well-kneaded. At the time of the preliminary work it should be laid on the ground and looked at. [IV.25]

Further work makes it as smooth "as the surface of a drum" and the meditator strives to produce a clay like that "in the stream of the Ganga (Ganges), which is the colour of the dawn," that is, neutral tannish (IV.26, 24).

The meditator's preparatory work of bathing, seating himself before the kasina, and encouraging himself by devout thoughts, has already been described. In an extended commentary Buddhaghosa points out the benefits that result from this preparation. It arouses the following powers and dispositions that in the end will produce enlightenment: energy, happiness, tranquility, concentration, and equanimity. These factors are adjusted to avoid. extremes lest the meditator become like a "too clever bee" that overshoots the flower and returns to it to find the pollen gone, or else like the "not clever enough" bee who also arrives too late, or like the too brash surgical student who hastily slashes with his scalpel clear through the lotus leaf on the water, or the timid person who, fearful, never lays scalpel on leaf at all. With self-knowledge and presumably with the help of the master, the meditator strives for "balanced speed" like the successful bee and "balanced effort" like the good surgical student. Neither too impatient nor too cautious, neither too optimistic nor too discouraged, the meditator "confronts the sign [i.e., the kasina] with balanced effort" (IV.51–73).

The next step is twofold: one gazes at the kasina (here functioning as a maṇḍala) steadily and at the same time repeats the word "earth" over and over again like a mantra until the "sign," "after-image," or "counterpart sign" of the kasina is developed. And what is this counterpart sign? To state it as simply as possible: "When ... it comes into focus as he adverts *with his eyes shut exactly as it does with his eyes open*, then the learning sign is said to have been produced" (IV.30; italics added).[8] That is: *the sign is the willed hallucinative image of the kasina*. It can be produced at will under all circumstances, with the physical kasina present or absent. This does not happen all at once. Buddhaghosa counsels the meditator in this same passage to keep working at it by repeatedly gazing at the physical kasina and repeating "earth, earth," and trying to remember the sight of the kasina when necessarily absent from it, or with eyes shut, as many as a hundred, a thousand, or even more times *"until the learning sign arises."*

Once the sign has actually arisen, the meditator "guards" it, that is, tries to strengthen and confirm it, as though "it were the embryo of a Wheel-turning Monarch" (IV.34). If he can produce it with eyes closed, while still seated in front of the kasina, he may get up and try to carry it with him back to his quarters. But if it vanishes "through some unsuitable encounter, he can put his sandals on, take his walking stick and go back to the place to reapprehend the sign there" seated before the kasina again "and striking at it with thought and applied thought" (IV.30). During this period of time he abstains as much as possible from any distractive activities or light conversation and continually lives with the sign in all that he does, though he is always accessible to monastic duties and the needs of fellow monks.

The goal is complete control of the kasina sign so that it can be produced in visual consciousness at any time, any place, and under all circumstances. "If he wills to see it far, he sees it afar. As regards seeing it near, to the left, to the right, before, behind, within, without, above, below, it is the same. It appears together with mind" (*PF*, p. 78). Obviously this use of the sign is not fully jhānic but preparatory for full jhāna. Even so it has the secondary meditative value of creating increased detachment within everyday activity and pointing on to final vipassanic detachment.

A further perfection is the so-called "extension" of the sign:

> The way to extend it is this: . . . He should first delimit it with his mind (by) successive sizes for the sign, according to . . . one finger, two fingers, three fingers, four fingers, and then extend it by that amount. . . . After that has been done, he can further extend it . . . (to) the verandah, the surrounding space, the monastery, . . . the village, the town, the district, the kingdom, and the ocean, making the extreme limit the world-sphere or beyond it. [IV.127]

Finally, it should be noted again that the extended kasina is progressively purified of gross materiality. In the earlier stages of the learning sign any "imperfections," that is, slight marks or irregularities in the original physical kasina, will be still present in its mental image, which in one sense is only a physically stimulated visual afterimage. But the counterpart sign when properly developed

> appears as if breaking out from the learning sign, and a hundred times, a thousand times, more purified, like a looking-glass disk drawn from its case, like a mother-of-pearl dish well washed, like the moon's disk coming out from behind a cloud, like cranes against a thunder cloud. But it has neither colour nor shape; for if it had, it would be cognizable by the eye, gross, susceptible of comprehension . . . and stamped with the three characteristics [impermanence, emptiness, and suffering]. [IV.31]

By the contemplation of this immaculate and incorporeal kasina the meditator attains the first jhānic level of awareness, rises by successive practice to the fourth jhāna, and thence "takes off" into the formless state meditations. Apparently, the meditator, in progressing through these states, uses the same basic sign-datum just described but advances by the successively greater subtilization of the total subject-object consciousness, particularly by the elimination of "materiality" from the object, that is, the sign. Thus:

> If he enters [the meditation, *jhāna*], often and goes out of it often and acquires facility in the practice of the first meditation, *jhāna*, he can . . . cause the arising of the second meditation, *jhāna*, and surpass the first meditation, *jhāna*. And again he thinks thus: "This first meditation, *jhāna*, is coarse; the second meditation, *jhāna*, is fine." And he sees the tribulations of the first and the merits of the second meditation. [*PF*, p. 100]

The "tribulations" of the first are its still uncomfortable nearness to the five hindrances (sense-desire, ill-will, rigidity and torpor, agitation and anxiety, and uncertainty), even though they have been eliminated in the preparatory stages, and to the muddying activity of the discursive intellect in its tendency to "initial and sustained thought" about things. And by similar perceptions of each lower level attainment as being inferior, the meditator goes up through all the levels, abandoning materiality completely in the fourth jhāna and taking up the "kasinas" of boundless (not kasina-limited) space and consciousness.

The jhānic states call for further description. The range of the translations of jhāna (from "musing" and "meditation" to "absorption" and "trance") suggests the problem. So too do the descriptions that seem on the one hand to suggest something approaching a hypnotic state in depth and yet on the other hand a species of clear, serene consciousness. One of the best summary comments known to me is the following:

> As far as *jhāna* is concerned it is by now amply clear that we are not dealing with an unconscious state. If we are to understand *jhāna* as being a trance state, it must be as a lucid trance. It is equally clear that it possesses the characteristics of trance. The mind does not perceive through the five senses and is incapable of speech from the first jhāna. By the fourth all bodily activities have ceased. The movement of the breath is explicitly mentioned and the heartbeat is doubtless implied. A form of catalepsy of the body is the rule in *jhāna*. Later texts elevate this to the status of a proposition: "The *javana* of absorption controls even posture (*iriyā-patha*)." [9]

Although suggestive, this leaves us with the problem of what a "lucid" trance is—a state without sense input and speech, and a deathlike rigidity of body, and yet some form of consciousness. Perhaps it is a form of that consciousness Easterners insist is without any object. But here it has been induced by concentrated attention on a single object till that object takes over the totality of attention. While agreeing it is not the same as unconsciousness—achieved only at the final end of the series in nirodha-samāpatti —I suggest the following: it is a state in which (as above) attention is locked in on one specific datum to the total exclusion of all others; for practical purposes and with respect to ordinary awareness, the subject is in full trance and operatively unconscious; the lucidity is actually a description of the immediately ensuing moments, when the mind reawakes to the world around it but sees that world in the mood of the just ended "higher" state of consciousness. The calm, undistracted, post-jhānic mind now sees clearly. This is the time of "review."

The post-jhānic review (*paccabekkhaṇa*) is defined as "the recollected mental image obtained in concentration or any inner experience just passed, as for instance any absorption (jhāna), or any super-mundane path, or fruition of the path."[10] Buddhaghosa writes thus about it:

> When he has acquired mastery in these five ways, then on emerging from the now familiar first jhana he can regard the flaws in it in this way: This attainment is threatened by the nearness of the hindrances . . . and its factors are weakened by the grossness of the applied and sustained thought. He can bring the second jhana to mind as quieter and so end his attachment to the first jhana and set about doing what is needed for attaining the second.
>
> When he has emerged from the first jhana, applied and sustained thought appear gross to him as he reviews the jhana factors with mindfulness and full awareness. [IV.137–38][11]

An analogous process takes place with respect to the immaterial (formless) meditational states. Thus the meditator, wishing to progress from the meditational base of boundless space (next above the fourth jhāna), reviews the boundless space attainment thus: "Then he should see the danger in the base consisting of boundless space in this way: 'This attainment has fine-material jhāna as its near enemy, and is not as peaceful as the base consisting of boundless consciousness' " (X.25). Thus the meditator proceeds up the ladder to the succeeding immaterial states, that is, those with bases of boundless consciousness, no-thingness, neither-perception-nor-nonperception, and finally nirodha-samāpatti itself.

The function of this process of post-jhānic review is to facilitate progress toward the next higher stage. On the one hand, the desirability of the progression is emphasized: thus the experience the meditator seeks to transcend is seen as impure, threatening, full of materiality, inferior, and so on. The more overt emotional qualities are progressively diluted so that only equanimity (detachment) remains, especially when the formless meditations are reviewed. On the other hand, the progression is analyzed. The means taken to produce the jhāna, its component factors, and its quality as an experience are all carefully examined in the light and feeling tone of the recent experience, so that the next steps to be taken will be clearer. This review is essential to further progress and its technical analogue is also present in the vipas-sanic progression to be discussed later.

Fringe benefits accompany the jhānic progression. *The Path of Freedom* enumerates the benefits of earth-kasina meditation:

> Twelve are its benefits, namely, the sign is easy of acquisition ... ; at all times and in all actions, mental activity is unimpeded; acquiring supernormal power, a man is able to walk on water just as on earth and to move freely in space; he gains the supernormal power of manifoldness, the knowledge of past lives, the heavenly ear and worldly higher knowledge; he fares well and draws near to the verge of the ambrosial [Nibbāna]. [P. 71]

The other fringe benefit is escape from pain. Not only do overtones of joy and bliss suffuse the body-mind, the joy and bliss also grow finer and less emotional as the meditator progresses, until in the fourth jhāna equanim-ity succeeds them all. Yet at the moment of entry into any *one* of the jhānas itself, the "pain-faculty" ceases "without remainder." The reason is that when one is in jhāna itself, the body is so "showered with bliss," so pervaded by equanimity, that pain simply cannot arise. Indeed in the fourth jhāna the refinement of feeling has become such that even the "neutral feeling," which is considered by Buddhism to be a third alternative to painful and pleasant feelings, does not arise. Here, Buddhaghosa rhapsodizes: "This crescent moon consisting in specific neutrality is utterly pure because it is not outshone by the glare of the opposing states ... and because it has the night of equanimity-as-feeling for its ally." The total content of fourth-jhāna awareness is "equanimity as feeling, and unification of mind" (IV.195).

What is happening here is now reasonably evident. Psychologically, the kasina meditational process has checked the input of all sense data and explicit feeling tones. The attention is locked in on the meditational subject, here the counterpart image, to the total exclusion of all conceptualizing activity. It is totally permeated by the transcendently flawless, nonphysical quality of that image. But that image is deliberately developed into a char-acterless and space-filling "form." It becomes a completely timeless, space-less, identityless (subjectless-objectless) awareness in which, as already noted, "all sense activity is suspended, ... there is no more seeing and hear-ing, no more perception of bodily impression and feeling." Whether it should be called trance or not is scarcely problematic, for there is no communication with others or input from the outside world as long as the state lasts.

And what is the relation of this consciousness to ordinary time-space consciousness, seen as an ongoing series of thoughts and feelings? It tran-scends ordinary consciousness, becoming a timeless and infinite awareness. And for the Buddhist meditator this has two important implications: first, being outside the time-space series during jhānic moments, the meditator does not perform any actions in thought, word, or deed that have kammic potential, either good or bad. And, upon returning to that normal time-space consciousness, the meditative overflow is bound to help produce good kamma. Second, those moments in which the body is showered by bliss or permeated by equanimity are taken to be higher and more blessed states of consciousness. And no doubt the tendency is to seek to make such moments more frequent and longer, thus excluding more of the ordinary states. If the meditator is properly purified of unwholesome states, says Buddhaghosa, "then he remains in the attainment even for a whole day, like a bee that has gone into a completely purified hive, like a king who has gone into a perfectly clean park. . . . So if he wants to remain long in the jhāna, he must enter it after (first) purifying his mind from obstructive states" (IV.125, 126).[12]

Formless-State Meditation Bases (Abstractive-Absolute Subjects)

As previously observed, the jhānic series leads naturally, even inevitably, into the formless or immaterial-base meditations, supporting the view that they are both yogic and here are incorporated by Buddhism into its own meditative structure. And as a "continuation" of the jhānic series the dynamics of this higher series of attainments are apparent on the surface: they constitute a thrust toward an ever more absolutized immateriality and complete abstraction from all space-time awareness. This process proceeds upward from the fourth jhāna, using whatever subject base has been used to achieve that level of attainment.

In passing, it should be observed that the fourth jhāna must be reached before the immaterial states can be achieved. This seems necessary because only at that level is the meditator capable of a perfectly equanimous state of awareness. The previous three states still involve emotion; but the general mood of the immaterial-state meditations is "peaceful," that is, without emotion, negative or positive. Only in this frame of mind can the meditator successfully "give his attention to it [the meditational subject of boundless space, boundless consciousness, etc.] and strike at it with thought and applied thought" (X.40).[13]

But there is a further complication concerning the relation of jhānas to the formless meditations that supposedly follow them. Theoretically, equanimity, breathing, and even the formless or immaterial states themselves are said to be *possible* bases for developing any of the jhānas (III.107). It may seem surprising that the "higher" immaterial states can be used as a basis for achieving the "lower" fourth jhāna. Thus the relation of jhānas to immaterial states is not simply and only that of progression *from* jhānas *to* formless states. It may be that this progression is only for the purpose of achieving nirodha-samāpatti; at any rate it is not essential for gaining enlightenment. Thus in the attainment of the fourth jhāna, which represents the full height of jhānic (yogic) attainments necessary for the Buddha's (and monk's) gaining of enlightenment, though *structurally* higher the formless states are *functionally* lower. That is, they may be attained without and apart from enlightenment, which comes only through insight (vipassanā), and they may be used as bases for jhānas. As we shall see later in detail, an immaterial state may also be a subject for the exercise of enlightening insight.

The jhānic (samādhic) adept would have no trouble using an immaterial (formless) state as a meditation base for attaining a jhāna, since he can use any and all states flexibly, easily going from one to the other in any desired order and skipping up and down the series at will. However, when Buddhaghosa discusses the attainment of the jhānas (IV), he mentions only the kasinas as a means of achieving the jhānas. Perhaps this was the more usual practice, at least for the beginner; and perhaps in the traditional mode of practice (and thinking) the formless states were considered higher than the jhānas in most contexts.

One reason for this is surely the nature of the kasina base. Having shape and color, the kasina is the visible and tangible presence of materiality to the human consciousness. And since the basic meditational movement here is away from materiality, the transcending of that which embodies it as meditation sign is the best possible springboard into the formless. Consequently, apprehension of the kasina at the fourth jhānic level is the only stage from which further progress toward complete formlessness can be made; at that stage the gross material object has been subtilized into a fine material object, that is, the kasina counterpart sign has been developed away from its flawed particularized basis into a transcendental luminous sublimation of itself.

But, says Buddhaghosa, "although he has already surmounted gross physical matter by means of the fourth jhāna of the fine-material sphere, nevertheless he still wants to surmount the kasina materiality *since it is the counterpart of the former*" (X.2; italics added). Thus is materiality, in consonance with both the yogic and Buddhist traditions, even in its most sublimated ghostly fourth jhāna form, viewed as contaminating and limiting. And how does one accomplish its full transcendence?

> So when he has become disgusted with (dispassionate toward) the kasina materiality, the object of the fourth jhāna, and wants to get away from it, he achieves mastery in the five ways. Then on emerging from the now familiar fourth jhāna of the fine-material sphere, he sees the danger in that jhāna in this way "This makes its object the material with which I have become disgusted," and "It has joy as its near enemy," and "It is grosser than the Peaceful Liberations." . . . When he has seen the danger . . . in this way and has ended his attachment to it, he gives his attention to the Base Consisting of the Boundless

Space as peaceful. [X.5; "Near enemy" refers to that limitation of the next lower level of awareness into which it would be easy for the unskillful to fall back.]

What follows here by way of procedure is to "spread out the kasina to the limit of the world-sphere, or as far as he likes." The meditator then "removes" the kasina (functioning as materiality) by attending to the surrounding space touched by it, regarding that as "space" or "boundless space." Repeating, mantralike, "space, space" the meditator now gives "non-attention" to the beginning, or limited, kasina and is liberated into boundless space. That is, the meditator "removes" the materiality of the kasina as a physically perceptible form, and considers the place where it *was* located in his awareness as space that is indistinguishable from the rest of the undifferentiated boundless space that surrounds it. Having removed the "materiality" of the kasina-occupied space, he now uses *that* empty space as his sign and develops the infinity-of-space consciousness. The apparent result is to apprehend all forms and their material base as empty space—apprehend them as being unreal in their particularity and difference from each other. "He is like a man who plugged an opening . . . with a piece of blue rag . . . and is looking at that, and then when the rag is removed by the force of the wind or by some other agency, he finds himself looking at space" (X.9–11).[14]

The ensuing development of the other three immaterial states is similar to the attainment of the one based on boundless space. Thus the next of the immaterial states is produced by concentration on the base of boundless (infinite) consciousness and is achieved as follows: after thorough mastery of the infinite space attainment, the meditator views the attainment as "not as peaceful as the base consisting of boundless consciousness," that is, the next higher one. His attention is now turned to the next higher state, saying "consciousness, consciousness" over and over and thinking concentratedly "with applied and sustained thought," "boundless consciousness, boundless consciousness." That is, consciousness is "perceived" as no longer being limited to the meditator's own body and its narrow visual range; it pervades the boundless space of the meditation just perfected. Since there are no "objects" in that boundless space to impede consciousness, to anchor it in any one place, this transition is both natural and relatively easy. Focusing his attention thus, "his mind becomes concentrated in access," and then after fixing the "sign" (not described) his "consciousness arises in absorption with the (past) consciousness that pervaded the [boundless] space" (X.25, 26). That is, he produces a jhāna-quality trance state based on boundless consciousness.

After this state is mastered in its turn, he proceeds thus: "Without giving (further) attention to that consciousness, he should now (advert) again and again in this way 'There is not, there is not' or 'Void, void' or 'Secluded, secluded,' and give his attention to it, review it, and strike at it with thought and applied thought" (X.33). "That consciousness" is the "boundless consciousness" just completed. The result is that "no-thingness" arises in consciousness and becomes the subject of meditation. Presumably this has its counterpart sign, though it is not described except to note that one can find occasions for the practice of it everywhere, such as seeing an assembly place empty of occupants. It is clear from this, and other instances, that during the long-term seeking to master a new state, its theme is pursued even when one cannot be in full meditation. That is, even between meditation and actual trance periods the meditator thinks about the meditational base at every possible opportunity and thus saturates both conscious and subconscious awareness with its theme—in this case "no-thingness."

"No-thingness" rather than "nothingness" describes this new awareness. It is diffused and has no objective content or "thing" in it—not even the object of unlimited space or unlimited consciousness. "Void" or sheer negation or "there is not" *any*thing is its appropriate mantra. Materiality, or material existence in its most rarefied form, empty space or ether, and "mind" as boundlessly spread throughout this space, are here completely denied.

In the next stage the base of having "no-thing" as its object is surmounted by the recollection that "perception is a disease . . . a boil . . . a dart" (X.40) and by the reflection that neither-perception-nor-nonperception is far more peaceful. The meditator now practices the sign (nature not specified) of this next attainment and repeats "peaceful, peaceful," reflecting that though no-thingness is peaceful, neither-perception-nor-nonperception is more peaceful. And so the meditator arrives at an attainment understatedly termed to be of "extreme subtlety," in which "the perception . . . is neither perception, since it is incapable of performing the decisive function, nor yet non-perception, since it is present in a subtle state as a residual formation" (X.50).

Obviously what we call consciousness in its ordinary sense, the power to perceive and consciously register a perception, is on the verge of disappearing. Even the rarefied "perception" of voidness is left behind; for in that sense voidness is an object over against a perceiving (cognizing) subject. This infinitesimal degree of subject-object, mind-material dualism is also to be transcended in a state that raises a real question about the existence there of consciousness in any form. What remains here *is* awareness in some sense, perhaps; it is in "a subtle state as a residual formation," that is, power, but not as a truly conscious-perceiving activity. Perhaps it is a completely objectless, absolutely minimal awareness. Buddhaghosa says that though he uses the perception terminology, it could also be said that there is neither feeling nor nonfeeling, nor "consciousness," "contact" nor any other of the components of ordinary consciousness.

This faint, but not quite blank residuum of perception itself, in which it is uncertain whether there is even awareness, let alone any discernible object, a semiconscious state at most, is all that is left to the meditator in this trance. But when we have come thus far along the meditational trance road the inevitable logical question, and perhaps the dynamic psychological one as well, poses itself: is there not a state still beyond neither-perception-nor-nonperception, one of *no* perception at all, in which even the ethereal remnants of the subject-object awareness are completely destroyed, and the subject-object distinction and experience dissolve into each other without remainder? There is. And its name is nirodha-samāpatti, or "cessation of perception and feeling." As the capstone of this series of states, it needs specific attention. But this must be deferred until a later chapter, in which we shall consider it as the climactic fulfillment of both the jhānic progression just described and the specifically Buddhist insight-concentration (vipassanā) that is yet to be discussed in detail.

4

The Jhānic-Related "Buddhist" Meditations

Perspectival

In turning from the yogic (jhānic-immaterial-state) chain of meditational progression by means of kasina development to more specifically Buddhist meditation subjects, we are in one sense going back down the scale of attainment. Buddhaghosa explicitly informs us that "the base consisting of boundless space has to be reached by surmounting one or other of the first nine kasinas, and the base consisting of boundless consciousness, etc., have respectively to be reached by surmounting space, and so on" (III.108).[1] But none of the subjects noted *here* leads any higher than to the fourth jhāna. Thus breathing, equanimity, and even the four immaterial states themselves, when used as lower-level meditation subjects, have only jhāna potential. Equanimity as object can be developed to the fourth jhānic level, but the other three divine abidings, namely compassion, loving-kindness, and altruistic joy, attain only to the first three jhānas; and body-part and body-foulness subjects take one no higher than the first jhāna. Yet, as has been observed previously, on the real scale of values—the Buddhist-Nibbānic, as contrasted to the jhānic-trance scale—they are actually higher.

In any case, before dealing with these "Buddhist" subjects of meditation, their relation to the jhānic-formless-state progression needs to be noticed. First, it may be observed again that even if these subjects carry one no further than the fourth jhāna, this is the level on which the Buddha passed into Nibbāna, and it is often spoken of in the scriptures as the typical level at which arahants achieved enlightenment. The higher immaterial states are therefore not *salvationally* necessary. Second, and corollary to this: there is a qualitative difference in the two areas. The jhānic initiated series of states is called the "abidings that are peaceful" [*MLS*, I, p. 35 (I.41)]; and the progressively attenuated objective content and subjective awareness, climaxing in total cessation of perception and feeling, certainly conforms to this description. But a substantial part of the content and flavor of the Buddhist subjects of meditation is not "peaceful"; it is a deliberate and intensive direction of the attention to the insubstantial and impersonal, as well as repulsive, aspects of being human. Such is the thrust of the body-part and body-foulness subjects, and to a lesser extent the breath meditation. These themes are obviously dictated by the Buddhist world view.

Third, however, the jhānic techniques of concentration can be used even with these "Buddhistic" subjects as meditation bases. Or to reverse the statement: these subjects are capable of jhānic-state production. Thus in the full Buddhist structure, the yogic-jhānic techniques and the more specifically Buddhist subjects are integrated in some way, even though there *is* a distinction in terms of history and import. For though there are precisely defined and unavoidable technical sequences, such as that between the kasinas and the formless states or between the formless states themselves, there is also the possibility of using the same concentration subject at different levels and in different ways. This is particularly true of the subjects we are about to consider that are capable of: a general low-level thematic use; use as objects to be developed in a semi-kasina manner; and use in a personal, existential and Buddhist-contextual manner to be noted later.

The order of consideration will be the following: (1) the four divine-abidings, or illimitables, which seem to be "peaceful" in essence like the jhānic abidings and are sometimes placed between the fourth jhāna and the formless states, though obviously they cannot function organically as concentration subjects in that position; and (2) the body-self concentration subjects, which lead on to vipassanā-type meditation.

The Divine-Abiding Meditations (Attitudinal-Dispositional)

The four divine abidings, or boundless states, are: loving-kindness (*mettā*), compassion (*karuṇā*), altruistic joy, or joy in the joy of others (*muditā*), and equanimity (*upekkhā*). Buddhaghosa says they are named "divine abidings," because they are "best" and "immaculate," that is, immaterial, like the gods of the formless, immaterial Brahma-realms of existence (*Brahma-lokas*)—the most etherealized levels of existence. Thus "meditators who associate themselves with these abidings, abide on an equal footing with the *Brahma* Gods." The sense of "boundlessness" no doubt is derived from this same base of the near-infinity of the gods in terms of time and space, as well as indicating the possibility of achieving the goal of complete universalization by extension of these attitudes to all beings in all universes. They are "the best in being the right attitude toward beings" (IX.105, 106).

These divine abidings obviously embody the higher reaches of Buddhist ethical values and at first glance may seem to be at variance with both the "world-denying" spirit of anicca-dukkha-anattā Theravāda Buddhism and the world-recessive jhāna techniques. These attitudes and motivations are urged upon Buddhist laity as proper and right. Certainly loving-kindness is better than hate, compassion than indifference, altruistic joy than selfishness, and equanimity than feverish anxiety, on any scale of moral values. So, practically and ethically, these abidings are an organic unity of disposition, with equanimity representing the maturity and balance of all of them in action. These abidings may be used as meditation subjects in the hope of relating the results to ongoing lay life.[2] But this is not all. Equanimity as the highest of the four abidings suggests the same progression found among the jhānas—a movement toward detachment and neutrality, toward cooling the emotional temperature of involvement with others. The movement here is from loving-kindness, compassion, joy in the joy of others to the calm cool of equanimity.

And when the abidings are specifically placed, as they are here, in the jhānic order of development, then this formal hierarchy becomes actually functional. Equanimity is "the outcome of the first three divine abidings" and can be likened to the gable rafters built upon the "scaffolding and framework of beams" of the other three (*PP*, IX.104). *The Path of Freedom* further states that the first three abidings cannot serve as a meditational base for the fourth jhāna attainment because "through constant dwelling on the sorrows (of others) one develops loving-kindness, compassion, and appreciative joy. (And so no equanimity is present.) Therefore the third meditation, *jhāna*, is attained and not the fourth" (p. 194). Or, as Buddhaghosa puts it, the meditator must perceive the "danger" in the three lower abidings, because "they are linked with attention given to beings' enjoyment and in the way 'May all beings be happy,' because resentment and approval are near [potentially active in the meditator's mind], and because their association with joy is gross. And the meditator should also see the advantage of equanimity because it is peaceful" (IX.88). And finally Buddhaghosa explicitly states of the abidings that each in turn in the exact order specified supports one of the formless states (IX.119, 120). Thus, whether in their internal order, when used technically as bases of concentration, or when contextually supportive of the higher states, the divine abidings are congenial to the Buddhist thrust toward rarefied states of consciousness and detachment.

Each abiding has its "near" and "far" enemy, that is, the state of mind or disposition that *seems* to be like it (near enemy) and its opposite (far enemy). Thus, in order, greed is the near enemy of loving-kindness and ill will its far enemy. Compassion has grief (privation of desired things) as near and cruelty as far enemy. Joy (in obtaining desired things) and aversion (boredom) are the near and far enemies of joy in the joy of others. And finally the false "equanimity of unknowing" (ignorant indifference) is the near enemy, and greed and resentment the far enemies of the true equanimity (IX.98–101). Both sets of attitudes are to be distinguished and avoided as dangerous in establishing the desired dispositions as meditation subjects.

Their complicated relationship to their own respective jhānic developments will now be examined. What is the relationship between the general order and mode of developing an abiding as jhānic *object*, in the kasina way, to jhānic-type realizations? Loving-kindness is used by Buddhaghosa as an example of this type of development, as the earth kasina was for the kasina development. Its basic purpose is to equalize all emotional attitudes toward others. Four classes of persons are recognized in this connection: oneself, dear ones, neutral persons, and the enemy. There is a proper order for meditation here. One begins with oneself, thinking and feeling "May I be happy and free from suffering" or "May I keep myself free from enmity, affliction and anxiety and live happily." Beginning with this natural, human desire as motive force, the meditator can then most readily desire the same thing for other beings (IX.8–10). Next this attitude is extended to a respected person such as a teacher, then to a dearly beloved one, then to a neutral person "as a dearly loved friend," and last "towards a hostile person as neutral." The reasons for this are apparent: it would be impossible to begin with a hostile person, because anger would immediately spring up. And for the opposite reason one would not begin with a beloved person: for a layman who had sought to develop loving-kindness by beginning with his wife "was fighting against the wall all night," that is, the wall by which he had separated himself from her. Loving kindness had turned into sexual desire (IX.12, 6). Although these four types are the main categories, some subclasses are mentioned such as the "respected person" in the case of loving-kindness, the "wretched" person for developing compassion (IX.78), and a "boon companion" in the case of gladness (joy in the joy of others) (IX.85). For arousing equanimity the neutral person is used. It is obvious that these are naturals for the first exercise of the desired attitude. A neutral person would range from a mere acquaintance, through seen and known persons, to all the multitudes of beings the meditator does not know.

The continuing process is described as the "breaking down of barriers" of distinctions between these classes of persons differently related to oneself, interpreted by Buddhists as a positive universalizing of the desirable ethical attitudes. All attitudinal differentiation toward others is to be neutralized. But to begin with, the equal participation of self, friend, neutral person, and enemy (in order) in the meditator's loving-kindness is sought. Many devices are legitimate as means to this end. For example, Buddhaghosa prescribes that the meditator eliminate resentment "by entering repeatedly into loving-kindness (jhāna)" toward an enemy and then, "after he has emerged each time, directing loving-kindness toward that person" (IX.14). As a means of profitably directing the abidings' attitudes toward other persons, any psychological device is allowable. The hostile person in all cases presents the greatest problem; and there are a dozen or so ways for overcoming hostility, such as the following: admonishing oneself by the example of the Buddha, observing the disliked person's admirable traits as well as one's own unadmirable ones, the harm done to oneself in harming another, possible good deeds done by the "enemy" to the meditator in former lives, resolving him (mentally) into a collection of body elements and hence seeing that he is no fit object of hatred, and so on. Obviously this is not done during the jhānic state itself, but before and after.

Thus does the meditator break down the barriers "by practising loving-kindness over and over again, accomplishing mental impartiality towards the four [classes of] persons" (IX.40). The process of breaking down barriers differs slightly from this in the case of the other divine abidings. Compassion begins with the unfortunate person, then proceeds to the dear one as though the dear one were unfortunate, to the neutral one as though dear, and to the hostile as though neutral (IX.81). With gladness, the progression is from boon companion, to dear, to neutral, to hostile persons in the above manner (IX.86). But in the case of equanimity the order is: neutral person, dear person, boon companion, hostile person, and finally oneself (IX.89).

The optimum result of this cultivation is described thus:

> Suppose this person is sitting in a place with a dear, a neutral, and a hostile person, himself being the fourth; then bandits come to him and say "Venerable sir, give us a bhikkhu," and on being asked why, they answer "So that we may kill him and use the blood of his throat as an offering," then if that bhikkhu thinks "Let them take this one, or this one," he has not broken down the barriers. And also if he thinks "Let them take me but not these three," he has not broken down the barriers either.
>
> Why? Because he seeks the harm of him whom he wishes to be taken and seeks the welfare of the others only. But it is when he does not see a single one among the four people to be given to the bandits and directs his mind impartially . . . that he has broken down the barriers. [IX.41]

The example for the specific process by which the abidings base is used will be taken from the use of compassion as a base rather than loving-kindness, because the manuals are more specific about it. In general, the method is the same for each of the four abidings. *The Path of Freedom* instructs us thus:

> What is the procedure? The new yogin enters into a place of solitude and sits down with mind collected and undisturbed. If he sees or hears of a person stricken with disease, or a person affected by decay, or a person who is full of greed, he considers thus: "That person is stricken with suffering. How will he escape suffering? . . ." That yogin by these means and through these activities develops the thought of compassion for these persons and repeats it. Having by these means and through these activities developed the thought of compassion and repeated it, he makes the mind pliant, and capable of bearing the object. Thereafter he gradually develops (compassion) for an indifferent person and an enemy. [P. 191]

The Path of Purification provides a more vivid instance:

> Therefore first of all, on seeing a wretched man, unlucky, unfortunate, in every way a fit object for compassion, unsightly, reduced to utter misery, with hands and feet cut off, sitting in the shelter for the helpless with a pot placed before him, with a mass of maggots oozing from his arms and legs, and moaning, compassion should be felt for him in this way: This being has indeed been reduced to misery; if only he could be freed from this suffering. [IX.78]

Then with this freshly seen instance, fit for compassion, provided with emotional drive, the meditator turns compassion to a dear one, a neutral person, and an enemy. We must suppose here in the beginning, and perhaps on the access-concentration level only, that specific persons are visualized toward whom one directs this compassion, loving-kindness, or joy.[3]

But when the method of development of the abidings is carried forward to the jhānic level further difficulties arise. The meditator, sitting properly, concentrates on the visualization of some person to whom he wishes to extend a divine-abiding attitude. In loving-kindness, beginning with himself, the meditator repeats in mantric fashion a phrase such as "May I be happy," or "May that person (or the residents of that house) be happy" (IX.8). Next, extending this to a respected person, such as a teacher, "of course, he attains absorption," that is, a jhānic level of concentration with loving-kindness as base (IX.11). And in every case a specific person must be in mind. For "If he loses the object, he cannot arouse loving-kindness" (*PF*, p. 187).[4]

But one difficulty is never clearly explained in the manuals: how does the *personal* object of any of the four abidings serve as a base for developing the jhānic counterpart sign? (That this *is* the case is certainly implied in the above "of course, he attains absorption.") A clear visual fixing of the appearance of the suffering respected, dear, or hostile person can be imagined and developed until it can be visually reproduced at will. But how would this be developed in the kasina manner? Would it be "purified" as with a kasina, that is, abstracted from all particularities, individuality, and be "dematerialized" into a shining, glowing counterpart sign? If this is the case, and the logic of jhāna developments suggests that it must be, a formless depersonalized "someone" to be compassionated in general would emerge as the meditational subject. In any case, the formula for producing the sign is as follows:

> Thus the sign and access are obtained by this bhikkhu simultaneously with the *breaking down of the barriers*. But when breaking down the barriers has been effected, he reaches absorption in the way described under the earth kasina without trouble by cultivating, developing, and repeatedly practising the same sign. [IX.43; italics added]

We are not thus helped toward an understanding of precisely what sign is being developed, but there is here a key phrase which, taken in conjunction with another reference to it, may clarify the general process. It is "breaking down the barriers." These barriers are the distinctions our attitudes make between people in classifying them as dear, neutral, hostile. According to the other passage it is the neutral person as object who breaks down the barriers. Although this is said specifically about equanimity, the highest of the four, and therefore may be more abstracted than the other abidings, the process in all of them is essentially the same:

> Therefore he should arouse equanimity towards the neutral person. . . . *Then through the neutral one* he should break down the barriers in each case between the three people, that is, the dear person, then the boon companion, and then the hostile one, and lastly himself. And he should cultivate that sign, develop and repeatedly practise it.

As he does so the fourth jhana arises in him in the way described under the earth kasina. [IX.89, 90; italics added]

Or perhaps it could be said thus: once the barriers are broken down the whole gamut of persons can be regarded as the same. No one, including oneself, has any claim for special regard or a distinguishing emotional attitude. And how is this barrier breaking actually accomplished? Perhaps either at access or jhāna level.

> Just as a skilled ploughman first delimits an area and then does his ploughing, so first a single dwelling should be delimited and loving-kindness developed in the way beginning "In this dwelling may all beings be free from enmity" . . . he can then delimit two dwellings. Next he can delimit three, four, five, six, seven, eight, nine, ten, one street, half the village, the whole village, the district, the kingdom, one direction, and so on up to one world-sphere, or even beyond that, and develop loving-kindness toward the beings in such areas. [X.103][5]

Is this extension merely an emotional one and only at access level? Or is there a visualization of multitudes of beings as the sign? This seems impossible. Is there then a spatial universalization of the initial person visualization, a "person" of cosmic extent? It seems that, kasina-like, there is only a depersonalized space expansion of awareness, with an accompanying feeling tone of "may all beings be happy." This technique is described as follows:

> And here, *may all beings be free from enmity* is one absorption . . . *free from affliction* is one absorption . . . *free from anxiety* is one absorption . . . *may they live happily* is one absorption. Consequently he should do his pervading with loving-kindness *according to whichever of these phrases is clear to him.* [IX.56; last italics added]

Thus it may be that the neutral person counterpart sign or, simply, the "expanding-space" sign, is developed with repetition of "May all beings be free from enmity," and so on, as mantric phrases, just as was "earth, earth" with the kasina jhāna. Whatever the precise nature of this technique may be, the general direction of the development is clear. Obviously it "cools down" and "thins out" feeling for and involvement with specific persons, with its movement from loving-kindness, compassion, and joy as lower-level-jhāna bases up to the equanimity-based fourth jhāna. The lower-level abidings, even *as* jhāna bases, have "danger" in them, because "they are linked with attention given to beings' enjoyment in the way beginning, 'May they be happy,' because resentment and approval are near, and because their association with joy is gross" (IX.88). It is true that there must still be a "personal" concentration object even at the fourth jhānic level. Buddhaghosa specifically says the fourth jhāna cannot be entered by means of a third jhāna produced by the earth kasina "because of the dissimilarity of the object." The fourth jhāna must be entered from a third jhāna produced on a "similar" object base, such as a person regarded with loving-kindness (IX.90).

But with an equanimity-based fourth jhāna, "neutrality toward beings" comes to prevail. The meditator sees the karmic truth that "beings are owners of their deeds," and both "resentment and approval subside." When equanimity "has reached its culmination, it makes beings its object by simply looking on" (IX.96, 123n.). There is more: the process of the progressive "pervasion" of the universe by the abidings. This may be done, as already noted, household by household in any of the eight directions (adding up and down to the horizontal compass directions, perhaps to include all possible worlds) so that his heart, filled with loving-kindness, compassion, or joy, is sent back and forth "in all directions like a horse in a circus ground" (IX.46). Or it may be done in terms of men, women, deities, Noble Ones (Path enterers), not Noble Ones, all human beings, and all those in "states of loss" (less than human level) (IX.50–52).

Despite the personal terms here, the whole is impersonal. All beings in the eastern direction cannot be concretely visualized, nor does the jhānic-kasina development of a countersign suggest it. And this "versatility" of extension is possible *only* to one in a jhānic state (IX.49), that is, one whose attention is turned away from the external world and exclusively locked in on some kasina-like object. We read in *The Path of Freedom* that he "encompasses all beings (with loving-kindness) and identifies himself with them" (p. 185). But again this cannot be person-to-person but rather in a mystical and abstracted loss of sense of separate identity, as though he were an essence somehow penetrative of all worlds.

There is finally an obscure but suggestive process by which the divine abidings as concentration subjects are melded with color kasinas and then made into supports for appropriate formless meditations.

> For beings are unrepulsive to one who abides in loving-kindness. Being familiar with the unrepulsive aspect, when he applies his mind to unrepulsive pure colours such as blue-black, his mind enters into them without difficulty. So loving-kindness is the basic support for the Liberation by the Beautiful . . . but not beyond that. . . . One who abides in compassion has come to know thoroughly the danger in materiality since compassion is aroused in him when he sees the suffering of beings that has as its material sign (cause) beating with sticks and so on. So compassion is the basic support for the sphere of boundless space, but not for what is beyond that. [IX.120]

The Path of Freedom adds a further specification:

> If one develops the mind of loving-kindness, all beings are dear to him. Because they are always dear to him, he causes his mind to consider the blue-green, yellow (or other) colour *kasina*, and attains to fixed meditation, *jhāna*, without difficulty. At this time the yogin accomplishes

the fourth . . . *jhāna* of the element of form. . . . At that time the yogin, depending on loving-kindness which he has developed in the fourth . . . *jhāna* of the element of form, surpasses that (element). [Pp. 195–96]

Apparently the kasina—here only in its color mode—stands for materiality as present in the world of form and is symbolic of the world of embodied (formful) being and beings, which is dangerous to detachment. This is transcended at the fourth jhānic level. Thus by finding color "non-repulsive," in Buddhaghosa's terms, it loses its material impenetrability and one masters and transcends the entire material realm by "entering into it easily" and proceeding on through it to the immateriality of boundless space, of which meditation on compassion is the "support."

The above Buddhaghosa passage goes on to state that altruistic joy is the "basic support" of the meditation on infinite consciousness because joy in others' joy is aroused by one's becoming conscious of *their* joyful consciousness; and equanimity is the "basic support for the base consisting of nothingness," because the meditator has become skilled in apprehending the nonexistence of what the usual consciousness deals with.

The Path of Freedom provides no real technical help here but does provide some illuminating alternative phrasings: the practice of the loving-kindness meditation enables a person to know "the tribulations of the element of form," because it involves seeing "the sufferings of beings" who have form. Hence the mind considers "the abandoning of forms" and passes on to formlessness, that is, infinity of space. By appreciative joy the person attains to "the un-attached sphere of the infinity of consciousness" and by equanimity "fulfils freedom from attachment" and, passing on to the sphere of no-thing as meditation base, "cannot be attached either to consciousness or infinity" (pp. 196–97). The *how* of this occurrence seems to be as follows: a meditator, having arrived at a third jhāna level by one of the three lesser abidings as a meditation subject, shifts into the equanimity mode to achieve the fourth jhāna. Here, of necessity, a change of object occurs; somehow the loving-kindness as base merges into the color kasina as base, and then the new base as a materiality sign is the vehicle for its own transcendence into the immateriality of boundless space. During this process loving-kindness shifts its function from object to serve as a supporting factor (accompanying feeling-awareness or implicit-concept), providing easy "penetration" by the mind into color materiality; but in so doing, it dematerializes and etherealizes itself. And successively, as described above, joy supports the concentration of infinite consciousness as object, and equanimity reappears as support to the no-thingness concentration.

The *what* of the process seems to be a progressive depersonalization and etherealization of the awareness of the beings toward which the abidings are directed until what remains is only a vague somethingness called "beings in all directions" that can be changed into a color kasina and rarefied into no-thingness. And it is noteworthy also that supernormal psychic powers—

to be discussed later—are portrayed as one of the important results of the abidings-concentration attainments. Thus these seemingly ethical and personal attitudes, in the process of their universalization, have almost totally lost their ethical-personal quality and have become an integral part of the yogic progression toward the attainment of cessation.

Body-Self Meditations

The term "body-self" requires some explanation. In the Buddhist view what is called body, essentially the *rūpa* or form factor, is one of five elements (*khandhas* or "heaps") composing the human being. The other components are feeling, perception, mental factors, and consciousness. Although each of these is a separate "group" or "heap," each is intimately and organically related to all the others in the human individual. The *usual* conception is that they somehow form the "self" or "person"; and experience of selfhood ordinarily includes them all as integral to personal existence. Hence the body-self, both as conceived and experienced, is the embodiment of the illusion of a genuine and stable self, the enslaving illusion from which human beings need saving.

In thinking of "selves" as body-mind unities, people are bound to their kammic destinies by this multiple strand. Or it may be put thus: body-mind (or body-self) *is* the world to which human beings are by nature bound. The experienced world focalizes itself and exists for us in the body-self. Therefore, says the Buddhist, it is in the body-self matrix that all our problems needing ultimate, that is, religious, solutions center, not in any externalized action upon an external world. The key to salvation is within the body-self organism.

Obviously then Buddhist meditation must be psychosomatically oriented. Physical and mental, or body and mind, experiences are modes of time-space "reality" focalized in the sentient being. Organically, physical and mental states overlap and interpenetrate and are almost indistinguishable. In the Buddhist view, body and mind are indissolubly linked in their kammic fortunes. Blessed mental states include, with no sense of spiritual defilement but rather one of fittingness and inevitability, overtones of "bodily" bliss— and the reverse. Without this double blessedness or cursedness, no spiritual state of the sentient being would be considered either blessed or cursed in the full sense.

In the Buddhist meditational tradition body and mind, or body and self, are trained together. As *The Path of Freedom* beautifully states it: "Thus that yogin sometimes controls the body with his mind, and sometimes the mind with his body. Depending on the body, the mind changes; depending on the mind, the body changes" (p. 213). Functionally speaking, the mental aspect of both bondage and release is primary. Quality of mind or awareness is the essence of saṃsāric bondage; and the key to release lies in the transformation of that awareness. And so long as self-awareness is of a fully integral unity of bodily and mental factors, a person is indissolubly bound to the saṃsāric continuance of that self in impermanence and suffering.

The body-self meditations are aimed at breaking up this sense of integral, stable selfhood so completely that no sense of selfhood can attach to any or all of the fragments. And the meditations are constructed to do this both in thought and experience but especially in experience. Thus, one of the concentrations is an exhaustive analysis of the body into its component parts, all of them impersonal and slightly repulsive. Another meditation is on the foulness of the body in its stages of decomposition. So too, as noted previously, the body may be seen as composed of the four elements: earth, air, fire, and water. In another concentration the incoming and outgoing breath is meditated upon, that is, watched detachedly. So also the dynamic aspects of the body, the body-in-action, may be thus dispassionately contemplated. And this last concentration, which begins with the more obvious and concrete (bodily) activities, may be extended and subtilized to include feelings, mind, and mind states.

It is evident that this discipline involves the basic Buddhist world view and that it differs from the yogic world view implied by the jhānic series. This Buddhist view comes into full experiential, existential focus when it is, as here, applied to the jhānas. The meditator realizes in his own body cells and subjective awareness that *all* his states, all of *him*, is but one particular time-space form of impermanence, impersonality, and unsatisfactoriness.

This awareness is achieved in a twofold manner: first, and obviously, by the intrinsic content of the concentration subjects; and second, by their being contextualized up to the saturation point by the contemplation of body-self in all its parts as specifically impermanent, empty, and full of misery. How is this possible while engaged in the single-pointed "nonconceptual" concentration of attention? First, it may be noted that in the preliminary stages, before the jhāna is entered into, the meditator is instructed to *think* in such terms. For example: "So does he, as to the body, continue to consider the body either internally or externally, or both internally and externally. He keeps on considering how the body is something that comes to be, or again he keeps on considering how the body is something that passes away."[6]

Second, even if unable to thus consciously think during the actual jhāna established on a body-self base, the meditator is instructed so to think *after* the jhāna. This will be explained later. And third, though the jhānic absorptions themselves may be *immediately* impervious to such conceptual activity, the constant immersion of the total meditative process in the mood context of impermanence, impersonality, and suffering clearly conditions the jhāna itself existentially. This is suggestively illustrated by a passage from *The Questions of King Milinda*:

"When the reasoning wisdom has effected that which it has to do, then the reasoning ceases to go on. *But that which has been acquired by means of it remains—the knowledge, to wit, of the impermanence of every being, of the suffering inherent in individuality, and of the absence of any soul.*"

"Give me an illustration, reverend Sir, of what you have last said."

"It is as when a man wants, during the night, to send a letter, and after having his clerk called, has a lamp lit, and gets the letter written. Then, when that has been done, he extinguishes the lamp. But though the lamp had been put out the writing would still be there. *Thus does reasoning cease, and knowledge remain.*" [Pt. I, p. 67 (II.2, 3); italics added]

Finally, it is significant that though these concentrations seem to rank relatively low on the formal meditational scale, as noted earlier, they contain the essence of that awareness which, when fully developed, finally releases and enlightens the meditator. They are spoken of highly in the sutras, almost as though no other kind of meditation existed:

> This, monks, is the sole way that leads to purification of beings, to the utter passing beyond sorrow and grief, to the destruction of woe and lamentation, to the winning of the Method, to realizing Nibbāna, to wit: The four stations of mindfulness. What are the four?
>
> Herein a monk dwells, as regards body, contemplating body (as transient) . . . as regards feelings (as transient) . . . as regards mind . . . as regards mind-states, contemplating mind-stages (as transient), ardent, composed and mindful.[7]

With only this text and the explanation of the same process found in the *Middle Length Sayings*,[8] one might well ask if it is a primitive form of Buddhist meditation without jhānic techniques. That would probably be too simple, although an intriguing answer. Or is it simply that the essence of non-jhānic insight, that is, vipassanā, pervades the total meditational structure? But if Buddhaghosa and some other canonical texts are to be believed, even here there is jhānic apparatus. In any case, in this context the body-self concentrations seem to be "amphibious" forms, belonging limitedly to the jhānic series, yet pointing beyond themselves to vipassanā and its promise of enlightenment. The jhānic and formless-state series, *as such and by itself*, is essentially yogic. In this form there is a seeking for each state as a "peaceful abiding" —which is the faint ghost of the achievement of pure immaterial selfhood (as in Sāmkhya-yoga) or of realized identity with an Absolute Self (as in later Vedānta). But when changing, painful, nauseous body states become the basis for jhānic attainments, there is clearly another principle at work. The yogic-jhānic techniques are now permeated by Buddhist values and being used as *Buddhist* salvational techniques. Hence, even though there may be an abstracted abiding in peace in the depths of the jhānic attainment, its basic character is an "*un*peaceful abiding." Or better, it is a learning to live peaceably with and in the full existential awareness of one's own impermanent, impersonal, pain-filled existence.

But to return to our main theme: the Suttas present the body-self concentrations in a certain general order which will be followed here—though it is not adhered to in our manuals. In the "Discourse on the Applications of Mindfulness," Sutta Ten of the *Middle Length Sayings*, the meditations are set forth thus: "contemplating the body in the body," which includes concentration on breath, physical activities, body components, the bodily presence of the four material elements, the decaying states of the body; "contemplating the feelings in the feelings"; "contemplating the mind in the mind"; "contemplating mental objects in mental objects," including the nature of "subjective desires," the five khandhas, the "six internal sense bases," the seven factors of enlightenment, and the Four Noble Truths. And what is the significance of the order? Obviously these contemplations travel from the body factors and activities ever more and more inward into the core of the "self" until the analysis and understanding penetrate to the base of one's awareness and being as an individual person.

Body-Part Meditation

As previously noted the body can be meditated upon as the embodiment of earth, air, fire, and water, or perhaps even as the five khandhas—though this is more an organizing principle for progression from body to feeling and thought. However, here we shall see the body analyzed into its thirty-two components. The canonical list is as follows:

> And again, monks, a monk reflects precisely on this body itself, incased as it is in skin and full of various impurities, from the soles of the feet up and from the crown of the head down, that: "There is connected with this body, hair of the head, hair of the body, nails, teeth, skin, flesh, sinews, bones, marrow, kidneys, heart, liver, membranes, spleen, lungs, intestines, mesentery, stomach, excrement, bile, phlegm, pus, blood, sweat, fat, tears, serum, saliva, mucus, synovic fluid, urine." [*MLS*, III, p. 131 (III.90)][9]

I would like to make two observations. First, like Nagasena's chariot, the body-felt-as-self is analyzed into a bagful of impersonal elements. This body, so beloved and cherished by the human individual, is here to be viewed as nothing more or other than these thirty-two elements. Second, the gruesomeness, the repulsiveness of these elements is implied in the terms used in this listing and is extensively delineated in the meditation manuals' setting-out of this method. Thus Buddhaghosa goes out of his way, it seems, to portray the body, even in its ordinary, undecayed state, as nauseously as possible. For example,

> Head hairs are repulsive in colour as well as in shape, odour, habitat, and location. For on seeing the colour of a head hair in a bowl of inviting rice gruel or cooked rice people are disgusted and say "This has got hairs in it. Take it away." . . . And the *odour* of head hairs, unless dressed with a smearing of oil, scented with flowers, etc., is most offensive. And it is still worse if put in the fire. . . . But just as pot herbs that grow on village sewage in a filthy place are disgusting to civilized people and unusable, so also head hairs are disgusting since they grow on the sewage of pus, blood, urine, dung, bile, phlegm, and the like. [VIII.85, 6][10]

Elsewhere we read that "the flesh of the calves is the shape of cooked rice in a palm-leaf bag"; "The flesh of the breast is the shape of a lump of clay made into a ball and flung down. The flesh of the two upper arms is the shape of a large skinned rat"; the large shin bone "is the shape of a shrivelled snake's back"; "The occiput bone is the shape of a lop-sided coconut with a hole cut in the end," and so on (VIII.97–100).

The mode of the meditational development of body-as-object is much like that of the kasina; any one specific body component may be used as the visual base of the meditation. The actual jhānic-style development of the meditation-sign is usually preceded by and perhaps accompanied with a repetition of the thirty-two elements, forward and backward as one series, forward and backward in four pentads and two sestads, "verbally in this way a hundred times, a thousand times, even a hundred thousand times . . . [so that] the mind is prevented from running here and there, *the parts* become evident, and seem like (the fingers of) a pair of clasped hands, like a row of fence posts" (VIII.56; italics added).[11] This repetition is so important that even "if one is master of the Tipitaka, the *verbal recitation* should still be done at the time of first giving it attention." Two elders practiced this repetition exclusively for four consecutive months, whereupon, says Buddhaghosa, they became Stream Enterers (VIII.49). Of course the verbal recitation is the beginning form, which later "goes inward" and becomes a purely mental recitation when attention thereon has been fully established.

Along with this, to facilitate his concentration, the meditator may pluck a hair or two from his head, put it in his palm (or go to a barbershop), and focus his mind by repeating "black, black" or "white, white." Thus gaining his sign (and we presume, achieving a counterpart sign power over it as with the kasina) he then sets it visually in its proper anatomical place, that is, within the total body, and having done so, he places it mentally in a context of repulsive associations, visualizing and feeling it as "black hair repulsive as to colour, shape, odour, and location" (VIII.83–88).

He may find it useful to take one item all the way through to a first jhāna absorption, and/or as one elder did, achieve successive first jhānas on *each* of the thirty-two components. In one sense it makes no difference, for any part can become the surrogate for the whole body, perhaps even trigger the counterpart sign of the whole body—though this last implies a previous multiple sign practice. In any case, when he has mastered this meditation, human beings and animals "as they go about are divested of their aspect of beings, and appear as just assemblages of parts" to him (VIII.140). All such meditations may be based on and applied to one's own body as well.

This type of meditation is still considered useful in some contemporary Burmese Buddhist circles. The formula is memorized by all novice monks, even short-term monks. The *Catu-bhūmaka-mahā-satipaṭṭhāna* (four-stage application of mindfulness) sect has this as its major mode of meditational practice. A contemporary Burmese author writes:

It is important to note that the meditation of "kayagata-sati" (mindfulness of the constituent parts of the body, i.e., from the head hair to urine) is the most eminent one amongst all other meditations that relate to the "Fourfold Satipaṭṭhāna." The "Suttas" show that the Lord has taught it as the most essential factor in the practice of the Noble Eightfold Path, and made all his followers of both the monks and lay people unexceptionally to learn and practice this meditation.[12]

Meditation On Body-Foulness

There are ten kinds of foulness obvious in a dead body which the monk may use as meditation bases: the body as bloated, livid, festering, cut up, gnawed, scattered, hacked and scattered, bleeding, worm infested, and skeletal.[13] To get such a meditation object he would go to a burial ground, seat himself at suitable distance from a body in one of these conditions, and observe it till the sight was indelibly fixed in his mind's eye.

It is recorded that one meditator found that the cemetery attendant had already thoughtfully arranged a meditation piece for him:

> Kāḷī, woman broad and swart of hue as blackbird,
> Now hath broken off a thigh bone, now another;
> Now hath broken off an arm, and now another;
> Now the skull hath broken off as 'twere a milk bowl,
> Made them ready and is seated.

We are further told how the monk, once arrived, used this array of bones in his meditation:

> He who witless doth not understand, but maketh
> Cause for life renewed, comes back again to sorrow,
> Wherefore he who knows creates no more new causes.
> May I ne'er so lie again with scattered members![14]

Some safeguards were taken. It was not suitable for one to gaze on the corpse of the opposite sex, unless it had become greatly decomposed, for fear lust rather than detachment would arise.[15] One should not go downwind lest his gorge rise, he vomit up his food, and become totally incapable of meditation. (Or if a downwind approach were necessary, he should hold his nose with the corner of his robe.) Sight contact alone was desirable. Still further, the meditator might need to encourage himself by thinking of his errand as that of "a pauper on his way to unearth a hidden treasure" or thinking "surely in this way I shall be liberated from ageing and death." And it was thought wise to inform a senior monk that he had gone to the cemetery, so that after a long absence someone might be sent to look after him.

The mode of using a body-decay state as a meditation subject is essentially like that used with the kasina. The meditator gazes fixedly at the particular corpse he is using as a subject until the counterpart sign arises, which sign he then carries with him, reproducing it at will when he is in the solitude of his own cell. In order to achieve this, the initial corpse sense-datum is expanded or added to as necessary for success in fixing the sign and producing the countersign. He may "delimit," that is, fill in the details of the corpse's appearance by noting the particular position of arms, legs, head, and specific portions of the body. And, in order to maximize the value of the sign, and strengthen his grasp upon it even when interrupted by others and threatened by absence from the scene, he fixes in his mind the route to the cemetery and the immediate surroundings of the corpse, bush by bush, anthill by anthill, and stone by stone. These he always thinks of in terms of their association with foulness. And as with the kasina he repeats, mantralike, appropriate words such as "This rock is the sign of foulness," or of the body with "repulsiveness of the worm-infested."

It is worth noting that even in his private pursuit of meditation a monk could not deny all social obligations. Even though returning to the monastery and trying desperately to hold on to the sign he has developed in the cemetery, he should not keep silence when asked by a layman what day it is, thinking "I have a meditation subject." The question must be answered even if he does not know, and "a legitimate welcome must be responded to" even though he may lose his precious counterpart sign. Nor does his busyness with meditation exempt him from monastery duties of receiving visitors, serving food, cleaning the premises, and so on (*PP*, IV.60). Part of the reason for fixing in his mind's eye the detailed features of the corpse, its location, and the way thereto, is to make the recall of his sign easier when thus distracted.

Presumably the foulness sign as it is developed—though it is not clearly so stated—changes like the kasina and becomes more generalized. We are told that in the case of a scattered body or skeleton, the counterpart sign brings the parts together into a perceptual whole, thus differing slightly from the original visual image. But even though the process begins with a dead body, and its sign becomes generalized by its meditative development, the goal is not to abstract it from life. One begins with a dead body only because therein the decay inherent in every living body is radically manifested. And that concrete beginning datum is generalized and etherealized solely for the purpose of making it flexible enough to apply to living bodies—which otherwise hide this, their true nature, from our awareness. Thus it is that the meditator is given illustrations of modes of applying the developed cemetery sign to other persons.

Buddhaghosa tells of the Elder Mahā-Tissa who, in looking at a woman's teeth one day, suddenly saw her whole body "as a collection of bones," that is, as the skeletal sign. On another occasion a novice meditator, who was also a royal attendant, while watching the king riding on an elephant, saw the king's body under the form of a corpse—in some one of the ten states of decay we presume (I.55, VI.88). The moral is that if the meditator is ardently developing his sign, it may suddenly and effectively blossom out for him, wherever he may be. Thus his daily life surroundings may become supportive of his intensive meditative periods, which in turn affect his perception of the objects and events in ordinary life.

Naturally the final application must be to one's own body. This is the most important result of this meditation. Only when one can and does do this has the discipline achieved its full purpose of existentializing repulsiveness-detachment in the meditator. However, this needs to be done carefully if it is to succeed. *The Path of Freedom* thus instructs:

> When a man wishes to separate from passion, he causes the arising of the perception regarding the nature of his body. Because, if he has the perception of the nature of his body, he can quickly acquire the perception of its disagreeableness and cause the arising of the after-image [counterpart sign]. If the perception of putrescence is increased, the sign which he has grasped in his body will disappear. If he loses the perception of his own body, he will not be able to acquire the thought of disagreeableness easily. Therefore he should not increase—(the putrescence sign). [P. 140]

What this seems to say is that the factor of nauseousness should not be so maximized that it overwhelms detachment and makes it impossible to hold on to the physical datum while etherealizing it into the counterpart sign for further development. But in any event it *must* be brought to bear on the meditator over and over again until it has done its work and become fully existentialized.

Meditations On The Dynamic Body-Self

This is one of the most interesting and far-reaching body-self meditations. There is a transition from passive body concentration, that is, on its parts and inherent decaying impermanence, to the far more difficult concentration on the body as active. It is a case of the actor trying to catch himself in action and seeing even this positive, dynamic aspect of selfhood as also the embodiment of impermanence, impersonality, and dissatisfaction. And even more difficult, and further reaching, the meditative center of attention proceeds ever more inward until the feeler and thinker contemplates his own feeling and thinking processes, catching them on the wing, as it were.

The general picture of the meditator in this type of meditation is that of a person sitting slightly aside from "himself" in all his activities, physical and mental, and coolly, detachedly watching them go on, as though completely outside himself in another person. Sometimes, with respect to breaths, the illustration used is that of a city watchman who counts the carts, cattle, chariots, and people of all sorts going in and out of the city gate. The same observational attitude can be extended to thoughts and emotions as well as breaths. Thus, with the detachment of a watchman, the meditator just

registers the arrival and departure of all self-activities from the grossest
physical motion to the most subtle emotional nuance or half-thought. The
modern Burmese name for it is "bare attention," which Nyanaponika Thera,
in *The Heart of Buddhist Meditation*, defines as follows:

> Bare Attention is a clear and single-minded awareness of what actually
> happens *to* us and *in* us, at the successive moments of perception. It
> is called "bare," because it attends just to the bare facts of a perception
> .... [It is] a bare registering of the facts, without reacting to them by
> deed, speech, or by mental comment ... of judgment or reflection.
> [Pp. 27f.]

In this context the actor is completely bypassed as an entity separable
from his own actions, physical or mental. The awareness is not of the quality
of "*I* am sitting ... breathing ... thinking," but "I am *sitting* ... *breathing*
... *thinking*." Or even better, attention and mental-mantra, that is, accompanying words said or thought, include only "sitting ... breathing ...
thinking." The question of what or who observes must be discussed later;
but here I will deal with the major types of body-self action as meditation
subjects.

Concentration on Breathing (ānāpāna-sati)   The breath-based meditation is
the most important of the body-action meditations. Not only is it highly
rated in the scriptures, but it is clearly Buddhaghosa's favorite among all
the methods. He devotes thirty praise-filled pages (English version) to its
use and development in *The Path of Purification*.[16] In contrast to the foulness
contemplation, whose subject matter is revolting at first glance and becomes
"peaceful and sublime only by penetration," breath meditation is "an
unadulterated blissful abiding" that is peaceful and sublime "in its own
individual essence too, starting with the very first attention given to it."
It leads to "the obtaining of bodily and mental bliss with every moment of
absorption" (VIII.149). He notes again that it is "foremost among the various
meditation subjects of all Buddhas, (some) Pacceka Buddhas and (some)
Buddhas' disciples as a basis for attaining distinction and abiding in bliss
here and now" (VIII.155).

When a monk has attained arahantship by the breath meditation "he can
always define his life term," that is, voluntarily decide how long he will
remain embodied before passing away into Nibbāna (VIII.242). And when
a meditator attains the fourth jhāna thereby (more rapidly than by some
other means) it can readily be made the basis of vipassanā meditation and
the meditator can soon attain arahantship (VIII.155). Yet there are problems:
it is difficult to practice except in complete seclusion; indeed, it is intrinsically
difficult, we are told, beyond other methods: "But this mindfulness of breathing is difficult to develop, a field in which only the minds of Buddhas, pacceka
Buddhas, and Buddhas' sons are at home. It is no trivial matter, nor can it be
cultivated by trivial persons" (VIII.211). It becomes increasingly subtle

with practice. Perhaps Buddhaghosa's overwhelming enthusiasm leads him somewhat inconsistently to praise its difficulty while recommending it strongly for the beginner.

The basic scriptural text for the breath-meditation is found in the "Discourse on the Applications of Mindfulness" (*MLS*, I, Sutta 10) and reads as follows:

> And how, monks, does a monk fare along contemplating the body in the body? Herein, monks, a monk who is forest-gone or gone to the root of a tree or gone to an empty place, sits down cross-legged, holding his back erect, arousing mindfulness in front of him. Mindful he breathes in, mindful he breathes out. Whether he is breathing in a long (breath) he comprehends, "I am breathing in a long (breath)"; or whether he is breathing out a long (breath) he comprehends, "I am breathing out a long (breath)."

The same is repeated with respect to a short breath. In summary:

> He trains himself, thinking: "I shall breathe in experiencing the whole body." He trains himself, thinking: "I shall breathe out experiencing the whole body." He trains himself, thinking: "I shall breathe in tranquillising the activity of the body." He trains himself, thinking: "I shall breathe out tranquillising the activity of the body." [*MLS*, I, pp. 71f. (I.56)][17]

With this as a basis, a considerable number of detailed methodological emphases have been developed, some dependent on the stage of the meditator's skill and others becoming the distinguishing feature of a particular master's special method. Thus there are many ways of counting the breath, and there is breathing without counting. There are varied emphases upon the strength and rhythm of the breathing. Sometimes the out-breath is emphasized more; and sometimes the breath is observed at the nose and sometimes at the navel. But all methods are basically derivative from the preceding text.

In a vivid metaphor Buddhaghosa describes the breath meditation as follows:

> Now suppose a cowherd wanted to tame a wild calf that had been reared on a wild cow's milk, he would take it away from the cow and tie it up apart with a rope to a stout post dug into the ground. . . . So too, when a bhikkhu wants to tame his own mind which has been spoilt by being reared on visible data, etc. . . . he should take it away from physical data . . . and bring it into the forest or to the root of a tree or to an empty place and tie it there to the post of in-breaths and out-breaths with the rope of mindfulness. [VIII.153]

As to the actual practice itself we are told, in a phrase illuminating for all meditative practice, that at first, "he should only breathe in and out and not do anything else at all, and it is only afterward that he should apply himself to the arousing of knowledge" (VIII.173). That is, here, as in all the jhānic-type meditative devices, the mechanics of the process are first mastered, and *then* the further contextualizing of the practice in the Buddhist world view takes place.

To aid the process the beginner breathes strongly and firmly at first in order to hold the attention steady—a strong stake to which to tie the mind-calf. And the post of breathing is further strengthened by counting breaths. But inevitably and desirably the breaths, as a body action, grow less and less gross with the stilling of the body and the growing power of attention, until "they become quiet and still when his body and mind have been discerned. When they are still then the in-breaths and out-breaths occur so subtly *that he has to investigate whether they exist or not*" (VIII.176; italics added).

But before this rarefied state is arrived at a long development is necessary. Eight progressively defined stages of methodology are distinguished.

Stage One: Counting   As an aid to weak mindfulness, the beginner counts in-breaths, out-breaths, or both, at beginning or end, with a minimum of five and a maximum of ten and then begins again. If the place is lost, the beginner starts again with one. More than ten would require a disturbing type of conceptual-remembering attention. This counting of the flowing current of breath stabilizes "just as a boat in a swift current is steadied with the help of a rudder" (*PP*, VIII.193).

The beginning meditator counts several times on each full breath, as it is followed in and out, repeating "one, one, one" and so on in mantric fashion (mentally, not vocally, no doubt) for the full period of exhalation and inhalation. He may begin the counting on either out- or in-breath, whichever is strongest. The meditator may be aware of the long breath as long and the short as short, as well as follow its course into the body and out again. But as skill is gained the counting is reduced to one number per breath and the attention fixed only on the point where the breath touches on nose tip or upper lip as it leaves and enters, with no concern for length or shortness of breath-pulses. At a still later stage, when the meditator has fully mastered the power of attention, it is completely centered just on the touch point with no attention at all given to whether the breath is long or short, coming or going, or even that it is breath.

And the meditator should count "until, *without* counting, mindfulness remains settled on the in-breaths and out-breaths as its object." It is only a device whose goal is to cut off "the external dissipation of applied thoughts" (VIII.191–95; italics added).

Stage Two: Connection   "Connection" is defined as "the uninterrupted following of the in-breaths and the out-breaths with mindfulness after counting has been given up." This adds nothing new. Awareness of continuity of the breathing process is best achieved by firmly and exclusively fixing the attention on the breath entry point, obviating both counting and following the course of the breath from nose to navel and back again.

The analogies used to illustrate the methodological necessity of thus fixing the attention on the breath touching the nostril are suggestive: a lame man swings his child by standing (and pushing) only at the swing's midpoint; a gatekeeper merely counts enterers and exiters but does not examine their baggage or inquire about their business; the sawyer fastens his attention and exerts his energy only at the point where the saw teeth make contact with the log (VIII.199–203). Obviously this type of attention is completely one pointed and eliminates explicit conceptual thinking—though the existential thought-feeling context is importantly present throughout.

Stages Three and Four: Touching and Fixing   These two steps are one process, that of so fully intensifying the one-pointed attention on one sensation (touch) at one point (tip of nostril, or upper lip) that the concentration sign can be gained and the first jhāna attained. Here the increasing shallowness and subtlety of the breath (inevitably with the continuation of breath meditation?) become a problem. Every other meditation subject, says Buddhaghosa, becomes more evident with use; only breath becomes less perceptible (VIII.211). If it becomes totally imperceptible, the meditator must fix it on the place where he last felt it and remind himself that only dead persons have no breath. This place of touch varies with the structure of the nose (VIII.209); therefore each meditator learns by experience where *his* individual point of breath contact is best felt.

When this awareness is stabilized the fixing can take place, that is, the achieving of a counterpart sign. Because of the increasing subtlety of the breath itself, this sign development is obviously most difficult. One might ask how there can be a sign (of the kasina-type) at all with only a single-point touch-awareness to work with. Buddhaghosa describes the varied breath-signs thus:

> When he does so in this way, the sign soon appears to him. But it is not the same for all; on the contrary, some say that when it appears it does so to certain people producing a light touch like cotton or silk-cotton or a draught. But this is the expression given in the commentaries: it appears to some like a star or a cluster of gems or a cluster of pearls, to others with a rough touch like that of silk-cotton seeds or a peg made of heartwood, to others like a long braid string or a wreath of flowers or a puff of smoke, to others like a stretched-out cobweb or a film of cloud or a lotus flower, or a chariot wheel or the moon's disk or the sun's disk. [VIII.214–15]

In view of what we have already seen of the process of producing and developing counterpart signs this is an interesting and possibly unique case. There seem to be two types of sign: the mere touch of the breath (with no visual image) and the "official" rough-touch and visual-image type. Second is the considerable variety of counterpart signs even within the two types (touch and visual). Buddhaghosa explains this variation on the basis of "differences of perception"; and a commentary note explains not too helpfully that the difference results from "the manner of perceiving that occurred *before the rising of the sign*" (VIII.216; italics added).

What then is the nature of the developmental process of the breath sign? In the next section Buddhaghosa warns that "the meditation subject reaches neither absorption nor even access" in one who does not clearly distinguish consciousness of out-breath, in-breath, *and* the sign. But if he knows these three things, as separate entities, he *can* develop the sign (VIII.217).

This points to a seemingly anomalous situation: what begins with a tactile base (breath touch) seems to issue in both tactile and visual signs. But how is such a change in sign quality brought about? Does it mean that once the attention achieves a certain (jhānic) level of concentration it can be shifted at will to another type or that it automatically shifts at certain stages? This seems to contradict the usual kasina-type of sign development (here used as model) in which there is simply a refinement of the original sense datum through all stages up to the fourth jhānic level.

It also raises the dual problem of whether, on the one hand, there are some who begin with touch and remain with it as a modified kasina-type sign, and, on the other, whether such a tactile datum can be developed into a sign. This development seems to be implied here; and some contemporary methods emphasize the continuing use of the touch datum—though always in the non-jhānic, vipassanā-type of concentration. There is no clear answer in the texts, hence the possibility of a tactile kasina sign cannot be flatly ruled out, but the following interpretation of the above quotation is possible: Because the breath sign *is* nonvisual and of increasing subtlety—so that it may totally disappear, as we have seen—the (visual) sign must be separated from its (tactile) base in order that it may be developed like a kasina.

In any case, when the sign has been aroused it is to be developed in somewhat the usual (kasina-type) way. And each person works on the sign that most readily appears to that person, for the particular means is of no real consequence. Having once aroused the sign the meditator continues the breathing process with the sign, and without giving attention to "its colour, or review[ing] it as to its (specific) characteristics (i.e., distractive particulars), he should make it grow and improve with repeated attention" (VIII.221). Growth and improvement presumably mean the brightening and beautifying of the closed-eye "cluster of gems" or whatever, as with the kasina crescent moon. (What it might mean with respect to touch is unclear. Does the touch of cotton wool on the lip change into a light?) But in the end the fourth jhāna may thus be reached.

Stages Five to Eight   These consist of observing the breath-meditation jhāna and turning away from it, of purification by the non-jhānic awareness of the jhānic state just experienced and destruction of all the remaining attachments even to jhānas, and lastly looking back by "reviewing knowledge" on all these jhānic attainments as stages now left behind (*PP*, VIII.198ff.).

Breath meditations continue to be highly esteemed even today as a means of mastering attention and gaining ultimate enlightenment: "If mindfulness or attention is firmly established on a part of the body, such as one out-breath and in-breath, it is tantamount to attention being firmly established on all things. This is because the ability to place one's attention on any object at one's will has been acquired." [18]

Body-in-Action Concentrations   These can be discussed briefly because they are similar to the breath concentration with the following exceptions: they can bring the meditator no further than to the first jhāna; they can be used during bodily activity when the meditator cannot, for some good reason, be observing his breath in seated meditation. Hence they are used in some modern methods—those oriented toward lay practice—as a substitute for the seated meditation. But at best, so far as jhānic attainments are concerned, such meditation is second level, keeping the attention relatively undistracted even when away from deep meditation itself and indirectly supportive of that meditation. As such the layman using a contact-with-matter tactile theme can work with this (at the non-jhānic level) in daily life. Thus:

> And moreover, bhikkhus, a brother, when he is walking is aware of it thus: —"I walk"; or when he is standing, or sitting, or lying down, he is aware of it. However he is disposing the body, he is aware thereof. And moreover, bhikkhus, a brother—whether he departs or returns, whether he looks at or looks away from, whether he has drawn in or stretched out [his limbs], whether he has donned under-robe, over-robe, or bowl, whether he is eating, drinking, chewing, reposing, or whether he is obeying the calls of nature—is aware of what he is about. In going, standing, sitting, sleeping, watching, talking, or keeping silence, he knows what he is doing.
>
>   So does he, as to the body, continue to consider the body, either internally or externally, or both internally and externally. He keeps on considering how the body is something that comes to be, or again *he keeps on considering how the body is something that passes away*; or again he keeps on considering the coming to be with the passing away; or again, conscious that "There is the body," mindfulness hereof becomes thereby established, far enough for the purposes of knowledge and of self-collectedness. And he abides independent, grasping after nothing in the world whatever. Thus, bhikkhus, does a brother continue to consider the body. [19]

No further comment is needed here except to observe the perpetual contextualizing of all these body concentrations by the awareness that "the body is something that passes away." A contemporary phrases the attitude that is sought:

> In the course of the practice, one will come to view the postures (of his own body) just as one unconcernedly views the automatic movements of a life-sized puppet. The play of the puppet's limbs will evoke a feeling

of complete estrangement, and even a slight amusement like that of an onlooker at a marionette show. By looking at the postures with such a detached objectivity, the *habitual identification with the body will begin to dissolve*.[20]

Feeling-Mental Objects of Meditation   The other three types of awareness, "feelings in feelings," "consciousness (mind) in consciousness," and "mental objects in mental objects" are briefly developed in our manuals though each receives considerable space in the *Middle Length Sayings* (Sutta 10), as the culmination of the body-awareness and breath-awareness series. But Buddhaghosa states that there is no *separate* method for developing these other types. Thus he ties them directly to the continued use of the breath as meditation base. With the breathing rhythm fully established and the attention centered expertly on the in-breaths and out-breaths, certain thought or awareness modes can be attached as indicated in the following:

> He trains thus "I shall breathe in experiencing happiness . . . experiencing bliss . . . experiencing the mental formation . . . tranquillising the mental formation. I shall breathe out experiencing . . . [the same]."

This is specified as the "contemplation of feelings in feelings," and the almost identical formula is used for: "experiencing the (manner of) consciousness . . . gladdening . . . concentrating . . . liberating (the manner of) consciousness"; as well as that described as "mental objects in mental objects" "contemplating impermanence . . . fading away . . . cessation . . . relinquishment" (*PP*, VIII.145).[21] But other phrasings are more helpful than this. Sutta Ten also reminds us with respect to "feelings" that feelings per se are not referred to here, only that in the Buddhist analysis feeling *tone* is pleasant, unpleasant, or neutral. When such feelings have arisen we may become emotionally attached to them; but the purpose of this meditation is, of course, to obviate emotional attachment. The phrase here might be read "contemplating feeling *as* feeling," that is, unemotionally noting that a pleasant, unpleasant, or neutral feeling has arisen, persists, and passes on.

The same Sutta explains "contemplating mind in the mind" as the observation of what we might call "mind-types" or "mind-sets." The meditator sees within himself especially, but also in others, the "mind with attachment . . . with hatred . . . with confusion . . . as distracted . . . become great . . . as composed . . . as freed" and also their opposites. And as before, so here too that observation is a simple noting of the presence of such mind-sets or mind-states without allowing any emotion to enter into the observation.

Finally, the "contemplation of mental objects in mental objects" might better be understood as "contemplation of mental contents *as* mental contents," or as a contemporary commentator puts it: "The object of observation is here the condition and the level of mind, or consciousness, in general, *as it presents* itself in the given moment."[22] Such contents are in five classes according to our Sutta: subjective desires and attitudes, such as restlessness, doubt, and desire for sense pleasures; the six "sense-bases" (five physical senses plus mind) or faculties on which mental processes depend; the five khandhas; absence or presence of "enlightenment factors"; and "mental objects from the point of view of the four ariyan truths."[23]

The seven so-called factors of enlightenment or mental states and capacities directly conducive to progress toward enlightenment are these: mindfulness (power of attention), investigation of the law (learning about the teaching), energy, rapture (joyful consciousness peaking in the second jhāna), tranquility, concentration (samādhi), and equanimity (the fourth divine abiding). These are always to be cultivated at all levels of effort, and together they represent the balanced meditative striving. But certainly at this juncture in the investigation of one's own feeling and thought processes, the presence and absence, as well as the weakness and strength of these factors in oneself, must be examined dispassionately and appropriate measures must be taken. Their state will reveal much to him about his progress toward Nibbānic awareness.

Two incidental features will be noted before I estimate the significance of these meditations. First, the Sutta followed here does not connect these last three "applications of mindfulness" (feeling, mind, and mental objects) with breathing. Feeling, mind, and mental objects are to be observed directly, whereas Buddhaghosa connects them with breathing. Nyanaponika Thera, in *The Heart of Buddhist Meditation*, makes this comment:

> The other three Contemplations of Satipaṭṭhāna (feeling, state of mind, and mental contents) are not taken up in a systematic way, but are attended to whenever their objects occur, either in connection with primary and secondary objects or within the range of general (all day) mindfulness.... When the mental objects appear in close connection with one of the bodily objects, it will be less difficult to discern their subtle nature. [P. 122]

He says that direct observation is profitable only for those meditators who have the jhānic skills. Buddhaghosa agrees with this but maintains the connection of feelings, for example, with breathing; as inevitable accompaniments of breathing meditation, they represent an integral part of the jhānic awareness of "feelings in the feelings":

> He attains the jhanas in which happiness is present. At the time when he has actually entered upon them the happiness is experienced *with* the object owing to the obtaining of the jhana, because of the experiencing of the jhana. [VIII.227; italics added]

In the same way, still in connection with breathing, "mind in mind" and "mental objects in mental objects" are contemplated—though "as" should perhaps be substituted for "in." The reason for this difference may be simply emphasis, more on *non*-jhānic vipassanā with Nyanaponika, and more on jhānic developments with Buddhaghosa. Consequently, Buddhaghosa ties it up with breath, which is the one and only body activity capable of high jhānic development.

Second, *The Book of the Kindred Sayings*, another canonical text, specifically refers to the semimantric repetition of the formula: "Again, Ānanda, at such a time a monk makes up his mind (repeating): 'Feeling the thrill of zest I shall breathe in: feeling the thrill of zest I shall breathe out'" [p. 287 (V.323)]. Apparently "repeating" was not an explicit part of the original text, but in the judgment of the translator the original warrants its use; and the explicit statements of Buddhaghosa about mantric repetitions used with other meditations confirm this.

The "Discourse on the Applications of Mindfulness," in conclusion of its discussion of the four applications to body, feelings, consciousness, and mental objects, states:

> Whoever, monks, should thus develop these four applications of mindful-
> ness for seven years ... for six years, five years, four years, three years,
> two years, for one year ... for seven months ... for six months, five
> months, four months, three months, for one month, for half a month ...
> for seven days, one of two fruits is to be expected for him: either profound
> knowledge here-now, or, if there be any residuum remaining, the state
> of non-returning. [*MLS*, I, pp. 81f. (I.62–3)]

That these are jhānic is taken for granted by the translator's commentaries that interpret the recurring phrase "I shall breathe (in, or out) tranquillising the activity of the body" [*MLS*, I, p. 72 (I.56), n.1] as indicating a jhānic level of attainment. But it is interesting that in all the subsequent applications of mindfulness to body-feeling-mental function, a *non*-jhānic or special jhānic application is constantly referred to. Here again the dual role of the jhānas is obvious. They are, in a yogic role, "peaceful abidings," as their body-tranquilizing nature suggests. But in their specifically Buddhist role they reinforce the teaching of the evanescent, nonintegral, dissatisfying nature of everything thus attended to.

This Sutta is primarily an encapsulated version of the meditation and subjects of meditation already discussed in this chapter: meditation on breath, body constituents, body foulness and decay, body action, feelings, and thoughts. All are given post-jhānic attention—an attention calmed and sharpened by the previous jhāna—factually, realistically, and detachedly, "precisely to the extent necessary to knowledge ... not grasping anything in the world" [*MLS*, I, p. 75 (I.58–9)]. But they are viewed also as fleeting and empty of satisfying reality: one contemplates "origination things" and "dissolution things" in body, feelings, and mind. Jhānic peacefulness is induced *in order* that the Theravāda view of all things as impermanent, empty of true reality, and unsatisfying, might be seen with greater clarity. Buddhaghosa states:

Liberating the (manner of) consciousness, he both breathes in and breathes out delivering, liberating, the mind from the hindrances by means of the first jhana, from applied and sustained thought by means of the second, from happiness by means of the third, from pleasure and pain by means of the fourth. Or alternately, when, having entered upon these jhanas and *emerged from them*, he comprehends with insight the consciousness associated with the jhāna as liable to destruction. . . . Hence it is said "He trains thus 'I shall breathe in . . . shall breathe out liberating the (manner of) consciousness.' " [VIII.232; second italics added]

The key phrase is "emerged from them," which means that the blessed states achieved by jhānic meditation must not only serve the overall purposes of meditation, but must themselves be submitted to the specifically Buddhist "critique" of insight or vipassanā. This critique is the fully existentialized realization that even blessed states belong to the impermanence of saṃsāra and must be "risen above," no matter how high and rare they seem to be. Or to put it otherwise: with this phrase, and what it implies about meditational method, we have crossed over the borderline from the inherited yogic meditational method into the truly Buddhist territory of an anicca-anattā-dukkha critique of *all* religious experiences and trance states.

5

Vipassanā Meditation

Vipassanā (insight) is the Buddhist heart of the Theravāda meditational discipline. As the technique for attaining Nibbāna par excellence, it is the living, existential essence of the Theravāda world view and the mode absolutely essential to achieving final salvation.

I have already spoken of the relationships between vipassanā and the jhānic mode of meditation. Here I will observe the essentially non-Buddhist concomitants that continue to cling to the jhānic-immaterial meditations and note the Theravāda apologia for this situation; analyze the manner in which, despite the presence of non-Buddhistic elements (as above) the Buddhist world view prevails in the final practice of meditation; and describe the vipassanā progression itself, both as dominant over the jhānic progression and as independent of it.

Yogic Concomitants of the Jhānic Attainments

One of the basic differences between the jhānic-immaterial series of attainments and their vipassanic context is their strong attachment to the world of kamma of which vipassanā is presumed to be the denial. That is to say, the jhānic-series attainment of higher states of consciousness is also, and at the same time, the attainment of freedom *in* and power *over* the world. This takes several forms. In delineating the Buddha's enlightenment, I noted that immediately prior to enlightenment the divine eye-power, the divine ear-power, and the ability to recall past births were attained. These are part of a set of psychosomatic powers that include, in addition, penetration of the thought of others' minds, knowledge of one's own approaching Nibbāna, and the Ten Magical Powers. These powers, attained by Gotama, are also promised to every successful meditator. Thus:

> Now, O Brothers, the monk enjoys the various Magical Powers, such as being one he becomes manifold, and having become manifold he again becomes one. Without being obstructed he passes through walls and mountains, just as if through the air. He walks on water without sinking, just as if on the earth. In the earth he dives and rises up again, just as if in the water. Crosslegged he floats through the air, just as a winged bird. With his hand he touches the sun and moon.... Even up to the Brahma world has he mastery over his body.[1]

Significantly, the development of these powers is given considerable space in our two manuals: about seventy pages in *The Path of Purification* and twenty in *The Path of Freedom*. Buddhaghosa classifies these powers as "direct knowledge" and considers them as "benefits" in this life. And as we might expect they are directly contingent on mastery of the various jhānic stages. He says that only one in a thousand can do preliminary work in kasinas, one in a thousand of these can "arouse the sign," and so on successively, one in a thousand, through the stages of "extending the sign," "taming one's mind in fourteen ways," up to the attainment of supernormal powers. Such a person must have mastered thoroughly eight of the kasina meditations and be able to proceed in and out of, as well as nimbly skip from jhānic state to jhānic state with the greatest of ease before even attempting to attain such powers (XII.1ff).[2] *The Path of Freedom* supplements this account with specific directions: the yogin resolves to attain a particular supernormal power. (Each one must be attained by a particularized effort; attainment of one does not help with respect to another.) He then resolves upon the "four kinds of endeavour," that is:

> He endeavours to preclude the arising of evil demeritorious states that have not yet arisen; he endeavours to reject the evil demeritorious states that have already arisen; he endeavours to cause the arising of meritorious states that have not yet arisen; he endeavours to increase and to consciously reproduce the meritorious states that have already arisen; and to develop them fully. [Pp. 212–13]

The "states" referred to here are the rebirth-producing states of mind.

Suppose then that the meditator chooses to develop the power to fly through the air. We have the following directions:

> Thus the yogin develops the four bases of supernormal power. His mind, being wieldy, responds to the body, and his body responds to the mind. Thus the yogin sometimes controls the body with his mind, and sometimes the mind with his body. . . . The perception of bliss and lightness adheres to the body. In that state he accomplishes and abides. . . . Thus having through mental culture made his body light, he, owing to the lightness of body, enters the fourth meditation, *jhāna*, and is mindful and tranquil. Rising therefrom, he knows space, and resolves through knowledge. Thus his body is able to rise up in space. . . . It is comparable to cottonwool blown by the wind. Here the new yogin should not go far quickly, because he might, in the course of his application, arouse fear. If he stirs up fear, his meditation, *jhāna*, will fall away. . . . He should go gradually. At first one *shaku* [foot]; then he gradually rises and applies himself. [Pp. 213–14]

And so on to a fathom's distance, and then on to still longer distances till he reaches gradually "the point he desires to reach." In response to a question about whether the yogin who loses his jhānic concentration while in flight will fall from the sky, the manual responds negatively in a way that suggests that, despite some occasional literalistic interpretations, a kind of astral-body projection is here in mind: "No. This begins from one's meditation-seat. If, having gone far, the meditation, *jhāna*, is lost, one reaches the sitting place. One sees the body in the first posture (and thinks): 'This is the possessor of supernormal power. This is his serenity-practice'" (*PF*, pp. 213f.).

How then shall we explain the large place given to the attainment of such powers in a discipline that is ostensibly committed to the disdainful, even "passionate" forsaking of the world of time and space and all its values? It may well come from the yogic-practice context in which Buddhism developed in India and perhaps the reinfiltration of those values after the Buddhist break with Brāhmaṇism had lost its revolutionary force. But it is also to be noted that Buddhism here betrays its own derivation from the Brāhmaṇical spiritual tradition. From the time of the writing of the Pāli Canon, it was taken for granted by Buddhists that genuine, Nibbāna-oriented attainments were always accompanied by expanded this-worldly powers. These two elements, perhaps somewhat inconsistently, were not inharmonious; this-worldly powers were considered to be confirmatory evidence of true spiritual attainment—though such powers are downgraded in the Canon itself.

But even here there are Buddhist factors. Thus the four "endeavours" indirectly relate to world escape (mokṣa, Nibbāna) in their attention to meritorious and demeritorious states. And Buddhaghosa also tries in the beginning of his treatment to give a good Buddhist reason for making such attempts: "When he thus possesses concentration so developed as to have both provided benefits *and* become more advanced, he will then *more easily perfect the development of understanding*" (XII.2; italics added). Of course, the "development of understanding" is the development of that wisdom (paññā) that leads to Nibbāna and is the goal of vipassanā meditation. And this line of reasoning, as we shall see later, is of a piece with the way Buddhism regards and employs the whole jhānic series.

Even though the Buddha is portrayed in the Pāli Canon as able to exercise any or all of the Ten Powers with perfect mastery, such attainments play a subordinate role in a genuine following of the Path. The powers can be mastered along with attainment of the jhānic states and perfection of character, but his disciples are cautioned not to seek to achieve personal advantage or to make converts on the basis of such wonder-working power.[3] Thus did the Buddha seek to "contain" the possibility of a burgeoning yogic technique of magical character as opposed to his own Nibbānic moralism. However, the tension remains within the Buddhist tradition. Fortune tellers still find platforms in Buddhist pagoda precincts and now and then a monk gains a reputation for his feats in this realm, even though he indulges in them with a bad conscience.[4]

One final kamma-saṃsāra connection with meditation is the automatic attainment of specific rebirth levels by means of attaining specific meditational levels (see Diagram 1). This meticulously worked out correlation of medita-

Diagram 1

The Thirty-One Planes of Existence
in the Stable and Vertical Universe
of Buddhist Tradition

NIBBĀNA

*No passage from Brahma Worlds to Nibbāna
save for Anāgāmins*

ARUPA-LOKA; IMMATERIAL SPHERES; REALM OF
FORMLESSNESS

No.	Name of Plane	Access by		Life-Span	
31	Neither Perception nor Non-Perception	Formless Meditations		84,000	kappas
30	Nothingness	,,	,,	60,000	,,
29	Infinity of Consciousness	,,	,,	40,000	,,
28	Infinity of Space	,,	,,	20,000	,,

RUPA-LOKA; REALM OF FORM; FINE MATERIAL SPHERE
(Planes 23–27 called Pure Abodes)

No.	Name		Access by		Life-Span	
27	Sublime Gods		Fourth Jhāna		16,000	kappas
26	Easily-Seeing Gods		,,	,,	8,000	,,
25	Easily-Seen Gods		,,	,,	4,000	,,
24	Untroubled Gods		,,	,,	2,000	,,
23	Effortless Gods (Anāgāmins reborn here)		,,	,,	1,000	,,
22	Gods without Perception		,,	,,	500	,,
21	Richly-Rewarded Gods		,,	,,	200	,,
20	Completely Lustrous Gods	(high)	Third Jhāna		64	,,
19	Immeasurably Lustrous Gods	(medium)	,,	,,	32	,,
18	Limitedly Lustrous Gods	(low)	,,	,,	16	,,
17	Radiant Gods	(high)	Second Jhāna		8	,,
16	Immeasurably Splendorous Gods	(medium)	,,	,,	4	,,
15	Limitedly Splendorous Gods	(low)	,,	,,	2	,,
14	Great Brahmas	(high)	First Jhāna		1	,,
13	Priests of Brahma	(medium)	,,	,,	1/2	,,
12	Retinue of Brahma	(low)	,,	,,	1/3	,,

*High, medium, low refer to degrees of mastery
of the Jhānic meditative technique achieved on earth.*

KAMA-LOKA; SENSUOUS WORLD; ELEVEN-FOLD REALM OF
PLEASURE

Seven-Fold Realm of Sensual Bliss

11	Gods who control pleasure	Good Kamma		9,216	million yrs.	
10	Gods who delight in fashioning	,,	,,	2,304	,,	,,

9 Satisfied Gods (Tusita Heaven)	,,	,,	576	,,	,,
8 Yama Gods	,,	,,	144	,,	,,
7 Thirty-Three Gods (Top of Mt. Meru)	,,	,,	36	,,	,,
6 Four Great Kings (Slope of Mt. Meru)	,,	,,	9	,,	,,
5 Human plane of existence (earth)			80,000 yrs. on down		

Four-Fold Realm of Punishment

4 Demon or Asura world	Bad Kamma
3 Ghost or Peta World	,, ,,
2 Animal world	,, ,,
1 Hells or purgatories	,, ,,

From Winston L. King, *A Thousand Lives Away* (Oxford: Bruno Cassirer, 1964), p. 113.

tional attainment stages with rebirth levels has a rudimentary Pāli Canon basis but is developed fully in later commentaries.[5] It is apparently taken for granted by Buddhaghosa. Such an attainment as one's rebirth into the twentieth plane of the Completely Lustrous Gods with a life-span of sixty-four immeasurable ages (*kalpas*) is a splendid consolation prize for one who is able to master completely the third jhāna but does not achieve total freedom from saṃsāra! And presumably such attainers, when reborn into human status again after the lapse of sixty-four kalpas, will retain their meditative capacities undiminished for another attempt to achieve Nibbāna. If such is the case, jhānic meditators seem to have the best of both jhānic *and* Nibbānic worlds.

The appearance of this relationship raises interesting questions. Did it develop because the early assurance of quick and relatively easy attainment of arahantship soon began to fade within the community of monks? Was it because of increasing lay influence within the Buddhist community? Did it come from a reyoginization of the Buddhist meditational discipline or simply from the development of the yogic methodology to its logical conclusions within a Buddhist context? All this is only speculative. But clearly the jhānic series of attainments in the Buddhist structure is double-faced like Janus: One visage looks out upon realms of kammic blessedness and increased psychic powers; the other contemplates the attainment of world-abandoning Nibbāna.

The Buddhist Vipassanā Contextualization of the Yogic Discipline

Attention has been called to seemingly arbitrary or forced connections made between various jhānic attainments and a variety of other items such as the attachment of a certain attitude or emotional "set" to a specific kasina color; the connection made between the divine abidings (loving-kindness, etc.) and the kasina-based series of formless meditations, as their "supporting condition"; the relating of the meditative attainments to specific rebirths in the higher realms, some of which are semi-Nibbānic; the insistence that nirodha-samāpatti (extinction of feeling and perception) is a this-life entry into Nibbāna, which is also defined as the absence of greed, hatred, and delusion; and Buddhaghosa's assurance that even the attainment of the Ten Magical Powers is, in the long run, conducive to the Nibbānic liberation.

But what is the full functional relation between the yogic and the Buddhist components of the meditational pattern as presented in the Theravāda structure? In the *jhānic* series the Buddhist elements are attached to the technical meditative apparatus but are not organic to it. They are forced into connection with the jhānic-formless scale of attainments and are in fact developed by its techniques (we are told). But the "Buddhist" end result seems to be almost a nonsequitur.[6] And what of the eightfold progression of jhānas and immaterial states, which is relatively integral to itself, proceeding to ever more rarefied perceptions and states of consciousness, climaxing in the cessation state? From beginning to end it can be achieved with a kasina-like technique. In such a series where is the need or place for the Buddhist elements?

The Buddhist elements are the following: some themes used at the access level, such as mindfulness on death; the body-centered meditations, including those on foulness, body members, and breath; and the four divine abidings. None of these is absolutely essential to the jhānic-formless series, but most of them *can* be used as kasina-type bases in this series. Diagram 2 outlines the situation. The Buddhist components, such as the divine abidings, stand in a dual relationship to the technical meditational series. From the *jhānic* side they are clearly junior partners fitted rather loosely onto the series, conforming to it in the mode of their employment, that is, developed by a kasina-like method of afterimage (counterpart sign) that seems different in quality from them. But they can be strengthened by, or even in some sense produced by, the development of the mental powers through the jhānic-formless techniques. The old yogic technique is fitted, readapted, and reinterpreted, and then the two sets of elements reverse their relationships: the Buddhist elements become dynamically determinative. Historically, according to my thesis, this contextualizing represents the Buddhist rejection and critique of Brahmanically tainted yoga, the staking out of the Buddhist claim to newness. Dynamically, as actually functioning in meditation, the jhānic elements as peaceful abidings become secondary to the Buddhist goal of understanding, as well as to detachment even from the peaceful abidings of the jhānic states themselves. Thus even though much space is devoted to the jhānic apparatus in the manuals because of its technical complexity, in the Buddhist world view and meditational context, the simpler and less extensively developed vipassanā apparatus is not thereby lessened in importance.

Diagram 2

Nirodha-Samāpatti

Kasina Mode of Development
Formless Meditations ⟵⟶ Divine Abidings:
                              As supports
                              As subjects
Jhānic States ⟵⟶ Body-centered Subjects
Access Concentration ⟵⟶ "Buddhist" Themes

I have earlier described the general Buddhist context of attitude and world view into which the yogic techniques are fitted and by which their Buddhist use is conditioned as "world-denying." Here I add two further specifications: a strong emphasis on ethical attitudes; and an intense insistence upon the anicca-anattā-dukkha theme that vipassanā embodies. The ethical disposition theme (sīla) is stressed at every stage of meditational development, no matter how far the subject of that meditation and its methodology may seem to be separated from ethical disposition matters. Whether such a far-reaching connection is psychologically natural may be questioned; but Buddhism considers ethics primary. Nibbāna itself is basically defined as the absence of greed, hatred, and delusion; and this remains its essence, no matter how overlaid by additional descriptions. Therefore any psychic attainment, even though very subtle and skillful, is suspect in Buddhist eyes unless at the same time it results in the strengthening of the moral character and the growth of such traits as benevolence, harmlessness, and serenity. Buddhist meditational perfection is presumed to be unattainable without an accompanying (and resultant) moral perfection; or otherwise put, meditative (samādhic) perfection, based as it is on morality (sīla), also results in the development and perfection of moral character.

This ethical concern is present at almost every turn in the scriptures, though it is bypassed in the meditational manuals in their eagerness to detail the jhānic methodology. Nonetheless, it is always implied. For example, the meditator is not exempted from social obligations merely by virtue of being a meditator. It will be recalled that the monk who had just got hold of his counterpart sign in the cemetery or in front of a kasina must answer greetings from laymen or other monks and do his monastic duties, even if he should thereby lose his precious sign. And, to be discussed later, the monk who had entered into the attainment of cessation was required to be willing to be brought out of it if the monastery council needed him, the master called, or his insensibility should result in harm to others or their property.

That is to say, the moral and humanistic values always precede the meditative—though it seems to have been allowable within limits for the would-be meditator to find a quiet place away from human contact to forward meditational effort, and though special meditational seasons are allowable and special personal vocation as an advanced meditator is recognized in the "forest-dwelling" monk who wanders lonely like a rhinoceros. It also is noteworthy that the divine abidings, the epitome of character transformation, are given a prominent place in the meditational series. They "support" the formless meditations, even though their connection to them seems tenuous at best and though they are not organic to the jhānic series.

Theravādins emphasize the anicca-anattā-dukkha theme even more than moral disposition. The meditational process set forth in the scriptures is saturated with this essentially Theravāda weltanschauung. The meditator must never be allowed to forget, no matter how peaceful or pleasant the meditational experience may be, that its primary purpose is to release its experiencer from the bondage of saṃsāra *and* of attachment to meditational states themselves. Here we can sense an intensive drive to impose Buddhist values on a somewhat recalcitrant methodology. To repeat, the meditational methodology as a yogic discipline was originally conceived as a way of achieving freedom and power *in* and *over* the world, whereas the Buddhist Nibbānic goal entails the use of meditation as a means of achieving freedom *from* the world and *all* its values, by detachment from them. The yogic discipline may lead to the sublimation of time-space values, but for the Buddhist, meditation must always achieve an alienation from even sublimated time-space values—though in the resultant discipline and Buddhist tradition there remains a certain tension.

The major embodiment of this world-denying emphasis lies in the choice of certain meditation subjects, even though some are subordinated to a jhānic, kasina-type technique of development. This embodiment begins even before the kasina-jhāna development becomes fully operative. The themes of the repulsiveness of food, the resolution of the body-self into its basic elements, the meditation upon death and the like cannot produce more than access meditation, but they are valuable conditioners. And at the full jhānic level there are the body-centered subjects that continually enforce the lessons of the impermanence and repulsiveness of all that has to do with the body and its processes in any way and the suffering (dukkha) entailed therein. A thorough reading of all the passages in *The Path of Purification* pertaining to the body would only strengthen this impression. The meditator must at all costs be alienated emotionally from the world of body-experienced, time-space existence. And when he advances to the more subtle meditations on elements of feeling and thought, the same process is carried on in appropriate form: the meditator seeks to perceive directly within himself the complete impersonality (anattā) and quick-silverish fluxing (anicca) of thought and subjective awareness, that is, of the spiritual and mental I.

But this last level of perceiving in the self itself the three marks of saṃsāra (impermanence, impersonality, and unsatisfyingness) means fully crossing over the line between yogic-jhānic meditation into a specifically Buddhist meditation, that directed toward Nibbāna attainment. This must now be considered as a discipline in its own right, the Buddhist discipline par excellence embodied in vipassanā.

Vipassanā as a Meditative Discipline

Vipassanā or insight has been defined as "the intuitive light flashing forth and exposing the truth of the impermanency, misery, and impersonality of all corporeal and mental phenomena of existence."[7] Specifically it is penetrative insight, a subdivision or special enlightenment-oriented variety of understanding (paññā, sometimes also translated "insight"). The full term for meditation thus directed is *vipassanā-bhāvanā*, or insight meditation, seen as the essence of the Buddha's own method of meditation and as productive of *Buddhist* enlightenment. It is often tied together with samādhi (*samatha-vipassanā*) since vipassanā insight can be produced only by calm concentration of mind. I will henceforth use vipassanā as a short form for "vipassanā meditation."

The focus and quality of vipassanā meditation are set forth succinctly by Buddhaghosa in his introduction to the last third of *The Path of Purification*. There he discusses "understanding" (paññā), which seems to be his usual equivalent for vipassanā insight. After a lengthy description of all of the modes and subjects of jhānic-formless meditations and the resultant magical power attainments, he then turns to understanding (paññā, vipassanā) with these words:

> Now concentration [jhānic power] was described under the heading of *Consciousness*. . . . And that has been developed in all its aspects by the bhikkhu who is thus possessed of the more advanced development of concentration. . . . But *understanding* comes next. *And that has still to be developed.* [XIV.1; last italics added]

The last sentence is the most significant of all: even though the powers of the jhānic series have been attained, something more remains. In other words, jhānic powers do not of themselves give the liberating, enlightening understanding that leads to Nibbāna.

And what is the nature of this understanding that remains for even the adept meditator? Buddhaghosa continues:

> It is knowing (*jānana*) in a particular mode separate from the modes of perceiving (*sañjānana*) and cognizing (*vijānana*). For though the state of knowing (*jānana-bhava*) is equally present in perception (*saññā*), in consciousness . . . , and in understanding (*paññā*), nevertheless, perception is only the mere perceiving of an object as, say, "blue" or "yellow"; *it cannot bring about the penetration of its characteristics as impermanent, painful, and not-self*. . . . Understanding . . . brings about the penetration of the characteristics and it brings about, by endeavouring, the manifestation of the path. [XIV.3; last italics added]

The phrase "manifestation of the path" will be interpreted later. Here the point of interest is the "penetration of its characteristics, painful, and not-self"—the leitmotif of vipassanā in its entirety. This penetrative knowledge perceives the true nature of all existent entities but has many natural human and deluded views to overcome in doing so. Chapter 22 of *The Path of Purification* deals with them at length. They are summarized in the accompanying table.

Insight-Knowledge	Deluded Views
1. Contemplation of Impermanence	1. Idea of Permanence
2. Contemplation of Suffering	2. Idea of Happiness
3. Contemplation of Impersonality	3. Idea of Personality
4. Contemplation of Aversion	4. Idea of Lust
5. Contemplation of Detachment	5. Idea of Greed
6. Contemplation of Extinction	6. Idea of Origination
7. Contemplation of Abandoning	7. Idea of Grasping
8. Contemplation of Waning	8. Idea of Compactness
9. Contemplation of Vanishing	9. Idea of Kamma-accumulation
10. Contemplation of Change	10. Idea of Stability
11. Contemplation of Unconditioned	11. Idea of Conditioned
12. Contemplation of Desirelessness	12. Idea of Delight
13. Contemplation of Emptiness	13. Idea of Adherence
14. Contemplation of Higher Wisdom about Phenomena	14. Grasping, Adherence to Idea of Substance
15. Contemplation of Knowledge and Vision according to Reality	15. Adherence to Delusion about Self and World
16. Contemplation of Misery	16. Attachment and Adherence
17. Reflecting Contemplation	17. Thoughtlessness
18. Contemplation of Turning-away	18. Entanglement and Clinging[8]

To this imposing statement of the necessity for seeing existent space-time entities as "they truly are" (impermanent, painful, and impersonal) in order to be freed of attachment to them I add from the many hundreds that could be quoted a few more that make the same point. The meditating disciple, with thorough mastery of the Four Noble Truths, reflects on the nature of "formations of existence," that is, existential formations within the body-mind:

> Thus do the formations of existence ever and again arise as something quite new. But not only are they something new, they are moreover of limited duration, like a dew-drop at sunrise, like a bubble, like a line drawn with a stick in the water, like a mustard seed placed on the point of an arrow, or like a flash of lightning. Also as . . . jugglery, as a mirage.[9]

In still another place Buddhaghosa insists that this perception of reality must be applied directly to personal experiences and faculties:

> In particular, even sublime internal materiality should be regarded as foul (ugly); feeling should be regarded as painful . . . ; perception and

formations as not-self because they are unmanageable; and consciousness as impermanent because it has the nature of rise and fall. [XIV.224]

In the Canon is a certain monk who, with specific reference to jhānic
states, judges them the same way:

> Consider the monk who, aloof from sense desires, . . . enters and abides
> in the first musing: whatever occurs there of form, feeling, perception,
> minding or consciousness, he sees wholly as impermanent phenomena,
> as ill, as a disease, a boil, a sting, a hurt, an affliction, as something alien,
> gimcrack, empty, not the self.[10]

One can be sure that he is near to the goal of vipassanā when

> his consciousness no longer enters into or settles down on or resolves
> upon any field of formations at all, or clings, cleaves, or clutches on
> to it, but retreats, retracts and recoils as water does from a lotus leaf,
> *and every sign as object, every occurrence as object, appears as an impediment.*
> [*PP*, XXII.4; italics added]

Several points are now clear. First, reality as intrinsically impermanent,
painful, and impersonal is "reality" or "existence" *as it is apprehended in
experience.* It is beside the point whether there is truly an objective physical
reality "out there" that our subjective senses apprehend and relate to in
thought and feeling. (Buddhism developed many theories about this, and
Theravāda inclines toward the "real" existence of component elements or
dharmas in an exterior world.) But experienced reality to whose "existent"
entities we are attached by thought and emotion is full of impermanence,
pain, and impersonality. And its basic nature is the "materiality" or "substantiality" by which it is present to our six senses, including the sixth mental
"sense" that conceptually apprehends "things." To "see things as they truly
are" means, most importantly if not exclusively, to see myself-as-experiencing
as I truly am—impermanent, full of pain, and impersonal.

Second, the main focus of vipassanā is upon self-as-experiencing. Thus a
"feelingful" adjective such as "painful" can be applied to it. It is not that the
material item (whatever it is) is per se full of suffering; it is my experiential
relation to it that is painful—which is the intrinsic quality of all experience
of anything whatsoever in the Buddhist view. Further, attachment to such
experience and its objects only prolongs that same painful experience,
rebirths without end. Hence the observance of the body-mind as it functions
in its environment is the central and almost exclusive focus of vipassanā—not
the nature of the world around one, even though that too, whatever it is,
is "non-self," that is, without reality core, and in permanent flux.

Third, the complexity of presentation found in the list of deluded states
of mind that must be overcome (and in Buddhaghosa's further and formid-
able elaboration of good and bad views, elements, factors, formations,
powers, and the like) may give the impression that vipassanā is as complicated

in its methodology as the jhānic attainments are in theirs, which is not the case. This extensive apparatus is primarily an intellectual tour de force: Buddhaghosa and his fellow theorists, who had the whole Abhidhamma analysis at their disposal, wished to be absolutely certain that nothing in all the range of existence or experience could be thought to be exempt from the dismembering, depersonalizing reductionism of vipassanā analysis. Otherwise it might become a hiding place for some subtle attachment, intellectual or emotional. And further, this wide array of items offers the meditation master an abundance of possible tools to use with meditators.

But in actual meditative practice, applying the understanding of the Four Noble Truths is relatively simple. Essentially and practically it is the direct intensive application of this viewpoint to every or any item of experience. To further simplify the process, each meditator is urged to find one form of meditative object best suited to him and develop it fully.

This principle has been noted already in jhānic meditations, for instance, in the meditator's choice of one particular body state that presents itself to *him* most vividly as a concentration object. This applies to vipassanā as well. Any phase of life or experience, seen under the analytical, reductive vipassanā lens, is suitable for an object. Some, such as breath and tactile or feeling objects, are considered to be superior; but bodily movements or thought processes can be profitably observed. The only requirement is that they must be seen in the vipassanā way.

Fourth, the level of mental, transic attainment here is much lower than on the jhānic scale. In vipassanā nothing higher than an access or neighbor-hood degree of concentrative attention is necessary. In other words, here one never attains, nor needs to attain, the locked-*in* attention to a meditative base that totally and absolutely locks *out* all other data. It is only relatively one-pointed.

On the other hand, there appears to be a carry-over from the jhānic state into the vipassanic awareness. Buddhaghosa states that upon emergence from any jhānic state, except that based on neither-perception-nor-non-perception (in which no such factors are available for inspection), the meditator analyzes the mental and material factors of recent experience; and also the character and quality of the jhāna just experienced have some relation to the quality of the Path attainment that may ensue (XVIII.3, 4; XXI.111–16). The mind quietened and sharpened by jhāna, by virtue of the concentration required for and in it, is now better able to achieve insight-knowledge. Thus the jhānic discipline of mind supports the vipassanic process, at least indirectly.

Thus it follows that a more varied content is allowed and may be related to any of the ongoing body-mind activities. The meditation "on the body in the body" is an excellent example of this. As discussed previously, the meditator is aware of lifting an arm, or of walking, of eating, and also, more subtly, of thinking and feeling (tactile sensations) even while these processes are going on within his body-mind self. The awareness is impersonal, as "thinking of lifting, lifting arm," and so on. To be aware of these actions as an embodiment of that which comes to be and vanishes (impermanence), as that which is restless and ever unsatisfied (painfulness), and as the progression of a series of causes and effects (impersonality) *is the essence of vipassanā.*

What vipassanā then represents in the final analysis can be stated thus: *Vipassanā is the total, supersaturated, existentializing of the Theravāda world view that all existence in personal and individual modes of being, intrinsically and ineradicably embodies impermanence, pain, and impersonality.*

Fifth, such a discipline of thought and emotional tone is obviously more widely adaptable than the jhānic discipline, which takes immense amounts of time—a whole lifetime one might say—in a setting specifically adapted to it. It is a monk's technique. But vipassanā, although certainly applicable to the monk's life and absolutely necessary for his Nibbānic attainment, can be applied much more readily to ordinary daily life than can jhānic concentration. It may need periods and special modes of intensive application to achieve some expertise and depth; but intrinsically it is capable of extension to all types of life and activity, not just to those of a monk. Hence by means of a vipassanā-type practice, even laypersons can (and do) participate in Nibbāna-directed meditation.

Since the vipassanā insight that everything—even jhānic states—is impermanent, painful, and impersonal provides the truly liberating knowledge (paññā), these questions arise: Why not use vipassanā directly and exclusively, bypassing the jhānic series entirely? Would not this be shorter, faster, more available to all, and more truly Buddhist as well? The contemporary meditational schools in Theravāda countries are increasingly answering yes to these questions. And they have a warrant from Buddhaghosa himself. He recognizes the "bare insight worker," the one without jhānic powers, as perhaps atypical, but clearly existent and orthodox. This person can become an arahant as well as the jhānic adept.

Sixth, the final implication is that the distinction between vipassanā as *context* (second point) and vipassanā as *method* (now being discussed) is fluid. In some sense vipassanā is always present as context everywhere in Theravāda meditation. The Four Noble Truths are basic Theravāda teaching whether one learns anything else at all. And this teaching specifically contextualizes the meditative process, even the jhānic practice, at every step, before, during, and after the trances themselves. Further, as a specific method, for monk or layperson, it continues to contextualize life and become internalized into a visceral awareness of every activity.[11] Hence vipassanā might be defined as *method*, thus: vipassanā *is then the method of contextualizing all body-mind activities—including jhānic states—by the Buddhist world view.* And its practice as a specific, separate technique is only a more intensive periodic application of its life view to a single chosen series of body-mind phenomena for the purpose of its ultimate extension to *all* of life.

A prime example of vipassanā as both context and method is the application of vipassanā directly to the jhānic experiences. It must be used with all such experiences for good reason: though the jhānic techniques are used in the Buddhist practice as an auxiliary means of achieving Nibbānic release from saṃsāra, and hence always implicitly in the anicca-anattā-dukkha context, the jhānic experience itself may give the false impression of already having achieved that release. The trance mode, rapt away from the flux of ordinary consciousness, as a "peaceful abiding" may seem to the meditator to be Nibbānic realization itself. Therefore the vipassanā method must be applied to the jhānic experience *especially*. The presumption is that it is applied by the meditator immediately upon emerging from a jhānic state to the state just experienced.

Buddhaghosa writes about jhāna attained on a breathing basis: "On emerging from the attainment he sees that the in-breaths and out-breaths have the physical body and the mind as their origin; and that just as, when a blacksmith's bellows are being blown, the wind moves owing to the bag and to the man's appropriate effort, so too, in-breaths and out-breaths are due to the body and mind" (VIII.223). That is, even blessed jhānic awareness is *not* beyond saṃsāra; it is dependent on impermanent physical processes.

He goes on to say of the meditator: "When, after entering upon and emerging from one of the two jhānas accompanied by happiness, he comprehends with insight [vipassanā] that happiness associated with the jhana is liable to destruction and to fall" (VIII.227). And in a passage already quoted, he generalizes this statement by suggesting that *any* consciousness "associated with" a jhāna is liable to destruction.

Nor do the formless meditations themselves, highest of all jhānic-type attainments, escape this judgment of impermanence. Thus we read in the *Middle Length Sayings*:

> And again, monks, Sāriputta, by passing quite beyond the plane of no-thing, enters on and abides in the plane of neither-perception-nor-non-perception. Mindful, he emerges from that attainment. When he has emerged, mindful, from that attainment he regards those things that are past, stopped, changed as: "Thus indeed things that have not been in me come to be; having been they pass away." He, not feeling attracted by these things, not feeling repelled, independent, not infatuated, freed, released, dwells with a mind that is unconfined. He comprehends: "There is a further escape." There is zealous practice for him concerning that. [III, p. 80 (III.27-8)]

The "further escape" for which the meditator must zealously practice is the attainment of cessation (nirodha-samāpatti), which I will describe later. But what does the "impermanence" of these states mean? Obviously they can endure only a relatively short time—even the cessation attainment was limited to seven days. However, "impermanence" refers not so much to temporal duration as to the lack of the true Nibbānic quality of complete release from saṃsāra. The meditator must realize through a vipassanā introspection that the trance-attainment is not yet utterly free of saṃsāric elements. There is more work yet to do. Both the entrance into and emergence from a jhānic state are subject to the insight awareness that is characterized by "equanimity about formations," that is, unattachedness to all mental or material features of existence including one's own self and one's (jhānic) states. Buddhaghosa speaks of "preliminary insight"—which seems to mean a deliberate entering into the jhāna with awareness that it is still saṃsāric in nature—and "insight leading to emergence" (XXI.111). Insight leading to emergence is harder to understand, given the fact that jhānic consciousness is "cut off," but the will-to-insight in which the jhānas are contextualized seems to infuse itself into the states themselves and to end them.

Path Attainment

Path (*magga*) is important in the Buddhist meditational experience. Path realization is the positive, confirmatory fruit of meditational success. Path attainment, even at its lowest level, represents the first genuine achievement of a direct experience of Nibbāna. It is also the attainment of "sainthood," that is, the absolute assurance of a breakthrough in the quest for final liberation. And it is necessary to keep in mind that this attainment of Path realization and sainthood is not to be found in the jhānic scale; nor is it directly conditioned by it but is strictly and only a product of the vipassanā discipline. That is, the jhānic expertise *may* be used to assist in vipassanā success in auxiliary fashion by increasing the power of concentration and enabling the meditator to transcend his usual modes of thinking and feeling with higher ones. But Path attainment as Nibbānic foretaste comes only after the experience of the impermanence-flawed quality of all meditative states *other* than Nibbāna awareness itself; then jhānic states play a role comparable to body components, for example, as meditation subjects to enforce the anicca-anattā-dukkha viewpoint. We have already observed that on this basis vipassanā may become a fully independent discipline in the case of the bare insight worker or dry-visioned saint. But most of our texts assume the classic jhānic-related mode of progress, as the following discussion implies.

The Path is thus defined:

> "Path" (*magga*) is a designation of the moment of entering into one of the four stages of holiness—Nibbāna being the object—produced by intuitional Insight (*vipassanā*) into the impermanency, misery, and impersonality of existence, flashing forth and forever transforming one's life and nature.[12]

This Path consciousness, as just suggested, represents a major breakthrough into another type of awareness, a "change of lineage" type of knowledge as it is called. *It is the ability to make Nibbāna itself the actual object of awareness.* Buddhaghosa uses a vivid analogy to describe what happens here. A man wishes to swing himself across to the opposite shore of a stream by means of a dangling rope. He takes a running start, grasps the rope, and swings across in three stages (*leaving* the hither shore, *inclining toward* the other shore, and *letting go* to land upon the other shore). The running start is "by means of the contemplation of rise and fall, etc."; grasping the rope is "seizing with [by means of] adverting to impermanence, pain, and not-self the rope of materiality fastened to the branch of his selfhood." The first third of the swing is consciousness based on the previous type of awareness; the second is swinging toward the Nibbāna-object shore; and the third, landing on the bank, is coming to the direct consciousness of Nibbāna itself (XXII.6).

The four levels of Path attainment or sainthood are described as follows:

1. There the monk after the disappearance of the three fetters has won the Stream [to Nibbāna] and is no more subject to rebirth in lower worlds, is firmly established, destined for full enlightenment. [*Sotā-panna* or Stream-Enterer]

2. After the disappearance of sensuous craving and ill-will, he will return only once more; and having once more returned to this world, he will put an end to suffering. [*Sakadāgāmin* or Once-Returner]

3. After the disappearance of the five fetters he appears in a higher [than human] world, and there he reaches Nibbāna without ever returning from that world (to the sensuous sphere). [*Anāgāmin* or Non-Returner]

4. Through the extinction of all Biases [cankers] he reaches already in this very life the deliverance of the mind, the deliverance through wisdom, which is free from biases, and which he himself has understood and realized. [*Arahant*, Arahat or Full-Attainer][13]

This Path attainment awareness can come to the meditator a total of four times, that is, once each time one of the four stages of Stream-Enterer, Once-Returner, and so on, is gained. Its quality and mode of entering are described at length by Buddhaghosa, for Path attainment, like a jhānic state, is sought deliberately. "He thinks, 'Now the path will arise.' Equanimity about formations after comprehending formations as impermanent, or as painful, or as not self sinks into the life continuum" (XXI.129).

That is, the meditator completely accepts, existentially, *especially* as applying to himself, the insight view of all phenomena (formations): they are impermanent, painful, and empty of true reality. When this has been internalized, the meditator is ready for the Path awareness that apprehends the non-phenomenal, non-saṃsāric element of Nibbāna. Thus:

As soon as . . . the thick murk that hides the truths has been dispelled . . . then his consciousness no longer enters into or settles down on or resolves upon any field of formations at all, or clings, cleaves, or clutches on to it, but retreats, retracts and recoils as water does from a lotus leaf, and every sign as object, every occurrence as object, appears as an impediment.

This is the Theravāda world view, as embodied in the Four Noble Truths, fully functionalized in the dominant awareness in this stage of meditational attainment.

> Then while every sign and occurrence appears to him as an impediment ... change-of-lineage knowledge arises in him, *which takes as its object the signless, no-occurrence, no-formation, cessation, nibbana,* which knowledge passes out of the lineage, the category, the plane of the ordinary man and enters ... (that) of the Noble Ones ... which is the culminating peak of insight—which is irrevocable. [XXII. 4, 5; italics added][14]

The Path awareness can occur only once at each level; but its result, which has the same experiential quality of directly apprehending Nibbāna as object, may be repeated at will. Thus:

> PHALA: lit. "Fruit, Fruition," i.e., Result, Path-Result, denotes those moments of supermundane consciousness which flash forth immediately after the moment of path-consciousness ... and which, till the attainment of the next higher path, may during the practice of Insight (vipassanā) still recur innumerable times.[15]

These moments of fruitional consciousness normally occur immediately after the moment of Path consciousness two or three times as spin-off "flashes" of Nibbānic consciousness. But they may be deliberately sought later. Those who have attained the Path may, like a king or deity desiring to experience bliss "attain the attainment of fruition whenever they choose" (XXIII.8). The process in fact repeats the seeking of Path consciousness, except that *now* the seeker has a new datum to put into consciousness—the datum of Nibbāna that was tasted upon Path attainment. "A noble disciple who seeks the attainment of fruition should go into solitary retreat. He should see formations with insight according to rise and fall and so on. When that insight has progressed ... then comes change-of-lineage knowledge with formations as its object." That is, he now beholds all phenomena as impermanent, painful, and unreal in the contrasting light of Nibbānic permanence, bliss, and reality. "And immediately next to it consciousness becomes absorbed in cessation with the attainment of fruition" (XXIII.10).

Although fruition is spoken of as post-Path-attainment "flashes" in the first instance, apparently when the "flashes" are deliberately sought on their own they can recur "innumerable times." In the opinion of Shwe Zan Aung they thus add up to a sustained "vipassanic jhāna": "Each being who has attained a lower Path spends his time enjoying the fruit of that Path, before he attains the next higher. The process of enjoying the fruit for an indefinitely prolonged time is termed 'sustained fruition (*phala-samāpatti*) which corresponds to sustained jhāna ... an unlimited number of apperceptive moments of fruition of the respective paths having as their object Nibbāna.'"[16] This is borne out by the statement of the late Thray Sithu U Ba Khin, founder of the International Meditation Center in Rangoon:

Therefore the real test as to whether one has become an Ariya lies in his ability to go into the fruition state (Phala) *as he may like. While in that state, he is oblivious of any feelings through the five organs of sense.* At the same time his body posture (Iriyapatha) becomes firm and tightened in the same way as one who goes into a Jhanic trance . . . An experienced teacher alone will be able to differentiate between the two.[17]

And it is corroborated by the following statement from another source:

The *Phala-samapatti*, which literally means the Attainment of Fruition, is a wonderful experience. While in this trance, the person concerned is oblivious of the world and of himself. While practicing the spiritual exercises of meditation, it has been necessary to make a special effort, to obtain constant awareness of mind. But during this *Phala-samapatti*, it is not necessary consciously or deliberately to make that special effort to obtain the sense of awareness. It is automatically present and constant in this peaceful and supermundane state of consciousness. In other words, it is a state of tranquility approaching the peace and blessedness of Nirvana. The duration of this Phala-samapatti depends on the *samadhi* or strength of the sense of awareness developed prior to the Phala-samapatti. The trance may last one or two or more hours. During this period, if the trance has been entered into while the person is in a sitting or standing position, the posture is maintained as if the person has been turned into stone. No rocking movement, or bending over, or falling down will occur to disturb the posture of the person. When he comes out of this Phala Samapatti, there will be physical comfort as well as peace of mind. The effects of the complete tranquility of mind during the trance last for some time after he has come out of it. These tranquil effects can be clearly felt. There will be no tiredness of the limbs, no stiffness, and no discomfort of the body.[18]

An interesting possibility suggests itself here: is this the point at which jhānic expertise has an effect? That is, the dry-visioned saint or bare insight worker who has no jhānic powers can attain Path consciousness and at least its attendant fruitional flashes. But can he or she achieve their sustained fusion into a jhāna-like trance? Or is that possible only for the jhāna practicer? At least one passage in Buddhaghosa's treatment of fruition (XXIII.3–15) ties jhānas to fruition: "And if the path he has arrived at had the first jhana, his fruition will have the first jhana too when it arises. And if the path has the second, so will the fruition. And so with the other jhanas" (XXIII.11).

Whatever the answer to this, jhāna-like language describes entry into and emergence from fruition. Moreover, fruition can also be made to last for a length of time by "the non-bringing to mind of all signs, the bringing to mind of the signless element, and the prior volition" (XXIII.12).[19] Apparently one may bring fruition consciousness into being by blanking out awareness of sense data and conceptual thought—method not specified; by deliberately cultivating the Nibbānic awareness experienced upon Path attainment; and by predetermining the length of time that one wishes to remain in fruitional "trance." (The extensive use of predetermination of trance-time will be met with again in the attainment of cessation [nirodha-samāpatti].) To *emerge* from fruition the opposite means are used: the predetermined time comes to an end (nonvolitionally now) and the meditator does not bring to mind Nibbāna or does bring to mind some object of awareness. Are these last two also fed into the initial preparation for fruition? Or does the meditator begin to think in these ways in the midst of a fruition "trance"? It is not clear that this can be done.

The actual progression from stage to stage of Path attainment is greatly facilitated by review or retrospection of the Path and/or fruition experiences (*paccavekkhaṇa*), the same sort of review as we have seen at work in the jhānic series. Buddhaghosa describes the process by which this retrospection of the experience just completed takes place on the Stream-Enterer level:

> At the end of the fruition his consciousness enters the life-continuum. After that, it arises as mind-door adverting, interrupting the life-continuum *for the purpose of reviewing the path*. When that has ceased, seven impulsions of path reviewing arise.... With the arising of these he reviews the path ... in this way, "So this is the path I have come by." Next he reviews the fruition after that in this way, "This is the blessing I have obtained." Next he reviews the defilements that have been abandoned, "These are the defilements abandoned in me." Next he reviews the deathless nibbana in this way, "This is the state (dhamma) that has been *penetrated by me as object*." [XXII.19; italics added]

Obviously the function of the review of Path and fruition moments is similar to the review in jhāna: to enable the meditator to progress to the next higher stage—this time on the vipassanic scale. The meditator clear-mindedly examines the Nibbānic experience just passed through while its experiential flavor still permeates his consciousness; he analyzes shortcomings remaining that hinder further advancement and which must be eliminated; he reviews the techniques used to achieve the Path awareness and the fruitions. Now he can proceed intelligently toward the next higher level of attainment. Mistakes are possible even here, which is another reason why review of *all* attainments is necessary. "Herein, *illumination* is illumination due to insight [vipassanā]. When it arises, the meditator thinks 'Such illumination never arose in me before. I have surely reached the path, reached fruition,' thus he takes what is not the path to be the path, and what is not fruition to be fruition" (XX.107). So too with other psychic accompaniments of vipassanā, such as knowledge, rapturous happiness, tranquility, bliss, resolution, exertion, assurance, and equanimity. The result is that the meditator's "course of insight is interrupted. He drops his basic meditation subject and sits just enjoying the attachment" (XX.123).

This suggests a point to be made again later: there is considerable qualitative affinity between jhānic-style states and vipassanā results—such as general well-being, peace, and equanimity—despite their differences and consequent tension in the meditational structure. In fact, using the term "serenity" (*samatha*), which is a synonym for samādhi and hence of jhānic states in general, Buddhaghosa significantly remarks: "This imperfection of insight usually arises in one who has acquired *serenity and insight*. Because the defilements suppressed by the attainments [jhānas, immaterial states] do not manifest themselves he thinks 'I am an arahant'" (XX.110; italics added). That is, *jhānic* peace is mistaken for *Nibbānic* peace. But

> when illumination, etc., arise, a skillful wary meditator who is endowed with discretion either defines and examines it with understanding [*paññā*] thus "This illumination has arisen. But it is impermanent, formed, conditionally arisen, subject to destruction ... to fall ... to fading away ... to cessation." ... So he unravels this thirty-fold skein of imperfections without falling a prey to wavering. He defines what is the path and what is not the path thus "The states consisting in illumination, etc., are not the path; *but it is insight knowledge that is free from imperfections and keeps to its course, that is the path.*" [XX.126, 128; italics added]

That is to say, there is ever the danger of mistaking samādhic (jhānic) peaceful abidings for the direct experience and knowledge of Nibbāna. Only the rigorous and continuing use of vipassanic review can avoid this danger.

There is one further question: How can Nibbāna be "perceived" or "penetrated ... as object," that is, directly known? Perhaps it is known only in negative terms, which embody the quality of freedom-from-saṃsāra even in their manner of statement, if we accept Buddhaghosa's "description": "Then while every sign and occurrence appears to him as an impediment, when conformity knowledge's repetition has ended, change-of-lineage knowledge arises in him, which takes as its object the signless, no-occurrence, no-formation, cessation, nibbana" (XXII.5).

It is difficult to envisage anything more devoid of "content" or a more essentially "objectless object" of consciousness, than this "signless, no-occurrence, no-formation, cessation, nibbana." As "signless," it is devoid of the "marks" (impermanence, impersonality, misery) that are the essence of all saṃsāric entities, even of all jhānic experiences. As "no-occurrence," it is beyond all temporal reference to quality; and as "formless," that is, imperceptible, it is inconceivable as well. As "no-formation," it does not have the quality of any state of ordinary (saṃsāric) subject-object consciousness. Yet *some* sort of consciousness (supermundane?) is implied, for Nibbāna is held to be the *object* of awareness and it can be retrospected. One can only say that it is so different in its quality that it is separate from *all other* experiences, even the jhānas.

This leads to a consideration of nirodha-samāpatti, the attainment of complete cessation. In this state the jhānic and vipassanic progressions reach a consummatory climax, the highest and fullest participation in

Nibbāna possible to a living human being. And in this process the relation of the yogic and vipassanic elements come into their most intensive and direct interaction. This progression of meditative states that fuse together the yogic and vipassanic essences in one climactic attainment will be the subject matter of the next chapter.

6

The Attainment of Cessation (*Nirodha-Samāpatti*)[1]

Its Ultimacy

When the meditator comes to those Path experiences in which Nibbāna itself is the object of meditative awareness (available in some degree to all four levels of Path attainment), even if it be only for a succession of fleeting moments, the end of the meditative road is coming closer. How much higher can one go than this? The only possible further step would be the quantitative increase and extension in time of the flashes of ultimate awareness and perhaps a fullness of quality that somehow transcends these flashes even in their extended form. And this is specifically what the attainment of cessation provides.

The Buddhist scriptures and meditation manuals leave no doubt as to the absolute ultimacy of this experience in either of the two series of meditational attainments. Two passages in the *Middle Length Sayings* make this position clear with respect to the jhānic progression. In the first passage the Buddha is represented as talking to Udāyin about the whole series of jhānas and formless concentrations. From the first jhāna to the state of neither-perception-nor-nonperception he surveys each attainment in turn with a critical eye. He says to Udāyin, in effect: "You may think, upon experiencing each one of these: 'This is the final attainment. There can be no better.'" But in emphatically eloquent words the Buddha goes on to urge:

> This is not enough! I say, "Get rid of it," I say, "Transcend it." And what is its transcending? ... a monk, by wholly transcending the plane of neither-perception-nor-nonperception, enters and abides in the stopping of perception and feeling. This is its transcending ... Now do you, Udāyin, see any fetter, minute or massive, of the getting rid of which I have not spoken to you?
>
> No, revered sir. [*MLS*, II, p. 128 (I.456)]

In the second passage the Buddha is questioning three monks, headed by Anuruddhas, about their attainment of cessation. They too have found by experience that in each of the eight states below that of cessation a still higher experience lures them on. But when the Buddha asks about cessation, whether they perceived yet another and higher one after *that*, they reply with one voice:

> Here we, Lord, *for as long as we like*, by passing quite beyond the plane of neither-perception-nor-nonperception, entering on the stopping of perception, abide in it, and having seen through intuitive wisdom, our cankers come to be utterly destroyed. . . . But we, Lord, do not behold another abiding in comfort that is higher or more excellent than this abiding in comfort.

To which the Buddha replies: "It is good, Anuruddhas, it is good. There *is* no other abiding in comfort that is higher or more excellent than *this* abiding in comfort" [*MLS*, II, p. 261 (I.209); italics added]. "Abidings in comfort" are jhānic-type states, sometimes termed peaceful abidings, as noted. Hence *nirodha-samāpatti* is the Ultimate Jhāna, so to speak.

But it is also at the same time something more. Thus writes Buddhaghosa: "*Why do they attain it?* Being wearied by the occurrence and dissolution of formations, they attain it thinking 'Let us dwell in bliss by being without consciousness here and now and reaching the cessation that is nibbāna'" (XXIII.30). Nothing could be clearer. Cessation is here-and-now Nibbāna. Thus the Ultimate Jhāna is also the Ultimate Fruition, the experience of experiences.

The experience is of course in time. It "arises" when the meditator enters into cessation, and "ceases" upon emergence from it. But the quality is timeless. When, as an arahant or non-returner—for no others can achieve it—the meditator attains cessation of feeling and perception, he knows "This is It; I am arrived." No further attainment practice is necessary, for there is nothing further to attain in this life. It is the maximum possible temporal extension of those Nibbāna realizations contained in Path and fruition awareness as well as the experiential ultimate, Nibbāna itself, tasted in one's present existence. In the words of Nalinaksha Dutt, "While in this trance he has a foretaste of Nibbāna which is going to be his permanently."[2] And Shwe Zan Aung makes an interesting distinction between cessation and the fruition moments:

> On waking from trance, apperception of the Fruition of the respective Paths invariably occurs for one thought moment, with Nibbāna as its object, before the resumption of the stream. The difference between the consciousness of sustained fruition and that in the process just described (*nirodha-samāpatti*) is that Nibbāna is merely intuited in the former, but partially enjoyed in the latter, when the person is entirely free from pain.[3]

Thus the preeminence of cessation over fruition awareness is perhaps one of degree rather than kind; but it *is* greatly superior just as the fullness of an experience is superior to its intimations and foretastes.

It is to be noted that this state is reviewed also:

The process is followed by one of review, in which one of the first two of the eight great moral classes in the case of the Non-returner, or of the eight inoperative classes in the case of the Arahant, follows representative cognition before the stream resumes its flow. It is evidently this post-cataleptic meditation that the Nibbāna-under-present-conditions, enjoyed erewhile, is remembered.[4]

While the glory of this pretaste of final Nibbāna still infuses consciousness, as in the case of the review of fruition moments, the meditator examines the experience just past and his own present awareness. If he is an arahant he can find no bonds that tie him to saṃsāra—those that have been are now inoperative. Seeing himself clearly in the light of Nibbāna, there is nothing to cloud the picture. He needs only to wait for his demise. With the anāgāmin there are still subtle bonds to embodied existence—but they allow a final birth in some higher-than-human realm if arahantship is not attained in the present human life.

The paradox here lies in speaking of cessation as an experiential ultimate. If all thinking and feeling completely stop, how can it be an "experience"? It cannot be such *during* the cessation itself.[5] It is a Nibbānic "experience" indirectly—by inference, by anticipation, and by "postexperience." As stoppage of thought and feeling, it is inferred to be Nibbānic. With cessation already predefined as Nibbāna-in-this-life, the meditator so views it when anticipating or preparing to enter it. And in the postexperience, it is felt as utter, irrefragable peace because of the feeling tone of the stoppage of thought just occurring and the prestoppage conception of cessation as Nibbānic.

Entering and Leaving Cessation

What are the techniques employed for passing from the "semiconsciousness" of neither-perception-nor-nonperception to the "unconsciousness" of the cessation of perception and feeling? In part the basic technique further extends that employed throughout the jhānic series: using the meditation subject of the now fully mastered state as a springboard into the next. Or more accurately, by "surmounting" or "abandoning" that subject, one takes the related but different subject next in line. Cessation must be intended from the beginning. With this final goal in mind the meditator runs expertly and rapidly up the successive steps and then, like a pole vaulter, launches himself toward the attainment of cessation from the base of the highest formless state.

He enters the first meditation, *jhāna*, and emerging from it peacefully, sees the impermanence, ill and not-self of that meditation, *jhāna*, immediately. Possessed of the knowledge of equanimity towards the formations, he enters into the second, the third and fourth meditations, *jhānas*, the sphere of the infinity of space, the sphere of the infinity of consciousness and the sphere of nothingness. Then emerging there-from peacefully, he sees the impermanence, ill and not-self of Right Concentration immediately, and being possessed of the knowledge of equanimity towards the formations, he enters into the sphere of neither perception nor non-perception immediately. *Then passing beyond two or three turns of consciousness, he causes the perishing of mind and enters the Unborn and Unmanifest.* [*PF*, p. 325; italics added]

The regular jhānic technique, described previously, is in part the tech-nique here also. That is, the base of neither-perception-nor-nonperception "is surmounted" by leaping from it as a concentration subject into *no*-perception, that is, the "perishing of mind" in nirodha-samāpatti. This is the standard kasina mode of progression. But the vipassanic methodology is just as integral to this progression as is the kasina-jhānic. After emerging from the sphere of nothingness, the meditator looks back, as it were, upon the total progression thus far and "sees the impermanence, ill and not-self of Right Concentration," that is, the non-Nibbānic character of all the seven steps taken thus far on the kasina-jhānic road. *Not* reviewing neither-perception-nor-nonperception is a methodological necessity, not a true exception to the vipassanā purview; for since he proceeds directly into *no*-consciousness, the meditator cannot be conscious of the immediately pre-ceding state in any way.

One further observation: even the "experience" of cessation is reviewed in a manner clearly affected by the vipassanā context. Thus, in the scriptures:

And again, monks, Sāriputta, by passing quite beyond the plane of neither-perception-nor-nonperception, enters on and abides in the stopping of perception and feeling. And having seen by means of intu-itive wisdom, his cankers are utterly destroyed. Mindful, he emerges from that attainment. When he has emerged, mindful, from that attainment he regards those things that are past, stopped, changed as: "*Thus indeed things that have not been in me come to be; having been they pass away.*" He, not feeling attracted by these things, not feeling repelled, independent, not infatuated, freed, released, dwells with a mind that is unconfined. *He comprehends: "There is no further escape." There is no zealous practice for him concerning that.* [*MLS*, III, p. 80 (III, 27–28); italics added]

There are several interesting accounts of the *depth* of nirodha-samāpatti in *The Path of Purification*:

The Elder, it seems, sent for alms into the village where his mother, a lay follower, lived. She gave him rice gruel and seated him in the sitting hall. The Elder sat down and attained cessation. While he was sitting there the hall caught fire. The other bhikkhus each picked up their seats and fled. The villagers gathered together, and seeing the Elder, they said "What a lazy monk!" The fire burned the grass thatch, the bamboos and timbers, and it encircled the Elder. People brought water and put it out. They removed the ashes, did repairs, scattered flowers, and then stood respectfully waiting. The Elder emerged at the time he had determined. Seeing them, he said "I am discovered!", and he rose up into the air and went to Piyangu Island. [XXIII.36]

Another story is told of a monk in nirodha-samāpatti all night long in the forest. A robber gang coming with their loot in the darkness mistook the seated meditator for a tree stump and strewed their stolen goods about him. After resting for a time they began to pick up their booty. But just as the first one to lay his booty down around the monk began to pick it up again, the monk came out of his cessation state, and the robbers were much taken aback. Indeed they were so impressed by this feat that they all repented and themselves became monks (XXII.33). Another monk in the state of cessation was taken for dead by some cowherds, who decided then and there to cremate him. But so powerful was the force of his previous concentration that not even a corner of his robe was burnt (XII.32)!

Whatever the historical value of these accounts, three features call for comment. First, the cessation can be maintained for extended periods of time. Buddhaghosa nearly always speaks of a seven-day limit for sustaining this condition, though he never flatly states that a person *can* not live longer than this. The *Buddhist Dictionary*, on the basis of a commentary, states that such concentration can go on for eight days or longer.[6] Second, to reinforce statements already made about the complete unconsciousness of this state, at least one passage in the Canon distinguishes this condition from death itself. In the attainment of cessation all bodily functions (including breathing), as well as verbal and mental functions cease. The only difference between the two is that in death, the life-force itself is exhausted, the vital heat has been extinguished, and the "sense organs are entirely broken asunder" [*MLS*, I, pp. 356–57 (I.296)].

Third, cessation can be broken out of by the meditator *if it is predetermined*. Nothing else could have awakened the monk surrounded by robbers' loot, except his own predetermination. And in order to avoid awkward situations like that of the elder around whom the monastery burned down, the monk about to enter this state is required to preset his mind to awaken in response to these four situations: avoidance of damage to others' property; when the community of monks calls for the meditator's presence to conduct business; when the Leader (originally the Buddha) calls the meditator; and the approaching end of the meditator's life-span. This last is presumably thought of as running out of strength because of the long period of non-nourishment and/or the fateful coming to an end because of past karma (*PP*, XXIII.35–42). But why *should* the meditator return to life in saṃsāra when experiencing the bliss of cessation? If, as anāgāmin, he has not yet attained to arahantship, he should be using his energies to attain that state, here and now. And further, to die while in this state deprives the community of valuable spiritual help: "For in the case of sudden death he would not be able to declare final knowledge, advise the bhikkhus and testify to the Dispensation's power" (*PP*, XXIII.42 n.). But what of the mind-set of one who emerges from cessation? "It tends toward nibbana ... 'his consciousness inclines to seclusion, leans to seclusion, tends to seclusion'" (XXIII.50).[7]

The Interaction of Jhāna and Vipassanā

One further central issue remains to be more fully discussed: the relation of the jhānic and vipassanic elements here intermingled. Their tension-stimulation, opposition-mutual support, and identity-difference symbiosis throughout the Theravāda meditative structure is present here in its most intensive form in the attainment of cessation, and is therefore of particular interest. The following questions will be considered: 1. How are the two elements combined for the production of the attainment of cessation? 2. What does each contribute to the process? 3. How do they affect each other?

1. How do jhānic and vipassanic techniques combine to produce nirodha-samāpatti? That they do so and must do so, Buddhaghosa makes clear in the following passage.

> *How does its attainment come about?* It comes about in one who performs the preparatory tasks by striving with *serenity* and *insight* and causes the cessation of [consciousness belonging to] the base consisting of neither perception nor non-perception. One who strives with serenity alone reaches the base consisting of neither perception nor non-perception and remains there, while one who strives with insight alone reaches the attainment of fruition and remains there. *But it is one who strives with both*, and after performing the preparatory tasks, causes the cessation of [consciousness belonging to] the base consisting of neither perception nor non-perception, *who attains it.* [XXIII.31; all but first italics added]

The key words, of course, are "serenity" and "insight." Serenity refers to the jhānic technique and eightfold series of attainments. Cessation is the true child of that process and cannot be achieved without its perfection up to the trance of neither-perception-nor-nonperception. Likewise the perfection of the vipassanic practice in anāgāmin and arahant attainments is absolutely necessary. Only those who have attained the Path can attain cessation. It cannot be repeated too often that *cessation is an integral blending of the two.*[8]

To establish this I will now directly observe the process leading to cessation. As noted, the meditator must intend to achieve it from the beginning, even when preparing to enter the first jhāna. And all succeeding steps are also to be thus undertaken.

> When a bhikkhu who desires to attain cessation has finished all that he has to do with his meal and has washed his hands and feet well, he sits down on a well-prepared seat in a secluded place. Having folded his legs crosswise, set his body erect, established mindfulness in front of him, he attains the first jhāna, and on emerging *he sees the formations in it with insight as impermanent, painful, not self.*

Thus proceeding similarly at every stage, he advances on up to the base consisting of no-thingness. Then,

> on emerging from that he does the fourfold preparatory task, that is to say about (a) non-damage to others' property, (b) the Community's waiting, (c) the Master's summons, and (d) the limit of the duration. . . .
>
> He then attains the base consisting of neither perception nor non-perception. Then after one, or two, turns of consciousness have passed, he becomes without consciousness, he achieves cessation. [*PP*, XXIII.32, 44][9]

Such is the interweaving of the jhānic and vipassanic elements, but the character of their interaction is not yet clear, especially in view of their tension with each other. For here, those jhānic-yogic elements rejected initially by the Buddha, continually downgraded as being too saṃsāric in the context of Buddhist meditation, are now combined with vipassanā to produce the highest possible vipassanic (Nibbānic) state!

There is the general Buddhist dictum that all *means*, however excellent and necessary to attainment of enlightenment, are to be abandoned when enlightenment has been attained. The vipassanic view of jhānas as still saṃsāric (produced in dependence upon body-mind factors and other variable elements) is certainly one form of this teaching. Hence the vipassanic downgrading of jhānas is not essentially a declaration of their evil or to-be-abandoned-Brāhmaṇical nature. It is only a declaration of the limits of all means.

But there is more. The two elements are akin internally, though they originally stemmed from different world views—one leading to a blissful union with Ultimate Reality (Brahman) even in this life, the other to a going out of/from all existence. But apart from differing goals and world views, the two processes (jhānic and vipassanic) *as processes* are quite similar.

To review: both seek states transcending ordinary time-space oriented, sense-informed consciousness. Jhānic "awareness" is for its duration locked away from ordinary awareness. And the continuing jhānic advance represents a progressive refinement of the subject-object nature of consciousness by the increasing subtilization of the object of awareness, until we reach neither-perception-nor-nonperception as an object base of consciousness. On the vipassanic side is the attainment (in the first of the Path achievements,

Stream-Enterer) of a direct awareness of "unformed nibbāna" as Buddha-ghosa puts it. The meditator's knowledge mode has a "change of lineage" into supramundane awareness. Thus, though the jhānic awareness, no matter how refined at its upper levels, differs from the vipassanic fruitions, both types transcend *ordinary* consciousness. That is, though fruition (direct awareness of Nibbāna) is attained by a level of consciousness (neighborhood consciousness) less transic than the jhāna, its fullness, that flashing moment of awareness, must also be "emerged" from, just as with jhānas. So also these moments may be repeated and sustained, as noted above.

Still further, both processes seek the ever deeper, fuller knowledge that in the end should lead to an "absolute" awareness. The yogic "parent" of the jhānic process sought a unitive awareness with Brahman, or a unitive awareness of oneself. That was its mokṣa or release. In its Buddhist adaptation, however, the process was deprived of its traditional goal, but the process itself was retained. Since the Buddhist goal is Nibbāna—which is Buddhist mokṣa—the jhānic process by definition must lead there also, if it is to contribute in any way to the Buddhist quest. But true to its yogic quality, as a meditational process it logically heads toward a state in which the total cessation of ordinary consciousness is accomplished—though with no Brahman realization as content. The vipassanic process, on the other hand, should head toward ever fuller experiences of Nibbāna. The flashes of Nibbānic awareness (fruition) even when sustained merely whet the appetite for a more sustained, in-depth "experience," in this life if possible. To use an earlier phrase, the "intuitive glimpses" of these fruitions should give way to "the partial enjoyment" of Nibbāna. And since Nibbāna is "the signless, non-occurrence, no-formation, cessation" (*PP*, XXII.5), what more appropriate form of its this-life realization can there be other than deliberately chosen, total cessation of consciousness?

An interesting confirmation of this inner likeness of the two types of meditative practice comes from a Buddhist source, the late U Ba Khin, founder and head of the International Meditation Center in Rangoon. He wrote about the relationship of jhānic and vipassanic meditation in a memo to me in 1960.

> The method whereby a student is changed to the course of Vipassanā after attainment of an appreciable degree of concentration [neighborhood concentration] is called the Vipassanā-yanika method. Where a student learns to go into Jhānic States and then takes the course of meditation in Vipassanā, he may be said to have taken the Samathayanika method. (This) method is not suitable for householders as Jhānic states are ordinarily meant for persons who live in seclusion . . . although the possibility of householders, *who have cleansed themselves thoroughly with Vipassanā meditation*, going into Jhānic states, should not be discounted. [Italics added]

The pattern of analysis followed thus far seems almost reversed: vipassanā prepares for jhāna, as though jhāna were the higher.

Whether U Ba Khin might have had a particular Pāli text in mind I do not know. But in any case at least one such passage speaks of the jhāna-vipassanā and vipassanā-jhāna order of meditations as alternatives. In *The Book of the Gradual Sayings* [pp. 162–63 (ii.156)], Ānanda states that there are four routes to arahantship: insight preceded by calm (samatha), calm preceded by insight, calm-and-insight coupled, clear-about-Dhamma one-pointed thought. The point seems clear: it is possible, though perhaps not usual, to work with jhānas and vipassanā in any order, provided only that vipassanā gets in its necessary work.

The procedure for going into jhānic states is further outlined in the letter as one of concentration on breath-at-nostril, becoming aware of points (or point) of light seen with closed eyes upon achieving one-pointedness of mind, mastery of this light so that one can "play with it mentally" by "placing" it wherever one wishes, and finally placing it at the base of the nose and then drawing it inward ("swallowing it") till it joins with "the inner light of the Mind." This will produce the first jhāna, and in turn the higher jhānas by means of drawing the light inward again and again.[10]

But the final comments are even more to the point.

> "Mind is intrinsically pure," said the Buddha. . . . While a person is in a Jhānic State, his mind is perfectly pure, i.e. free from any taint of impurity and out of the field of sensuality. If Brahman or God were taken as the personification of "Intrinsic Purity," then such a person could be said to be in union with Brahman or God.

It seems, then, that despite the breakaway of Buddhism from Brāhmaṇism, the rejection of its goals and partial-critical use of common yogic elements and methods, the deep inner likeness of the two traditions and their meditational methods persists, so that "heretical" Buddhism can still use the common techniques. Stephan Beyer, in writing about the trance of cessation (nirodha-samāpatti), states it thus:

> The Buddhist trance of cessation is in many ways a logical extension of the gradual sensory withdrawal of the four trances: all the so-called formless trances were worked into the standard structure of the contemplative process as part of the practice of calm and considered preliminary exercises to the application of insight. . . .
>
> There are many parallels between this Buddhist trance and the procedures of classical Yoga. Despite deep clashes in metaphysical superstructure, there is considerable similarity in the ultimate experience of enstatic disentanglement from the world. The trance of cessation is structurally equivalent to the final *samādhi* of the yogic texts: both are states wherein all thoughts and feelings cease; neither relies upon the external support of a meditative object; both culminate a sequence of withdrawals from sensory experience, and both are the highest happiness that can be achieved in this life. The yogic word for salvation is "isolation," and though the Buddhist texts do not use the term, it is an apt description of ultimate transcendence.[11]

Or to put it differently: After centuries of using yogic and vipassanic methods together, what could keep them from coalescing in some final climactic experience—called Nibbāna-realization in the Buddhist context? In the words of Dutt:

> The object of Jhānas is to bring the mind into such a state that it will be above worldly pleasure and pain. It can be effected by dissociating the mind completely from all worldly matters. This is achieved by means of the trances, the highest of which is the *Saññāvedayitanirodha*. From the foregoing discussion about the highest trance, it is evident that Nibbana is psychically *Saññāvedayitanirodha* provided that the adept complies with the other necessary conditions of Arahanthood.[12]

But of course "Arahanthood" is the product of vipassanā.

2. What does each meditational discipline contribute to the process? This is difficult to answer because of the close melding of the two, but certain features stand out. The jhānic side contributes a technique. Even for the non-jhānic vipassanā meditator, his method appears to be a jhānic product. The neighborhood concentration level of awareness is the first step toward full jhāna. Still further, as earlier suggested, the jhānic expert is perhaps able to give a depth and continuity to fruition moments that make them a vipassanā-jhāna—a sustained fruition.

This depth and continuity are crucial for the attainment of cessation. Even though each of the eight preceding stages (jhānas and formless meditations) is "interrupted" by vipassanā flashbacks to keep them on their *Buddhist* road toward Nibbāna, it is the jhānic technique of using one jhānic state as springboard into the next higher one that propels the meditator finally into cessation.

Likewise, it is the depth of jhānic concentration, not that of the vipassanic, that enables the meditator to maintain cessation over considerable periods. This jhānic depth and force of concentration both projects the meditators into cessation and holds them there till the predetermined time is over. Thus jhānic force holds the meditator in Nibbāna (in this life)!

The vipassanic element is also necessary, though on the surface it seems less *functionally* essential. It seems to contribute no technique to the progression, yet it is absolutely necessary to the final stage of cessation. How can this be? Is terming jhānic cessation "Nibbāna" anything more than putting a Buddhist cloak of Nibbānic terminology on a jhānic result? The tentative answer to this includes the answer to the third question, which follows.

3. How do the jhānic and vipassanic elements affect each other? The answer involves the totality of Theravāda meditation, though here I will keep it primarily within the confines of the nirodha-samāpatti technique. Obviously the designation of cessation as Nibbāna participation provides a powerful motivation for jhānic progression. To "experience" Nibbāna-in-this-life in its utter cessation of all turmoil or painfulness "for as long

as we like" was surely immensely attractive to those brought up in the Brāhmaṇical and early Buddhist traditions! Stcherbatsky's comment is to the
point here:

> We will better understand the Solution [Nirvana] at which the Buddha
> arrived, if we take into account a specific Indian habit of mind, its
> idea of Quiescence as the only real bliss which life can afford. The
> Buddhist Saint (*arya*) regards the life of the worldling as an unhappy
> existence of constant turmoil. His aim is to escape from the movement
> of phenomenal life into a state of absolute Quiescence, a condition
> in which all emotion and all concrete thought is stopped forever. The
> means of attaining this Quiescence is profound meditation (*yoga*), the
> technique of which was developed in India at a very early date.[13]

More important, however, is the depth and power exerted by the Buddhist context of meditation upon the jhānic elements. The Buddhist jhāna,
though derived from that yogin tradition common to Brāhmaṇism and
early Buddhism, and reinfluenced as yogic in the taking over of the formless
meditations, has been "deyoginized" and thoroughly "Buddhacized."
Some tensions remain, but they are now (in the Buddhist context) *creative,
intradisciplinary* tensions, not antithetical practices. The jhāna is no longer
merely or truly yoga but a new Buddhist creation similar to yoga.

What makes the Buddhist jhāna different from the Brāhmaṇical-Hindu
yoga is the interfusion of the transcendent, wholly other Nibbānic element
into the discipline and techniques of meditation itself. This was observable,
for example, in the movement from vipassanā to the jhānas suggested by U
Ba Khin. Purification by vipassanā is necessary *before* undertaking the
jhānas. And vipassanā-purified jhāna—with its ultimate goal of Nibbāna—is
not the same as a yogic trance. Though it has general similarities with yoga
in the form of being cut off from the ordinary give and take of subject-object
sensory experience, the interfusion of the Nibbānic element, as goal and as
experiential datum, is an important, decisive difference. That is to say, the
Negative Unconditioned of Nibbāna is not the same as the positive *neti-neti* of
Brahman-awareness—so the Buddhist has always maintained.[14] And the
jhānic (yogic) practice is steeped from beginning to end in Nibbānic values
—first as aimed at, later as experienced.

One obvious point of the Nibbāna influence upon jhānic techniques is
the posttransic vipassanā review of jhānic states already noted. Thus the
jhāna in Buddhist usage can never be an end in itself. Only as reviewed and
hence subordinated to the quest for Nibbāna can yogic techniques be used
in Buddhist meditation. This jhāna-cum-vipassanā, jhāna-cum-Nibbāna
goal is the Buddhist transformation of Brāhmaṇical yoga.

But still further, when Nibbāna as object of awareness comes into meditation with the Stream-Enterer attainment, the distinctively Buddhist
Wholly Other—the signless, no-occurrence, no-formation, cessation—
directly affects and qualifies every meditative act thereafter. The jhānas

of one who has perceived Nibbāna *directly* cannot be the same as those of one who has not. Their lesser depth of reality and ultimacy of experience are now apparent even as they are used. Their role can never be anything more than instrumental to the deepening of Path fruitions, the attainment of cessation in this life, and of final Nibbāna when this life ceases.

This instrumental use of jhānas is most clearly evident in the techniques used to attain cessation. There, as noted, the jhānic attainments are totally subordinated to Nibbānic values. The meditator takes them up only with the deliberate intention of using them to attain cessation without lingering in their enjoyment—now seen as paltry compared to the (Nibbānic) fruitions. Mercilessly and immediately, the meditator subjects them to the anicca-anattā-dukkha analysis of vipassanā. Rapidly proceeding up the eight-step jhānic ladder the meditator plunges into nirodha-samāpatti, scorning all other attainments. Nibbāna is triumphant. Its unconditioned absoluteness blots out all means, lesser experiences, and other values in its full realization.

> While in this trance he has a foretaste of Nibbana which is going to be his permanently. He acquires ... knowledge of the destruction of his impurities and of the consequent attainment of emancipation. His mental faculties then become so clear that he understands with a moment's thought all that is happening around him. He is now possessed of full illumination, i.e., he is enlightened.[15]

Yet, an ambiguity still clings to nirodha-samāpatti. For example, how can supposedly superior states of consciousness (jhānas) lead on to unconsciousness (cessation)? Is this the fully mystical assertion that the completely ineffable is fullness of knowledge? And/or is cessation the maximization of the fruition awareness of "the signless" which overtops the jhānic awaremess by nonawareness? Is fruition-awareness the objectless awareness of Eastern mysticism, here identified with total unawareness and designated as that absolute realization *beyond* all consciousness?

There is also cessation's ambiguity by association, so to speak. Cessation is no doubt a good in its own right. But there are "this-worldly" fringe benefits too. Thus Buddhaghosa in a section entitled "What are the benefits of concentration?" lists cheek by jowl such benefits of jhānic meditation as these: the ability to "dwell with unified mind the whole day"; "by being without consciousness for seven days we shall abide in bliss here and now by reaching the cessation that is nibbana"; development of magic powers so that "having been one he becomes many." And he encourages ordinary lay people by saying that the development of the power to achieve preparatory access meditation "ensures an improved form of existence in the happy destinies of the sensual sphere." In closing he exhorts:

> So wise men fail not in devotion
> To the pursuit of concentration;

It cleans defiling stains' pollution,
And brings rewards past calculation. [XI.120–26]

The Path of Freedom is even more explicit. In specific answer to the question "Why is it (the trance of cessation) developed?" the author replies:

For the sake of happiness in the present. This is the Noble Individual's last immovable concentration. *And again, for the sake of supernormal magical power, one enters into the whole range of concentration . . . It is (entered also) for the sake of protecting the body.* [P. 324; italics added]

Thus even in the climax of its progression, in the highest state of all, the classic Buddhist meditation pattern remains an ambivalent product of present-life benefits, and of its own negative vision of reality as it truly *is*, impermanent, painful, and impersonal—as well as the experience of the highest bliss possible to a living being.

7

Contemporary Theravāda Meditation in Burma

The Age for Vipassanā

The Evil-Age Motif

The classic Pāli Canon structure of meditational progression is intended primarily for the monk, who, it is assumed, will follow the jhānic progression toward Nibbāna at least to the fourth-jhāna level. Vipassanā understanding of all experiences and states, including the jhānic, as impermanent, painful, and impersonal, is to be directly applied to the jhānic states subsequent to their attainment. And the jhānic and vipassanic progressions together lead on to the crowning attainment of cessation.

But since the vipassanā understanding (wisdom) is the quintessence of the insight leading to Nibbāna, as well as the sine qua non for that final liberation, it is implied in sacred scripture that vipassanā alone *could* be a discipline sufficient for salvation. By the time of Buddhaghosa (c. A.D. 500) at least, the implied had become the explicit, even though it is sparingly alluded to in *The Path of Purification* by the term "bare insight worker."

What was implied in the Canon and mentioned by Buddhaghosa as a second-grade possibility has in the twentieth century become central for popular Theravāda Buddhism. Today many meditation centers for laity, laity-become-monks-and-nuns in their retired years, and for monks also, follow a vipassanā-oriented meditational discipline. And a kind of consensus exists that the modern age and modern people are best suited to vipassanā as an independent spiritual technique for achieving enlightenment, largely bypassing jhānic-style practice.

The jhānic practices are by no means dead or necessarily dying. The accepted tradition is too strong for that—though I think that few members of the contemporary Saṅgha, particularly in the cities, actually spend much time in meditation.[1] And lay-oriented meditation centers dedicated to vipassanā do encourage limited jhānic practice. Some secluded monasteries, such as those in the Sagaing Hills, follow the classical pattern and emphasize meditation. There is also a "hidden" elite among the monks, adept *both* in jhānic and vipassanic attainment and instruction—though other meditation masters might be described as "bare insight masters," to vary

Buddhaghosa's phrase slightly, that is, vipassanā-only practicers and teachers.[2] But the teaching of vipassanā as a self-sufficient method regardless of the master's attainments occupies the center of the stage today in Theravāda meditation in any case.

What are the reasons for this relatively recent development? Is it the result of a conscious desire to "reform" the traditional meditational pattern and make it more purely "Buddhist," that is, reduce the importance of the yogic (jhānic) elements inherited from India? This does not seem to be consciously an issue; the original welding of Brāhmaṇical and Buddhist elements is now so many centuries old that the thought of the jhānic elements as non- or less-Buddhist than vipassanā would simply not occur to a Theravādin. Hence contemporary vipassanā movements are self-consciously and thoroughly Theravāda and traditional, and are completely indisposed toward either doctrinal or practical innovation. Vipassanā is popular today for historical and practical reasons.

The first set of reasons is scriptural and traditional. The Buddha once prophesied the coming decline of the Dhamma and Saṅgha. The words were spoken to Ānanda in response to his thrice-spoken plea that women be admitted to the Saṅgha: "If, Ānanda, women had not been allowed to go forth from the home to the homeless life into the discipline of Dhamma . . . for a thousand years would Saddhamma have lasted. But now, Ānanda, . . . just for five hundred years will Saddhamma last."[3]

On this basis, with the passing of the centuries there have appeared many variable estimations (ranging all the way from 500 to 1000 to 2500 and to the now prevalent one of 5000 years) of the time during which Buddhist piety and practice will progressively decline from their original splendor and in the end totally disappear from the earth. Thus according to one scheme, in the first 1000 years the attainment of the level of insight open to Buddhas is possible, as well as knowledge of the four Paths. There is thereafter a successive decline in spiritual attainment, one stage at a time, till in the fifth 1000 years, only the Stream-Enterer (sotāpanna) stage is possible. Such, in the opinion of some today, is the level of our present age, though the chronology does not jibe with the thousand-year scheduling. Other schemes speak of ages of eminent practices: for example, the Buddhists of the first 500 years excel in resolute energy, the second in meditation, the third in scripture, the fourth in the founding of monasteries, the fifth in quarrels and the disappearance of the Dhamma altogether. Still others speak of the gradual disappearance of scriptures, first the Abhidhamma, then the Vinaya, then the Suttas, and finally even the Saṅgha itself.[4]

With this tradition there have been many repeated readings of "the signs of the times" to see where one's own age might be located in this timetable of decline. Frequently, as at present, there has been an overriding sense of living near the end of the Buddhist era—a form to be found also in the recurrent Japanese Buddhist teaching of *mappō*, the last Dharma age. Precisely what the "end" will be like and when it will come remain mysterious.

Other traditional motifs compound this sense of doom. A general context of *cosmic* decline is found both in scripture and tradition. In the *Dialogues of the Buddha* there are two suttantas entitled "War, Wickedness and Wealth" and "A Book of Genesis," which set forth a Buddhist cosmology, adapted from Brāhmaṇical sources (pt. III, Suttantas 26, 27). Its pattern is a cyclic fall from a light-filled, virtuous world where beings lived for 80,000 years to a low point with a maximum ten-year life-span. With life-spans now at six or seven decades we are obviously in the last, evil Kali age, rapidly plunging down toward the historical nadir. In *The Path of Purification* (XIII.30ff.) this process of decline and final destruction by fire, water, or wind is graphically described in amplified form as a cataclysmic end of most material universe systems. These modes of destruction are linked to a general moral decline—and a sense of moral decline can, of course, be easily documented in any age by its contemporaries.

Still one further popular note of pessimism may be added. Reading the scriptures reveals a contrast between the Buddha's day and our own: *then* there were hundreds, perhaps thousands of monks who had achieved arahantship; now there are few if any arahants. And many further contemporary evidences of Buddhist decline can be adduced: monks in general are not as devout as they used to be; young people are less interested in Buddhism; Western science has turned many Buddhists away from faith in the Buddha-way; many people of "Buddhist" upbringing do not even know the basic Five Precepts, and so on almost ad infinitum. Surely Buddhism has declined and the end of the age is near!

There are also some optimistic notes. In the scriptural passages describing the descent of the universe to its nadir of a ten-year life-expectancy, there is the promise of an upward swing because of people's repentance and the fact that a lower point could scarcely be reached. Buddhaghosa says (*PP*, XIII.34) that usually just before a world cataclysm, devas from the higher realms come down to exhort people to repentance (and meditation?), and the "sinners" respond in great numbers.

So too there is the prospect of the coming of Metteyya (*Maitreya*) Buddha, the fifth and last Buddha of this great world epoch of whom Gotama Buddha predicted:

> Among such humans, brethren ... there will arise Sankha, a Wheel-turning king, righteous and ruling in righteousness, lord of the four quarters, conqueror, protector of his people.... More than a thousand will be his offspring, heroes, vigorous of frame, crushers of the hosts of the enemy. He will live in supremacy over this earth to its ocean bounds, having conquered it not by the scourge, not by the sword, but by righteousness.
>
> At that period, brethren, there will arise in the world an Exalted One named Metteyya, Arahant, Fully Awakened, ... a Buddha even as I am now.... He will be accompanied by a congregation of some

thousands of brethren, even as I am now accompanied by some hundreds of brethren.[5]

The precise relation of this Golden Age of Metteyya Buddha to the general cosmic upswing just mentioned is not clear; probably they embody a Buddhist historical and a Hindu cosmological tradition respectively, which were never fully fused in the Buddhist scriptures. But in any case, and interestingly, the Metteyya hope apparently supports meditation. That is, it works harmoniously with the generally negative sense of world decline and Buddhist decay to actually strengthen the contemporary enthusiasm for meditation.

This occurs as follows: if on the one hand a person ought to improve his spiritual status by meditation in view of the impending total disappearance of Buddhism—during many centuries perhaps before Metteyya finally comes to renew the Dhamma—he ought on the other hand to seek to be reborn as a human being in that Metteyya epoch. In the living presence of a new Buddha the opportunity for achieving arahantship will be much better than in this decadent age when spiritual vitality is low everywhere and in everyone. And many Buddhists today do make the hopeful vow to seek to be reborn in the Metteyyan age. What better way can there be to insure this than by present ardent meditative effort? For present Buddha-Dhamma time is running out, and it is extremely difficult to be born as a human being,[6] let alone as a properly prepared one in an infrequent Buddha era! To successfully pinpoint such a birth in the less than century-long lifetime of a historical Buddha (Metteyya in this case) fantastically multiplies the negative odds. But sufficient good kamma produced by meditation might bring this off.

We have a near contemporary statement by the Ledi Sayadaw, of this double motif that draws precisely the meditative conclusion. He has already said that in any age morality (sīla) and mental concentration (samādhi) are possible. But, "outside of a Buddha Sasana [read "Buddha Dhamma Age"] one does not get the opportunity of even hearing the mere mention of words associated with *paññā*, though an infinite number of '*sunna*' (world-cycles) may elapse." Paññā is that vipassanā-type understanding of all things as impermanent, painful, and impersonal process. He goes on to say:

> Hence, those persons of the present day who are fortunate enough to be born into this world while a Buddha Sasana flourishes, if they intend to accumulate the seeds of *magga-ñana* and *phala-ñana* for the purpose of securing release from worldly ills in a future existence within a future Buddha Sasana, *should pay special attention to the knowledge of the* paramattha *(ultimate realities), which is extremely difficult to come across.*

The "ultimate realities" here alluded to are consciousness, mental factors, material qualities, and Nibbāna. That is, paramattha knowledge is insight into the empty-flux of the body-mind self (vipassanā again) *and* the positive flashes of Nibbāna awareness. If this Path-fruition is impossible, meditators should at least attain the first knowledge—insight into the impersonality of their own bodies, composed of earth, air, fire, and water elements; for even this much will enable them to "obtain a sound collection of the seeds of paññā."

Good morality will help one to be born when Metteyya appears—which will be the *second* small world-age after this one.[7] Bad morality might project one into a hell, and once arrived there an infinite number of hellish rebirths is very likely. *But absolutely essential for maximum benefit in the Metteyya Age is the presence of the previously gained "insight-seeds" just noted.* If people lack "insight into the nature of Material Qualities, Mental Qualities and Constituent Groups of Existence . . . . they cannot attain Enlightenment, *even though they hear the discourse of the next Buddha in person.*"[8]

Historical Results in Burma

This multifaceted sense of urgency motivated at least some of the Saṅgha to seek simplification of the traditional meditational apparatus, which seems, with its growth and development, to have become daunting even for monks. And indeed most persons in this evil age are not fully capable of meditation! A further (eventual) result of this search for simplification was to extend the possibility of meditation to the layperson, for almost the first time in recent Theravāda history.

To be sure there never was an absolute prohibition of lay meditation in Theravāda tradition; but practically speaking it was confined to the monks, because only their mode of life was suited to the attainment of jhānic skills. And, in general, laypersons did not think of themselves as capable of that direct seeking of enlightenment for which the monk's life was specifically designed. Of course, devout laypersons had always come to pagodas and temples on sabbath days for special "austerities" and pious exercises, but seldom if ever for actual meditation—certainly not in the later centuries. Indeed most monks themselves probably did comparatively little actual meditation and hence could not have guided their "parishioners" even if they had wished to.

One of the initiators of a gradual relaxation of the monkish "ban" on lay meditation and at least an indirect mover toward a simplified method was the Ledi Sayadaw, from whose major work I just quoted. In his concern for all Buddhists to work toward their final salvation while there was time and opportunity, he urged that any and all should at least *begin* meditation at their present level. Thus:

> Even in the case of hunters and fishermen, it should not be said that they should not practise *samatha vipassanā* (Calm and Insight) . . . unless they discard their avocations. . . . Hunters and fishermen, on the other hand, should be encouraged to contemplate the noble qualities of the Buddha, the Dhamma, and the Sangha. They should be induced to

contemplate, as much as is in their power, the characteristic of loath-someness in one's body. They should be urged to contemplate the liability of oneself and all creatures to death.[9]

Not only did he encourage lay meditators, but he himself appears to have had several lay disciples. It was a second-generation lay disciple of his, U Thein, who established the Māha Bodhi Vipassanā Center at Mandalay in 1947 and became a teacher of meditation to both monks and nuns as well as laypersons. So also Thray Sithu U Ba Khin, late founder of and meditation master at the International Meditation Centre in Rangoon, was his spiritual descendant and used his general method.

Another important stream of influence in simplifying meditational method and extending its practice to laymen was from U Narada, thus described by a contemporary Western-born monk living in Ceylon:

As far as the writer's knowledge goes, it was only at the beginning of this century, in Burma, that the Way of Mindfulness, in its singular features, has been sharply outlined again, and practiced accordingly. At that time, a Burman monk, U Narada by name, bent on actual realization of the teachings he had learnt, was eagerly searching for a system of meditation offering *a direct access to the Highest Goal without encumbrance by accessories.* . . . In the course of his quest, coming to the famous meditation-caves in the hills of Sagaing, he met a monk who was reputed to have entered upon those lofty Paths of Sanctitude (*ariya-magga*) where the final achievement of Liberation is assured. When the Venerable U Narada put his question to him, he was asked in return: "Why are you searching outside the Master's word? Has not the Only Way, Satipaṭṭhāna, been proclaimed by Him?"

U Narada took up this indication. Studying again the text . . . he finally came to understand its salient features. The results achieved in his own practice convinced him that he had found what he was searching for: *a clear-cut and effective method* of training the mind for highest realization . . . .

We propose to call it here the "New Burman Satipaṭṭhāna Method." We call it "new" only in so far as it has started a new tradition in this ancient Way of Mindfulness.[10]

"Satipaṭṭhāna" refers to the applications of mindfulness; and the scripture referred to by U Narada's respondent is Suttanta Ten of the *Dialogues of the Buddha.* That suttanta, to which reference has been repeatedly made, is a discourse in which the Buddha instructs the monk how to give attention, with increasing subtlety, to his physical body, to its dynamic qualities, and finally to his own feeling, thought processes, and thought content—under the aspect of their impermanence, painfulness, and impersonality. In a word it is a vipassanā manual; and when taken to be the "Only Way" to enlightenment it becomes a mode of "direct access to the Highest Goal without encumbrance by accessories" (jhānic attainments) and the "clear cut and effective method" itself, that U Narada was seeking. As developed in Burma it is sometimes called the method of "bare attention" and is defined by Nyanaponika Thera thus:

> Bare Attention is the clear and single-minded awareness of what actually happens *to* us and *in* us, at the successive moments of perception. It is called "bare," because it attends just to the bare facts of a perception as presented either through the five physical senses or through the mind. . . . Attention is kept to a bare registering of the facts observed without reacting to them by deed, speech, or by mental comment . . . . Any such comments (as) arise in one's mind . . . themselves are made objects of Bare Attention, and are neither rejected nor pursued."[11]

And it is always to be contextualized by the vipassanic awareness of anicca-anattā-dukkha:

> After the practice of Bare Attention has resulted in a certain width and depth of experience in its dealing with mental events, it will become an immediate certainty to the meditator that *mind is nothing beyond its cognizing function.* . . . By way of one's own direct experience, one will thus have arrived at the great truth of No-soul or Impersonality (anattā; Skr. anātma) showing that all existence is void of an abiding personality . . . or an abiding substance of any description.[12]

This rediscovery of the "Only Way" to enlightenment in the scriptures themselves—seemingly independent of the Ledi Sayadaw's influence—also influenced Theravāda meditation in Burma, Thailand, and Ceylon. Although not displacing the jhānic practices entirely, the "new" minimal method of vipassanic bare attention to one's own body-mind became another force for the revival of meditational practice that could, and finally did, include laypersons. How could meditation be made simpler? The only "equipment" needed was oneself and one's own powers. In addition, the bare-attention method (vipassanic in nature) could be worked into daily life activities—an ideal layperson's method, so to speak.

So it was with monks themselves seeking "clear cut" methods, some notable ones among them encouraging lay meditation, and the "rediscovery" of vipassanā as a method in its own right, that actual centers for laypeople came to be established perhaps forty years ago.[13] After World War II the trend toward lay meditation became a tide, especially in Burma, resulting in the establishment of hundreds of centers, many operated by monks and a few (including the International Meditation Centre at Rangoon) by laymen. This sudden movement was fueled by at least three factors: some desire to do intensive meditation, long frustrated by its institutionalized monopoly by the Sangha; the new emphasis on the "easier" vipassanā methods, forwarded by the Ledi Sayadaw and U Narada, as noted; and the great uncertainties and distresses produced by the war and its aftermath.[14] This "revolution" was more readily and widely effected in Burma than in either Thailand or Ceylon, in part because of the ease with which the Burmese Sangha may be entered, even temporarily for a few weeks' meditation, and left, at any age or stage.[15]

Some Contemporary Burmese Meditation Methods

General Features

Before entering into a description of some contemporary meditation centers and their methods, some general characteristics of the modern methods may be noted. First, as suggested earlier, they are all emphatically vipassanā, largely bypassing the jhānic practices. Vipassanā is thus viewed as a fully sufficient and independent methodology for making progress toward enlightenment—and importantly in these last Buddha-age days as producing good rebirth kamma. The popular "new" methods emphasize strongly the inherently contrasting yogic-jhānic and vipassanā practices. For the jhānic tends toward direct body-mind control and the actual cutting off of ordinary sensibility and thought, but the vipassanic specifically seeks to be a method of sheer observation of body-mind in activity, thought, and feeling. Its "control," such as there is, is thus auxiliary and indirect, a fruit and by-product of vipassanā practice.[16]

Second, the traditional Buddhist ambiguity toward jhānic skills still exists even in laity-oriented vipassanā centers. And the reasons for continuing to gain jhānic skills are much the same as always, even though they are now supposedly of secondary importance. The increase of the concentrative powers of the mind, developed in the jhānic discipline, is viewed as a positive aid to the total meditative effort. Also it must be confessed that though various psychic-power accompaniments of meditative practice are recognizably not organic to Buddhist meditation as such, most Burmese Buddhists admire them. And benefits such as the curing of disease or mental disturbances and being able to enter into deep samādhi to avoid sea or air-sickness[17] are valued adjuncts of contemporary meditation, whether jhānic or vipassanic.

However, a more important reason for the continued cultivation of jhānic-yogic powers in Theravāda meditation circles is different from any of these and comes much nearer the reason already given for the attainment of cessation by Buddhaghosa: "Why do they attain it? Being wearied by the occurrence and dissolution of formations, they attain it thinking 'Let us dwell in bliss by being without consciousness here and now and gaining the cessation that is nibbāna'" (*PP*, XIII.30). Among the modern meditators of whom I speak there is seldom if ever any belief that they are near *such* an attainment. Yet the ability to produce the jhānic counterpart signs in the kasina manner is supportive assurance of progress in meditational power, a tasting of levels of awareness beyond the ordinary and an experiential confirmation of the attainment of the higher Nibbāna-tending factors. Even though it is not a genuine Path awareness, in some sense even a low-level jhānic attainment is the bright shadow of Nibbāna itself. It is at second or third remove but nonetheless a token of better things to come.

Thus one may hear meditators among themselves comparing notes about how a kasina-form counterpart sign, or a breathing counterpart sign, has appeared to them and how it can be made to "move" or "grow" or be developed. In this way do the would-be saints encourage themselves and each other! In fact *The Path of Purification* itself says that even at the *access* concentration level the jhānic sign first appears (IV.32–34). Hence some jhānic-type sign *should* be possible even for vipassanā meditators. And in at least one school of meditation, to be discussed later, the appearance of such signs indicates a sufficient depth of concentration to begin genuine vipassanā practice.

Third, contemporary emphasis in meditation is almost exclusively body-mind centered—natural to vipassanā—and concentrates especially on breath and body-feeling (*vedanā*). As noted, breath meditation is highly rated in the scriptures and by Buddhaghosa; but its new and dominant position in contemporary practice means that the emphasis has been shifted from the predominantly visual bases, present in the traditional kasina-jhānic practice, to the tactile. Attention is given to the "touch" of breath at the nostril or the rising-falling "touch" sensation in the abdomen. Further, this may be, and often is, extended to *all* touch sensation—especially suitable to a layperson's low-level practice in ordinary life.

The emphasis on feeling (vedanā), which does not completely exclude breath or touch attention, concentrates awareness on the momentarily dominant feeling, often a bodily irritation or pain, or the discomfort induced by the meditation itself, or even a particular touch sensation. Thus one attends to what is most immediate and "real" to the body-mind at that moment—a constant reminder of its true (anicca-anattā-dukkha) nature.

Finally, rivalry exists between meditation centers, or more properly between their adherents in the laity. In comparisons such virtues as "deeper," more "difficult," or "faster"—especially faster—are attributed by each group to its master and center. The discussion is usually not acrimonious or sharply sectarian but bears witness to the feeling that one's own teacher or method is best for the speaker at any rate. There is considerable shopping around in the exercise of the ancient right of a pupil to seek that master who provides the most help. Thus a Burmese friend told us that he and his wife had been following the Sunlun method but found that too hard. They then turned to the guidance of Ashin U Okkata Sayadaw at his center near Hmawbi. In any case, all these masters and their followers consider themselves to be firmly orthodox Theravādins faithfully practicing Buddha's way.

The following selection of meditation "schools" is somewhat arbitrary, limited by my knowledge and the available sources. But those selected typify the main trends in contemporary Burmese practice.

An Adaptation of the Ledi Sayadaw Method

The late Thray Sithu U Ba Khin (1898–1971), was a disciple of a disciple of the Ledi Sayadaw (Saya Dala Thet). U Ba Khin thought of himself as a continuer of the Ledi Sayadaw's efforts to encourage meditation among people of all classes and kinds, especially among laypersons.[18] As a devout Buddhist layman, U Ba Khin was fully persuaded that vipassanā was the quintessence of the Buddha's teaching and that it could be practiced in connection with daily work. (He himself held numerous positions in the Burmese government, including that of Accountant General, and carried on this full-time work while acting as head meditation master at the International Meditation Centre.) So practiced it had both practical benefits—better performance of secular duties by virtue of applying onepointedness of mind to the business at hand, more harmonious relations with others, healing of bodily and mental ailments—as well as being the way to finally attain Nibbāna. He had, at an earlier period and for a considerable time, followed an intensive meditation practice, though as a layman. During the early part of his occupancy of the Accountant General's office, he set up noon hour meditation sessions (vipassanic) in his office. In time this led to the formation of the Vipassanā Association of the Accountant General's Office and finally to the founding of the Centre in 1952 and the subsequent construction of appropriate quarters for it in a Rangoon suburb.

In his firm conviction that vipassanā was the final cure for all human ills, he sought to open the Centre to all people of every and no faith. He was especially concerned to provide a place of meditation for foreigners as well as Burmese. And because he spoke English well, he could admit English-speaking persons of all nationalities to his meditation courses—usually ten days in length. Meditators were not asked to renounce their faith if it was other than Buddhist, but only to indicate that they desired to attain "Nibbānic peace within" and to agree to keep eight of the Buddhist Precepts while in the Centre.[19]

The Centre continues its work under some of those who assisted U Ba Khin during his lifetime, and attracts some foreigners as well as many Burmese. A disciple of his, U Goenka, who calls his work "vipassanā in the U Ba Khin tradition," teaches numerous foreigners and nationals at several places in India and has recently set up a permanent Centre near Bombay. So too U Ba Khin's adaptation of the Ledi Sayadaw's method is taught at several places in the United States, Europe, and Australia by his American disciples.

Notwithstanding the creation of an U Ba Khin tradition, U Ba Khin's methodology is more difficult to describe precisely than some other teachings[20] because he never wrote out a detailed manual and he was not a narrow traditionalist—though he was a completely devout Theravāda Buddhist in thought and feeling. As a pragmatist he perceptively adapted his method to the needs and characters of his disciples. This, plus his immense charisma, yielded a "method" that, although generally in the vipassanic mold, was more of a master-disciple personal relationship than a cut-and-dried technique.

The best way to present his mode of meditational teaching is to reproduce here an account of a long-time European Buddhist who undertook to meditate under U Ba Khin. This is taken from a pamphlet entitled "Personal Experiences of Candidates (Buddhists and non-Buddhists)" printed by the Vipassanā Association in Rangoon, sometime after 1954, pp. 1–15:

The case of Mr. A

Mr. A was here in Rangoon on a business tour during the latter part of December 1952. He took advantage of his short stay in Burma by coming in contact with Sithu U Ba Khin and obtaining from him a practical course in Buddhist Meditation. His experience is narrated in a brief statement made by him on the eve of his departure from Rangoon. This, together with the explanatory remarks thereon of U Ba Khin, will give the reader a clear and concise account of the course of training in practical Buddhist Meditation being given at the International Meditation Centre, Inyamyaing, Rangoon.

Statement of Mr. A.:

Experience of a state of purity of Mind (Samādhi) and of Vipassanā under the leading and with the help of my Guru Sithu U Ba Khin, Accountant General of Burma.

Being a Buddhist for about 18 years, having been a member of the Sangha (Buddhist Monks) during one year in Mongolia and Tibet, where I practised many meditations (so-called White Magic), I must and wish to state with all my heart, that I never experienced or even heard about the meditation as is being done under the direction of Guru Sithu U Ba Khin. I came to Rangoon on a business trip for seven days only, but managed with the help of said Guru to reach the Samādhi and Vipassanā in this short time, which I myself (and nobody else) would have believed possible.

After only two preliminary meditation lessons of half-an-hour each, I saw the light clearly within me: meaning, that the Mind becomes powerful and bright, freed from disturbances, pure and serene. The technique is rather simple, concentration on the breath leading to one-pointedness; but the Guru can better inform you about that. After some developed meditation on Saturday-night (20th December 1952), Vipassanā was started at 10 o'clock in the morning of Sunday, 21st December 1952. I concentrated on the burning in my body—concentrated with other words in Dukkha (Suffering)—felt the burning inside till I felt myself almost burning like steam on the surface of water. Then I had to concentrate the total heat, total suffering, on the central part of my body until the suffering grew even unbearable. At the last moment when I felt myself about dying, it was as if my heart was pulled out of my body and at the same moment—wanting eagerly to be freed from

Dukkha—with a sudden but a small flash of light, I was out of it and felt a refreshing coolness and delight, which words cannot describe. It is an escape and a refuge from all daily trouble, too great to be understood, when not experienced. And the great bliss is that every one can achieve this state; provided he has a pure mind at least for the time of concentration, has the right intentions, attentiveness and concentration, and anyhow tries to live as pure as possible.

Another necessity is, that he has no fear whatsover and a complete faith in his Guru. I hope with all my heart that Guru U Ba Khin will have many followers and disciples in the near future, who can be helped by him as much as I have been.

Rangoon, 22nd December 1952, –Sd/– (A)

Explanatory remarks of Sithu U Ba Khin on the statement of Mr. A dated 22–12–52.

Mr. A and myself had a preliminary discussion as to the method to be followed for practical Buddhist Meditation and he agrees with me that the best course towards progressive realisation of the Truth is to follow strictly and diligently the three indisputable steps of Sila, Samādhi and Pannā of the Eightfold Noble Path laid down by Buddha in the Dhamma Cakka Pavattana Sutta.

Step I.   Raise the standard of Morality to the prescribed minimum (Silā);

Step II.   Develop the power of concentration to one-pointedness of Mind (Samādhi);

Step III. Gain insight into the ultimate realities of nature within one's ownself (Pannā).

2. I have no reason to doubt the moral qualities of Mr. A who has impressed me very much on first contact. Accordingly, I put him straight away on a course of Ānāpāna Sati. He did very well in the initial course. And in just a few hours of solid work he was able to develop his power of concentration to one-pointedness (Samādhi). In fact by the time I needed him for the change of the course of training to Vipassanā, he could keep the Light (Patibhāga-Nimitta) before his Mind's eye for quite a long time and had begun to play with it. I should say he is a man of no small Paramī.

3. We know from science that everything that exists in the Universe is composed of electrons, all in a state of perpetual change or flux. The Karaja Kāya—the Coarse body—of our own selves cannot therefore be an exception to the rule. Mr. A knows this. He knows, too, what Nāma, Rūpa and the Kalāpas are, together with their composition, characteristics and tendencies. With the powerful lens of Samādhi which he has developed, he should now be fit for the introspective and analytical study of the true nature of Rūpa and Nāma.

4. Just at the right moment, soon after 10 o'clock on Sunday, the 21st December 1952, Mr. A was called upon to focus his whole attention searchingly into his ownself, from point to point, to examine and to feel the changing process—the radiation, the vibration and the friction—caused by the whirling movement of an infinite number of kalāpas (electronic units). The human body, as it were, is a sum total of innumerable millions into millions of kalāpas, each breaking down simultaneously as it arises. A Kalāpa is akin to—but infinitely smaller—than a visible spark. In reality, the human body is nothing but atomic energy, conditioned by forces of one's own deeds, words or thoughts. Thanks to all the Devas who have guided us in our work, Mr. A got the thread of it almost instantaneously and in a few minutes he began to have a sharp sense of feeling of the radiation, then of vibration and then again of the friction of electronic units within, which spread like wild fire to all parts of the body in the course of just one-half of an hour. He was encouraged not to relax but to keep on feeling with greater intensity and to keep on knowing with a clearer sense of perception. He knew also that, feeling (Vedanā), perception (Sanna), Volitional energies (Sankhāra) and Consciousness (Vinnana)—the four Namakkhandā—are also fleeting, passing away and dying out along with Rūpa. He was then advised to make an analytical survey of the whole being both in respect of Nāma and Rūpa in terms of the doctrines of Anicca (Impermanence), Dukkha (Suffering) and Anatta (Absence of Ego-centralism). Lest he entertained any doubt as to what was happening, he was asked to examine the body temperature of his own-self and others nearby which were just normal. The fact is that as he proceeded with the meditation, he had a better and better telescopic view of the Ultimate Realities (Paramattha Dhātu). Meanwhile he was explained how the predominating factor of tejo (radiation) in a kalāpa is responsible for the burning sensation, how the non-stop replacement of wasting kalāpas by a continuous influx of food property (nutrient) creates vibration, how the breakdown and replacement of these kalāpas (electronic units), individually and collectively, causes friction and how a telescopic view of the true nature of these things can be obtained by one who owns the powerful lens of Samādhi.

Samādhim bhikkhave bhāvetha.
Samāhito Yathabhutam pajanati,
Oh Monks! Develop the power of concentration.
He who has the power of concentration can see
things in their true state.

5. Just before noon, Mr. A was feeling intensely the heat of radiation. Not only that, he was also seeing sparks of light emitting from all over the body.

"Yes, Mr. A, are you quite convinced now that human body is composed of electrons, all changing fast and yet never coming to an end, and that there is no such thing as substantiality in it?" I remarked.

"I am quite convinced of that," was the reply.

"In that case," I said, "Fix your attention to these sparks of light and think that they are also impermanent and subject to the law of Anicca."

He did so and those sparks of light were suppressed and eliminated. I explained later these were "Obasa," one of the ten Upakkilesa (Defilements) and that if they were allowed to remain long, piti would creep in and the course of meditation would be diverted.

6. But for a break of about half-an-hour for lunch in the room adjacent to the Meditation Chamber, Mr. A was on the course again; for he was already engrossed in it and he knew that "continuity of practice is the secret of success." As he proceeded with the meditation, he could think of nothing but Dukkha in all its variety. At times, it seemed as though he were struggling, with words of "Dukkha, Dukkha" or "Suffering" in a low tone. After an elaborate explanation of what he was experiencing with reference to the teachings of Buddhas, I said:

"It is the realisation of the Truth of Suffering by actual experience —the real and not the imaginative—which will lead you to the Extinction of Suffering (Dukkha-Nirodha)."

"The attachment to Self has been so strong that you will not discard it unless the 'Suffering Within' which you feel is stronger."

"If you get out of Dukkha, you also get out of Nāma and Rūpa. If you can get out of Nāma and Rūpa, you will surely get out of the Samsara."

"Suffering arises from Kilesā, the origin of Dukkha. Kilesā is just like fire, it burns. There will be burning within, for so long as there is fuel of Kilesā to burn. Burn it all by a contemplative meditation of Anicca, Dukkha and Anatta, without relaxation, and you will surely come to the end of Kilesā."

"It is really an endurance feat. Forbear it until you are firmly convinced of this Truth of Suffering and until you become truly afraid of, disgusted with, and disinclined to Nāma and Rūpa which are identified with Dukkha."

"Think, then, of Dukkha-Nirodha, the end of Suffering. Long for it. Just transmit your thought to it. Mind you, the escape is from the centre."

(Such were my instructions. The words used might not be the same but the sense is there.)

7. It was already 4 o'clock in the afternoon. Some of my disciples had also turned up for meditation. Mr. A was at that time in a lying posture. I advised him to sit down with his legs crossed at one corner of the room and encouraged him to go ahead, ever mindful of Dukkha and eager to get out of it.

All was quiet in the meditation room. The silence was however broken by Mr. A at 16 minutes past four.

He gave me to understand he was suddenly relieved of the burning heat by a stream of coolness which was most refreshing. He felt as if he was re-born.

I was really very glad, called, "Sadhu" three times and congratulated him on his success.

After a spell of 5 minutes or so, I said:

"Well, Mr. A, please come forward, Let us have another try."

He came forward and was seated just in front of me. With instructions suitable to the occasion, I asked him to collect himself again and to go into the fruition state (Phala) with a vow to rise up just after 5 minutes. He did so without any difficulty. There was no such burning as was experienced by him throughout the day. Just a radiation to remind him of the true nature of things inside, i.e., Anicca, Dukkha & Anatta.

I was not satisfied with that as yet. I wanted to be doubly sure. So I made him go into that State again for another 15 minutes. I am glad to say that he got through this test also quite successfully.

8. We had achieved our objective. Mr. A was really very pleased and grateful. He had still plenty of work to do in Rangoon. I should not therefore detain him any longer. He must have rest for the remainder of the day. I therefore sent him back to his hotel with instructions to see me the next day at 6 o'clock in the afternoon.

When we met again on the following day, we had a quiet discussion on certain aspects of the Dhamma as well as on matters personal. As desired by me, he joined with my other disciples in meditation and went into the state of "Nibbanic Peace Within" for 15 minutes. He rose up just in time.

To my mind, Mr. A has fulfilled the requirements of the Eight-fold Noble Path.

Sīla: During the course of training, there was no occasion for him to break the three fundamental requirements of Sīla, viz., Sammā Vācā, Sammā Kammanta & Sammā Ājīva.

Samādhi: By Sammā Vāyama and Sammā Sati, he has acquired "Upacāra Samādhi" (Neighbourhood concentration). He was able to keep the Patibhāga Nimitta for a length of time.

Panna: By Sammā Sankappa, he has understood the true nature of things and has realised the Truth.

9. In practical Buddhism what really counts is the realisation of the Truth. Whatever may be the Kamathāna method adopted, it must be in the order of Sīla, Samādhi, Pannā of the Eight-fold Noble path. Go step by step along this path and you will still be in the confines of any Kamathāna system, because the real essential feature in Buddhist Meditation is to get to the origination and dissolution of Mind and Matter in his body. For instance, the course followed by Mr. A is in accord with the fundamental requirements of Ānāpāna Sati Sutta or of Ānāpāna section of the Mahāsatipathāna Sutta. It also accords with the treatise in the Pārājikan Athakathā for the realisation of the Truth

by an analysis of the "Kalāpas" in the body with the lens or Samādhi obtained through Ānāpāna Sati. Let us now see also how it fits in with the seven stages of Purity (Visuddhi) in the Visuddhi Magga (the Path of Purity).

1. Sīla Visuddhi	: Mr. A can be said to have complied with it during the course of meditation.
2. Citta Visuddhi (Purity of Mind)	: He has developed his concentration to one-pointedness (Citta-Ekaggata).
3. Ditthi Visuddhi (Purity of Understanding)	: There is every evidence from the course of meditation that he has known by experience the true nature of Nāma & Rūpa.
4. Kankhā Vitarana Visuddhi (Purity of escape from doubt)	: Realising that Nāma & Rūpa are in a state of perpetual change, he is freed from all doubts as to Self-entity whether of the past, present or future.
5. Maggāmaggananadassana Visuddhi (Purity of knowledge as to which is the right or wrong Path)	: When defilements appear, he is able to overcome them, i.e., he can differentiate between right & wrong Path.
6. Patipadanānadassana Visuddhi (Purity of knowledge of the right course)	: He has no doubt, for what he has succeeded, as to the prospect of reaching the goal and that it is now just a question of time.
7. Nānadassana-Visuddhi (Purity of the Eye & Wisdom)	: He knows for himself what a change has occurred when passed through the stream of Sotāpanna.

10. Ketam Samāpajjanti. Ariya pana sabbe pi Samāpajjpanti.
   Who can go into states of Peace Within?
   All Ariyas can go into states of (Nibbanic) Peace Within.
                    (Visuddhi Magga)
Therefore the real test as to whether one has become an Ariya lies in his ability to go in to the fruition state (Phala) as he may like. While

in that state, he is oblivious of any feeling through the five organs of senses. At the same time, his body posture (Iriyapatha) becomes firm and tightened in the same way as one who goes into a Jhanic trance. As between Jhana and Phala there are great variations in the mode of entry and exit. An experienced teacher alone will be able to differentiate between the two to the satisfaction of a disciple. Mr. A has satisfied these requirements. Shall we call him an Ariya?

(Sd/-BA KHIN)
12–1–53

The Mahasi Sayadaw's Meditational Method

The Mahasi Sayadaw ("Mahasi" means "Big-Drum") is the popular name given to U Sobhana Mahāthera (right reverend Mr. Sobhana). Born in 1904 in north-central Burma near Shwebo, he was ordained a novice at the age of twelve, and at twenty he became a fully ordained monk. He studied the Buddhist scriptures and then taught in a monastery until in his twenty-eighth year, he met and trained in meditation under U Narada. At thirty-seven, after further monastery teaching, he introduced courses in Satipaṭṭhāna Meditation at the monastery in his native village of Seikkhum. Eight years later, in 1949, Prime Minister U Nu and the Buddha Sāsana Association brought him to Rangoon where he established a meditation center called Sāsana Yeiktha. The Rangoon center has had many meditators during the course of the years since, and there are more than a hundred "branch" centers in Burma that follow this same method, as well as others in Thailand and Ceylon.[21] I will describe the general features of Mahasi Sayadaw's method and the viewpoint underlying it and then present the beginning steps and basic pattern as portrayed in an official manual of the center.

First, it should be clearly understood that this method is primarily vipassanā. In his "Translator's Foreword" to *The Progress of Insight* Nyanaponika Thera writes:

> This approach road to the ultimate goal of Buddhist meditation is called *Bare Insight* because insight into the three Characteristics of Existence is made use of exclusively here, dispensing with the prior development of the full concentrative absorption (jhana). But nevertheless . . . here too a high degree of mental concentration is required for perseverance in the practice, for attaining to Insight-Knowledge, and for reaping its fruits.

Thus, even though based on *The Path of Purification*, this method only casually refers to, and does not actually use, jhānic techniques. However, Mahasi Sayadaw seems to envisage a *near*-jhānic quality of transic awareness at the higher stages of fruition consciousness when Nibbāna itself becomes the object of awareness. He writes:

> One should also set one's mind resolutely upon the further task: to be able to repeat the achievement of Fruition Attainment, to achieve

it rapidly, and, at the time of achievement, to abide in it for a long time, say for 6, 10, 15 or 30 minutes, for an hour or more. [P. 24]

And, indeed, there are some phrasings here that use the term "cessation" (nirodha):

> If the power of concentration has reached perfection, the Fruition consciousness will, repeatedly, get absorbed in cessation by way of Fruition Attainment. The mind can thus reach absorption even while one is walking up and down, or while taking a meal, and the Fruition Attainment can remain for any length of time as resolved. During the Fruition Attainment, *the mind will abide only in the cessation of formations, and will not be aware of anything else.* [P. 24; italics added]

Obviously this is not the full, deathlike nirodha-samāpatti; but it *is* an intense awareness of the Nibbāna-like cessation of all phenomena. There is definitely a non-jhānic "absorption" quality here too; for this attainment occurs in the midst of activity and presumably the activity goes on afterward. Thus there is no suggestion that the walker suddenly sits down upon becoming "absorbed." Probably the walking (as with eating or any other activity) becomes almost automatic, with no attention paid to it; and/or the walking itself becomes a reinforcement of the so-called absorption which is being experienced here.[22] It never becomes a blank no-thought trance.

Second, the *direct* knowledge or experience involved here is repeatedly emphasized. This is *not* "knowledge derived from ratiocination" (p. 6). The meditator sees "the three characteristics once or several times by direct experience" (p. 9) within his own body-mind, whence it is then possible to generalize to all existence. Again, "it should be borne in mind that this refers only to understanding arrived at through direct experience, by one engaged in noticing only; it is not an opinion derived from mere reasoning" (p. 16).

Corollary to this, the fundamental and persisting subject of the meditator's attention is his *own* body-mind awareness. In the beginning in particular, strong touch-awareness is primary. The reason for this is that at first "it is difficult to follow and to notice clearly all bodily and mental processes that incessantly appear at the six sense-doors. Therefore the meditator who is a beginner should first notice the perfectly distinct process of touch" (p. 2). This can be observed in the form of "sitting . . . touching"[23] or particularly in the feeling of the abdomen's "rising, falling" in breathing. Breathing, as the official directions make clear, is the central means for focusing attention, though at the Mahasi Sayadaw centers the walking meditation is interspersed with seated, breathing meditation.

The official (beginner's) manual states:

> The disciple should keep on with this exercise of knowing the movements of the abdomen as "rising" and "falling." It may be mentioned that it is necessary to make a mental note of each movement as "rising" and

"falling" so as to keep time with each movement. The disciple should on no account repeat by mouth. The disciple should avoid breathing deeply or quickly with a view to making the movements more clear. If he tries the method of breathing deeply and quickly the disciple will soon feel tired and will not be in a position to proceed with his exercise. It must therefore be emphasized that the disciple should proceed with his exercise of knowing the movements of his abdomen as they occur in the course of normal and natural breathing.[24]

This is in some contrast to the forced ("rough") breathing method used by Sunlun (see next section).

The manual describes the proper procedure for the walking meditation:

While walking it is important to know completely every movement in each step, from the beginning to the end. The same procedure should be adopted when he is taking a stroll or walking exercise to and fro. The disciple should try and make a mental note of each step in two sections, such as, "lifting," "putting," "lifting," "putting"; on his getting a sufficient practice in this manner, he should then try and make a mental note of each step in three sections, such as, "lifting," "pushing," "putting" or "up," "forward," "down."[25]

The same pattern can be extended to *every* action, breaking it up into smaller and smaller "impersonal" units, until the meditator is aware of each act as a series of psychosomatic action moments, *not* as an act that *he* (as a person) *does*.

As the meditator becomes adept, the happenings in his own body-mind become perceptible in ever more subtle forms. Body processes are broken down in terms of how thoughts and sensations rise, persist, and disappear, then what constitutes a "thought" or "feeling" and then the conditions for "thought" or "feeling" arising are observed. So too the consciousness that accompanies physical processes will *itself* be observed:

Similar to that appears the dissolving and vanishing, moment by moment, of the bodily processes noticed. And the dissolution of consciousness noticing these bodily processes is apparent to him along with the dissolution of the bodily processes. [p. 15]

The taped practice manual—again on the beginner's level—states that

at times he may expect and wish for a good result. In such case, he should proceed with the contemplation, such as "expecting," or "wishing." At times he might try to remember or think of the way or manner of his having carried out his training. In such cases, he should proceed with the contemplation of "remembering" or "thinking." At times he may be trying to examine whether the object of contemplation is Rūpa (matter) or Nāma (mind). In such cases, he should proceed with the contemplation, such as, "examining," "examining." At times he will feel sorry because he does not find any improvement in his contemplation. In such cases, he should proceed with the contemplation, such as, "sorry," "sorry." At times he may feel happy when he thinks that his contemplation is improving. In such cases, he should proceed with his contemplation, such as, "happy," "happy." In this manner he should make a mental note of every moment of mental behaviour as it occurs, and then proceed with his contemplation of "rising" and "falling."

Third, what then of the stray thought or distracting sensation? Follow it momentarily with the attention, else it will undermine the quality of attention to be given to the main subject, breathing or walking. The manual advises thus:

> If however, he happens to look on intentionally at an object he should at once make a mental note, such as, "seeing," "seeing," two or three times, and then proceed with his usual contemplation of "rising" and "falling." If any person (either male or female) happens to come in sight, he should make a mental note, such as "seeing," "seeing," two or three times, and then proceed with his usual contemplation of "rising" and "falling." If he happens to listen to any voice, he should make a mental note, such as, "listening," "hearing"—"listening," "hearing," and then proceed with his usual contemplation of "rising" and "falling." If he happens to hear loud sounds, such as barking of dogs, speaking, songs, etc., he should at once make a mental note, such as, "hearing," "hearing," two or three times, and then proceed with his usual contemplation of "rising" and "falling."

What is the result? The meditator realistically gives the stray thought or feeling attention and it then goes away—just like a child who bothers one until it gets attention. This is especially so with pain: "On noticing the respective painful feeling repeatedly, twice, thrice or more, the meditator will see that it gradually grows less, and at last ceases entirely" (p. 9).

Fourth, it is taken for granted that the "bare" attention exercised here is a "Buddhist" bare attention—a mode of awareness that specifically focuses on the impermanence, impersonality, and painfulness of all experience, totally discounting as unreal any sense of permanence and pleasure. The precise purpose of this meditation, as in all vipassanā, is to indelibly impress upon the consciousness of the meditator these fundamental Buddhist truths, until they are internalized as an existential mode of thinking and feeling. Thus, "when that knowledge has come to maturity, the meditator understands thus: 'At the moment of breathing-in, there is just the rising movement of the abdomen and the knowing of the movement, *but there is no self besides!*'" (p. 7; italics added). And,

> After noticing these manifestations of Brilliant Light[26] and the others, he goes on continuously as before with the act of noticing the bodily and mental processes. . . . While thus engaged in noticing, he gets over the

corruptions relating to brilliant light, rapture, tranquillity, happiness, attachment, etc., *and his knowledge remains exclusively with the arising and passing away of the processes noticed.* [Pp. 13–14; italics added]

The "corruptions" referred to here are the delight that the meditator is tempted to take in his meditative attainments. The final goal is for the meditator to become so aware of "the misery in conditioned things" that his or her mind "is entirely disgusted with them." And having thus experienced disgust with transitoriness "there will arise . . . a desire to forsake these formations or to become delivered from them." At this juncture, his consciousness engaged in noticing, seems to shrink from the object noticed . . . and wish to escape it (p. 17). The meditator who once took delight in forms and conceptual entities will come to the point where "his mind will delight in the *cessation* (of the phenomena)" (p. 15; italics added).

Fifth, spontaneity in the process of meditation and the consciousness that arises from it increases. Thus in the fifth of the eighteen stages, "Knowledge of Dissolution": "When that Knowledge of Arising and Passing Away becomes mature, keen and strong, it will arise easily and proceed uninter-ruptedly *as if borne onward of itself*" (p. 14; italics added). Attention, Buddhist bare attention, becomes almost automatic with practice: "If he resumes the practice of noticing with the thought: 'Now I will do it vigorously again!', then before long the noticing will function efficiently *as if borne onward of itself*" (p. 20; italics added).

Here, as in the Ledi Sayadaw's practice, many jhānic qualities are paralleled, and the jhānic flavor in vipassanā is present even though jhānic attainments have been specifically forsworn. At the fourth stage, for example, in the "Knowledge of Arising and Passing Away," there is the arising of elements reminiscent of the jhānic development of a breath kasina and of the joy and rapture of the first two jhānas themselves. If the meditator can "keep exclusively to the *present* body-and-mind process—then as a result of Insight (the mental vision of) a *brilliant light* will appear to him." This takes different forms and lasts for different periods. So too, along with increase of awareness, faith and tranquillity there arise "rapture" and "happiness."

> There arises also *rapture* in its five grades, beginning with minor rapture. When Purification of Mind is gained, that rapture begins to appear by causing "goose-flesh," tremor in the limbs, etc.; and now it produces a sublime feeling of happiness and exhilaration, filling the whole body with an exceedingly sweet and subtle thrill. Under its influence, he feels as if the whole body had risen up and remained in the air without touching the ground or as if it were seated on an air cushion, or as if it were floating up and down. [Pp. 10, 11]

But here too, as with the jhānic blessedness, the meditator must not think the goal has been achieved. Rushing out to tell others about this great joy is also inappropriate. Delight in these delights is a "corruption," as noted above. Nonetheless, it is an auxiliary confirmation of progress toward supramundane knowledge.

At the higher levels, a nonsensuous, peaceful awareness arises, which is *not* to be thus brushed aside. At the eleventh stage of "Equanimity About Formations" joy is replaced by an "exceedingly peaceful and sublime clarity of mind." To use Buddha's words about his own enlightenment, such joy does not "impinge on the mind" and its clarity [*MLS*, I, p. 301 (1.247)]. In this state "he cherishes no desire nor hate with regard to any object, desirable or undesirable, that comes into the range of his sense doors, but taking them as just the same in his act of noticing, he understands them (that is to say, it is a pure act of understanding)" (pp. 19–20). And in the end, according to the manual, it produces advancement on the Path: "The disciple, who is thus occupied fully with his contemplation through-out the day and night will be able to develop his concentration in order to gain the desirable state of Udayabbaya Ñāṇa (initial stage of the fourth degree of Insight) in no long time, and other higher stages of Vipassanā-Ñāṇa up to the Final Achievement."

The Sunlun Method

The Sunlun method takes its name from the Sunlungukyaung Sayadaw who originated it; and he in turn derived his name from the cave monasteries (gukyaung) near Sunlun village in middle Burma near Myingyan,[27] where he attained arahantship according to his disciples.

Sunlun Sayadaw was born in 1878 as Maung Kyaw Din. After a very sketchy monastery education, he was an office boy in a government office for about fifteen years, during which time he married. At the age of thirty he took up farming. Worried by his continuing prosperity—a sign in Burmese folklore of near decease—he consulted an astrologer and resolved on a pious life. Two fortuitous personal encounters turned his attention to vipassanā breathing meditation, and without any real knowledge of the Buddhist scriptures, he began to concentrate his total attention on the touch of breath when meditating, on the touch of his hand on the plow or chopping-knife handle, or on the touch of his feet on the ground when walking during his daily work.

He began to see signs of progress. Colored lights and patterns flashed before his eyes during seated meditation. He pressed on more vigorously than ever. He also encountered the increase of unpleasant or painful sensations but—again instinctively—took these as *desirable* fruits of the practice. Concentrating on these pains and also increasing the vigor of his breathing in meditation, he broke through to higher attainments. According to his disciples he became a Stream-Enterer mid-1920, achieved Once-Returning the next month, Non-Returning the following month, and then resolved to become a monk.

After much resistance the wife agreed. But even then she asked him to sow a final crop of peas before he left. U Kyaw Din set out for the fields. But even as he was broadcasting the seeds he felt the great urge to renounce the world. So setting his cattle free he put the yoke up against a tree and going to the village monastery he begged the monk there to accept him as a novice in the Order. He next betook himself to the caves nearby and practiced diligently until in October, 1920 he attained the final stage of the arahant. [p. 7]

As his reputation spread he attracted disciples for instruction in vipassanā meditation along the lines he had worked out empirically. According to our source, when he was examined by monks, his answers fully accorded with the Pāli scriptures. He died in 1952, but his method is perpetuated in a center in Rangoon.

Like all vipassanā meditations, the purpose of the Sunlun method is to destroy the sense of, and attachment to, the personal I; it is the experiential confirmation of the reality of impermanence-impersonality-misery as the essence of I-ness. But the essence of the Sunlun method is the radical simplicity and fierce intensity with which it pursues this goal. It bypasses most definition, is uninterested in detailed specification of the stages of attainment, and presses on with burning zeal and indefatigable energy toward the goal of freedom from rebirth. It is impatient with gradualist and indirect approaches; here and now are the place and day of salvation: "Many are the occasions in which the yogi indulges in self deception. Though he *should* practice intensively he deceives himself that the goal of liberation can be won in a leisurely manner. Though he *should* sit still, he deceives himself that a slight shift or movement can do no harm" (p. 10; italics added).

Within the Theravāda tradition, the Sunlun school observes, are many varieties of achieving mindfulness, such as the kasina, body-foulness, four-element, and body-activity meditations. Recommended in the scriptures as applications of mindfulness these can be employed profitably by contemporary meditators: "The yogi may legitimately employ them to gain the concentration he needs" (p. 3). And the founder himself said that no one should adopt the Sunlun method who did not find it congenial. Nevertheless, Sunlun Shin Vinaya goes on to suggest that "perhaps it would be a wise approach for the yogi to seek to employ and practice that exercise which will lead him *all the way* to the final goal he seeks. That goal is liberating vipassana insight knowledge" (p. 3; italics added). In other words, since vipassanā *must* be practiced in the end in order to achieve Nibbānic liberation, why not walk on the "high road to vipassana" (p. 4) at once and avoid all time- and energy-wasting lesser means? For the earnest vipassanā meditator—and who can realistically choose any other method in our hurried age of feeble spirituality?—there is neither time nor energy for acquiring the jhānic skills:

There are also the ways of escape offered by methods which result in tranquility: these are the ways of jhana. The dross of sensuality is removed, anger is pacified, agitation is stilled, the mind quietened, and joy and bliss realized. There is development of the mind but the results are temporal and temporary. They take place within the thirty-one worlds and the reward is consumed when the force of the original causative act is spent. True liberation is won only through knowledge of the real attained in the moment of supramundane insight. Only true liberation is both transcendental and permanent. [P. 22]

Any successful method of meditation requires the absolute elimination of all concepts. Sunlun is especially insistent on this point. Concepts are the work of the "I," which is to be destroyed, and because they are the substance of the world of ordinary (illusory, attaching) experience, they must be shunted aside temporarily for the purpose of directly experiencing "reality." Thus:

> Insight (vipassana) is the elimination of concepts (pannati) to pene-
> trate to the real (paramattha) for the winning of knowledge (panna).
> Therefore the chief characteristic of the right method should be its
> power to gain immediate and direct access to the real (p. 18).

> When the awareness is guarded with mindfulness *thoughts are locked out*,
> they cannot intrude. No opportunity is offered for the formation of
> concepts, images or ideas. [P. 6]

Concepts and ideas are the usual modes of handling "reality" in the human consciousness; and so strong is this habit that even in the midst of meditation we may find ourselves relating to them rather than reality itself. For example, there are four ways of meditating on breath: by counting breath, by noting if the breath is long or short, by following the breath in and out, and by fixing attention just on the touch of breath. All of these fasten attention on the point of breath contact at the nostril. But, says Sunlun, the first three, which are jhānic, that is, samādhi or samatha types, actually employ the *concept* of number (counting), *image* (long and short breaths), and *idea* (in and out motion) and are therefore at one remove from the reality of the experience itself. Only in the fourth is there sheer sensation without any trace of ideation.

But even here, when presumably attending to sensation alone, the ghosts of conceptualizing still haunt the meditator: "Only the fourth method where the touch alone is taken in its bareness performs the vipassana practice. Yet even this practice can be adulterated with samatha. If instead of being aware of the touch in its bare actuality . . . the yogi makes a mental note of it, then for that moment he has slipped into the old habit of forming a concept or an idea" (p. 5). But *what* reality is the Sunlun method so anxious to experience directly—for the word "reality" occurs frequently even in this short work of thirty-four pages? Thus:

> Sunlun makes direct, immediate contact with reality. It cannot afford
> the time and effort required to build a conceptual bridge to approach

reality. . . . When there arises an ache it immediately catches hold of the fact of the ache; it does not formulate the concept "aching, aching" and then return to the *fact* of the ache. [P. 27; italics added]

This is in obvious reference to Mahasi Sayadaw's method. Again,

reality is to be grasped in the actual moment of occurrence. If mindfulness cannot be awakened to take place simultaneously with the moment of occurrence . . . then reality would have died away . . . and any consciousness of that past event would be only the result of a glancing back at it, an after thought . . . a memory, a mentally created image of the touch, a replica of the real. [P. 18] [28]

One more quotation will make plain the nature of reality and the Sunlun concern with it:

Is it not necessary that we handle the processes with the gloves of concepts and ideas? This is the answer: If it were true that it is necessary to handle the processes with the gloves of concepts and thoughts, *that processes could never be got at directly*, then there can be no path to freedom and no liberating knowledge. *But because it is possible to get at processes directly as they are in themselves there is vipassana and the winning of intuitive liberating knowledge.* [P. 4; italics added]

The reality the meditator contacts through bare touch is *not* that real whose knowledge is "attained in the moment of supramundane insight." *That* real might more properly be termed the Real of Nibbāna, sighted when the Path first comes into view. But the reality that touch awareness minus all conceptualization makes contact with, is the anicca-anatta-dukkha quality of all existent items. "Knowing" touch nonconceptually, that is, by bare awareness, shows all concepts of subject-object, I-other, and so on, to be totally unreal. The reality known here is the reality of the unreality of all our ideas, concepts, and images. And this knowledge is absolutely essential to deliverance from saṃsāric unreality.

But is conceptualization totally evil? No, but it is of use only *after* the event. "Discursive knowledge of scriptural texts and philosophies may well aid the meditator after the event of meditation when he wishes to conceptualize the knowledge of the real he has won in the course of meditation, but, coming before the event, such theoretical studies tend to get in the way of the meditator" (p. 20). A good method of meditation for today, according to U Win Pe, should possess the following characteristics:

(1) Penetrating immediately and directly to the real;
(2) Overcoming the urge for sense gratification;
(3) Promoting bodily and mental health;
(4) Raising the threshold for noise;
(5) Self-energizing;
(6) Not requiring discursive knowledge;

(7) Productive of quick results;
(8) Capable of being practiced in conjunction with other duties;
(9) Suitable for the sluggish intuition;
(10) Distinguishing between means and ends; and
(11) Leading to true liberation. [P. 22]

The Sunlun method eminently fills these requirements.

Three of the Sunlun Sayadaw's sayings summarize the central features of the method. First, "Be rigorously mindful of the awareness of touch." As implied in previous quotations, touch, bare touch, is the methodological kingpin of the Sunlun technique. The locus of primary attention to touch is breath-touch at the nostril. During meditation the attention is to be fully and exclusively focused on the touch sensation itself, with no counting, no thoughts of whether it is coming in or going out. Even the mental mantra of "breath, breath" is unallowable. The reality of touch sensation alone fills the awareness. A secondary mode of touch awareness is the tactile awareness arising, or possibly arising, when the body touches the items of daily occupation. Sunlun is therefore particularly "capable of being practiced in conjunction with other duties," since touch is *always* present in a sentient being.

It is in connection with this maximization of touch as the ideal subject for awareness that Sunlun emphasizes "rough breathing." The breath at the nostril is a subtle sensation and may almost fade away from consciousness, except for the adept. Hence Sunlun, eminently practical and efficient, urges a strenuous breathing that serves as an obvious present center of attention, prevents dull and passive sitting in meditation, and raises the threshold for outside noise interference—particularly useful in our increasingly noisy world. It also tends to result in considerable pain at some stages, an important facet of the Sunlun method to be discussed below.

Second, "Do not rest when tired, scratch when itching, nor shift when cramped." Here Sunlun separates itself from most other methods, in particular from the Mahasi Sayadaw's method. Thus:

> It has been suggested that if, during the practice of mindfulness distractions should arise, the mind should follow after them to take note of them. Theoretically it should be possible to follow each distraction to grasp it mindfully. However, in practice, it is extremely difficult for the distracted mind to be mindful of whatever distracted it. *If it had been powerfully concentrated it would not have been distracted away from its originally selected object of meditation.* [P. 32; italics added]

This last sentence is a practical statement of the outstanding feature of this method: its concentrated intensity. The object of contemplation must be so specific and easily attended to, that by means of it one *can* shut out absolutely all other objects and all competing sensations and thoughts. The strategy is not to follow them and then come back, but to keep resolutely to the original object, touch. Hence in Sunlun when attention wanders, it must be rigorously turned back to breath touch, the breathing made more vigorous, and the onward course pursued with teeth-clenching intensity.[29]

U Win Pe, conversing with me in 1971, used the following suggestive analogy: the Mahasi Sayadaw's method of mentally following distracting thoughts for a little is like trying to pound each of many grains of rice as they lie scattered somewhere on the floor about one. The Sunlun method is to concentratedly pound all of the grains together in a mortar until they are all crushed. He went on to recommend intensive two- or three-week meditation sessions during which the meditator might go as long as eight or ten hours at a time, *without break or change of position*. A break of position, say from one hour of sitting to an hour of walking and back again (as in Mahasi Sayadaw's center), breaks the concentration at each time of change. Even the *most* moderate pace at the Sunlun center usually consists of four two-hour periods during each day, with longer periods if possible.

Third, "The uncomfortable truly is the norm; the comfortable will set us all adrift on the currents of samsara." It is possible to be so blessed with *pāramī* (perfections) from the good deeds of past lives that the meditator who "treads the pleasant path . . . can gain ariya knowledge without undergoing pain" (p. 11). But the meditator ought not to avoid pain in meditation in the hope of being one who can take pleasant sensation for a meditation base. For Sunlun the *increase* of pain is a propitious sign; strenuous breathing with total concentration almost inevitably brings the meditator to the point where pain becomes the dominant awareness. If there is no such pain, concentration may lack the proper depth and power. It is therefore suggested that after a time of vigorous breathing the meditator should deliberately hold the breath as long as possible to see what sensations *do* arise, and when they arise that the meditator should attend to the strongest one.

"Strongest" usually means the most painful. Some Sunlun meditators report that after a few days of periodic rough-breathing concentration, intense, seemingly unbearable pain arises at some point in their bodies, varying with the individual. What does one then do? Concentrate attention totally on the pain; do not cringe away from it. Buddhism holds that pain is painful only because it pains *me*. It is my identification with the pain—How it hurts *me*!, How painful it is (to *me*)!—that makes it hurt. If the meditator can break this identification and "generalize" the pain—being aware of the *sensation* of pain only, of "pain" as occurring somewhere—then gradually it will lose its power. Indeed some report that when the nettle of pain is grasped boldly, it will finally disappear altogether, sometimes suddenly:

> Let us say the unpleasant sensation arises. The yogi keeps mindful of it until the unpleasant sensation is consumed. Thereby the cause is killed in effect. He does it again and again until with perfect proficiency he finally manages to kill the cause in the cause.

Again:

> When the mind has penetrated into the sensation the meditator will no longer feel that "I" am suffering. These conceptual notions will be

replaced by a simple, clear awareness of sensation alone. And because the idea of an "I" which suffers has been removed, the meditator will not feel the discomfort of the unpleasant sensation. The sensation which a few moments ago was felt as pain or burning will now be felt by the meditator as only an intense sensation without the element of identification. [P. 28]

At this point one further question may be asked: Aside from the long-range, presupposed goal of all such seeking—arahantship—what level of experience can be expected as a result of "success" in a two-week intensive effort? U Win Pe suggested in conversation that "the knowledge of arising and passing away" (*udayabbayānupassanā-nāṇa*) was a practically realizable goal. (This is the fourth of the eighteen levels outlined in the Mahasi Sayadaw's method.) Apparently when one has achieved this level, though it is not *per se* the nonbackslidable Stream-Enterer level, it seems that a deep and fully established awareness of this within one's own body-mind experience represents a progression not easily reversible. And, it was emphasized, *this* awareness may be readily kept alive or increased even in the midst of a layperson's active life by a continuing attention to physical touch in all one's activities.[30] Touch is the sense surrogate of the total realization of anattā-anicca-dukkha, a continual encapsulated reminder.

Conclusion

Two questions remain. First, does the Sunlun method genuinely conform to the supposed vipassanā pattern of *observation* (only) of the fluxing process that comprises the person—and by extension, the whole world—or is there here a jhāna-type *control* and *production* of subjective phenomena by the rough-breathing and held-breath technique? This is reminiscent of the techniques rejected by the Buddha [*MLS*, I, pp. 297–30 (I.242–46)]. And the answer is not absolutely clear, for the line between these two types of method seems indistinct in Sunlun.

It may well be that the distinction between "observation" and "control" is neither ultimately important nor ever clearly defined in Buddhist meditation as a whole. Even detached "observation," the vipassanā ideal, can never occur without a distinct will to do so and without the continual direction of body-mind in certain channels. Yet the *professed* methodology of Sunlun is specifically observation and not control. Forcing the pace of breathing and the subsequent holding of the breath while observing what goes on within, it is said, only reveals more clearly than is possible in any other way those inner processes in their true nature. This is similar to studies of that exaggerated or abnormal behavior which, it is believed, more clearly reveals the hidden dynamics of ordinary behavior than would ordinary behavior by itself.

Thus, in the Sunlun context, holding oneself rigidly in one position for a long time starkly reveals the true nature of the body-mind "self":

Pain is unpleasant, ache is unpleasant, cold is unpleasant. Within the unpleasantness of all these there is an element of discomfort. It is this element of discomfort which is the basis of all composite things. The meditator who feels fatigue in his limbs and wishes to alter his position or whose mind being confined to the narrow point of touch wishes to be let loose among sensual objects, desires escape from the discomfort of his posture and confined mind. [Pp. 20–30]

Second, what is the nature of the specific mode of enlightenment-bringing awareness concentrated on by Sunlun? It is deliberately intensified awareness of pain, dukkha. In the words of U Win Pe, Sunlun emphasizes "the efficacy of dukkha to overcome dukkha." Other teachers, such as U Ba Khin at the International Meditation Centre, tended to use impermanence (*anesa* in Burmese pronunciation) as the main tool, but the level of attainment there aimed at seems not to have been as high as with Sunlun. In any case, with Sunlun, feeling (vedanā), and especially *painful* feeling, is made central in awareness. And if it is not central enough, it is to be deliberately made so by the methodology noted above. The concentration on pain must be so intense that it blots out all other mental content, even the *thought* of anicca-anattā-dukkha, from the conscious mind. (This thought is "there" saturating the subconscious even if not consciously present!) To *think about* sensation or pain in any way compromises the reality of the experience itself and makes it something other than vipassanā. Thus, "Know whatever arises, as it arises, when it arises, in the bare fact of its arising. Be mindful of just this. Let no thoughts of 'me' or 'mine' interfere. . . . *Do not consider that this is anicca, this dukkha and this anatta*. All thinking, reflection and consideration are conceptual. They are not vipassana" [p. 26; italics added].

Sunlun then has a double compression: that of the historic Buddhist methodology of meditation and that of the modern sense of paucity of time and capacity. As I have noted throughout, vipassanā represents the quintessence of the Theravāda Buddhist interpretation of the human condition: saṃsāra is essentially impermanent, empty of true reality, and pain filled. Salvation is to be accomplished by the full existentializing of this knowledge. Sunlun compresses this into a practice of maximum intensity, forcing the pace and deliberately intensifying the innate (but glossed over) painfulness of all sentient existence. Thus only can human beings be brought to a true, release-bringing knowledge. On the other hand, modernity also exerts its compressive influence. This is a busy, hasty, distracted age in which spiritual pursuits have little place and most people scant time for the inner life. Such an age needs a rapid, even superrapid method without technical complications and available to practice in daily (secular) life. Sunlun devotees believe their method to be this. It contains the absolute essence of Buddhism and makes it practicable by means of the sense of touch that constantly pervades our physical life. All that is then needed is the resolute will.

Appendix
"A Buddhist Pilgrim's Progress"

The following account condenses the second part of a two-part article that appeared in *The Guardian Magazine* (Rangoon, Burma) in the February 1963 issue (pp. 13–19), by Daw Khin Myo Chit. Used by author's and *The Guardian*'s permission.

I had done my first sitting with U Sasana as my meditation master. I had promised him to do three sittings as a trial. When I went home from the monastery after the first sitting I felt well and fresh in spite of the strenuous nature of the sitting. However, that night I woke up shivering with cold, my body feverish. Since my husband and my son were still at the monastery I was all alone in the house.

I remembered what U Sasana had told me: "Whatever happens to your body or mind there is nothing for you to do but to be mindful of them. You will need the strength to be mindful. To gain that strength breathe hard and be mindful of the touch of the air on the nostril. When you have enough strength to tackle your bodily pains be mindful of them till they are no more."

Since I had no one to help me, I had to find strength from within. I sat up and breathed as hard as I could ignoring the feverish sensations. Even as I breathed fever subsided and I began to perspire. In a few minutes I fell into a restful sleep. In the morning I felt well and fresh. There was not a hint of fever.

I went about doing the usual household chores and went to the monastery. I reported to my meditation master what happened last night and went on with my second sitting. There was not much difference with the first. There always came a moment while breathing hard when I felt I could not go on. With the meditation master's encouraging words I rallied my strength to go on only to find myself able to breathe on and enjoying myself too. In this way I finished the three sittings I promised.

My meditation master just said: "Now you know what it is like. If you feel like doing the practice go on. If you feel otherwise, do as you please." My husband and my son came home from the monastery. After reorganising our worldly life we felt we should continue the practice.

With the blessing and consent of our meditation masters we did try to practise at home and found out something about ourselves. That something we discovered was not at all flattering—that is, we would not or could not do the practice properly without the supervision of the meditation master.

After having done a few sittings under the supervision of the meditation master we knew the standard of perfection to be attained at each sitting. If we did well in the breathing session observing the rules—without changing position when cramped, without pausing when fatigued, without letting any bodily sensation interfere with the breathing—we could tackle the unpleasant sensations that arose in the second half of the sitting. Sad to say we always broke the rules. Without any one to watch over us we cheated and never did well when we practised mindfulness over the sensations. As a result of cheating we failed to get the feeling of peace and well being after the sitting. After overcoming a great disappointment in our own untrustworthiness we had to face the unflattering truth about ourselves and go to the monastery to practise under the watchful eyes of the meditation master.

We went to the monastery once a week for two sittings. A month or two later I began to have difficulty in breathing. After a minute or two of hard breathing I was seized with a severe contraction in the chest. Although I could overcome such a crisis by rallying my strength to breathe harder, at other times I could not do the same with this one. My meditation master told me to breathe harder but things got worse. As I struggled hard to get over the crisis my body trembled and my neck swelled as if bursting.

I could not get over the crisis even though my meditation master kept on telling me to strive more. I felt he was asking me to do the impossible. As I struggled I seemed to have found a way to get round if not to get over the crisis, to find some place of shelter instead of bravely running through the blazing pathway.

Like an animal trapped in a burning forest trying to find a place of shelter, instead of breaking through the blazing pathway I found a way to shirk the painful sensations that rose in me while breathing. As I was trapped in the throes of pain, I could not breathe even softly. Disobeying the meditation master who reminded me to breathe harder to get over the crisis, I found myself holding the breath automatically.

As soon as I held my breath I experienced a sensation of floating like a light feather in the pleasant wide open space. The meditation master's voice reminding me to breathe hard seemed far away. I fell into a trance during which I saw a huge pool of liquid whose colours changed into hues of a rainbow as they swirled round. It was a wonderful sight beautiful beyond description. All my pains were no more.

When I told my meditation master of my experience he said that trances and visions were not to be encouraged, for they were more of a hindrance than help in my task. They would not bring me any nearer to the Truth I was seeking.

Somewhat discouraged I tried to obey the meditation master. Even though the spirit be strong the flesh was weak. When faced with the unbearable pains I would not or could not get over them; it was especially difficult to obey the meditation master when I had found a way to get round the pains and fall into a pool of ecstasy.

My First Retreat to the Monastery

My meditation master advised me to come to the monastery for a week's retreat, so that I could get over the crisis. I was reluctant to do so. I put off as long as I could giving lame excuses. One day something happened. Coming home from the monastery after our weekly practice, I threw myself on a bed. That moment everything went blank and my body seemed to be no more. Nothing seemed to be left of my body except the heart beat. Even the heart seemed to be no more, only the throb was there. Without the burden of the body the heart throb was pure ecstasy . . . nothing like I had ever experienced before.

When I was jerked back to the every-day world by someone calling me to dinner I felt sorry for the loss. Since that time I kept thinking of the ecstasy that I had gained and I wondered if I could make it last as long as I wished. Perhaps if I went to the monastery for a week's retreat I might be able to do it?

So I decided to go to the monastery for a week's retreat. During the time I had to practise four times a day.

Is This the Truth I Seek?

On the third day of my retreat I had an extraordinary experience. As I began my practice at seven o'clock in the morning, breathing had become easier. I was no longer hampered by any critical pains. When the time came for the practice of mindfulness of bodily sensations I had no pains at all. Only the pit-a-pat of the heart remained. My mind withdrawn from pleasures of the flesh was clear of passions, worries, anxieties and all the perilous stuff that weighed the heart. My mind became a virgin pool, clear and serene. Various shapes of irridescent colours danced beautifully on the mirror-like surface annihilating all that is made of flesh and senses into calm tranquility. I realised then how vain were the pleasures of the flesh when compared with this. Sensual pleasures cloy but then this joy increased every moment of enjoyment. This sweet rest, peace and tranquility, I thought, might be the Truth I was seeking?

I Found the Answer

I began the next session with eagerness expecting to get the same experience. I breathed as hard as I could. But after a few moments I was caught up by a severe contraction in the chest. My throat became parched and dry. Suddenly a death rattle rose up and down my throat. My body shook and trembled and my heart seemed to be a lump of lead. Everything seemed to have gone dead except the death rattle in my throat. I had no breath left in me. When I tried to open my eyes a great shroud of darkness had fallen over me. I could not open my mouth to cry. I felt suffocated as if I was enveloped in the smokes of hell. A deep feeling of frustration came over me. I felt let down by all that I had put my trust in. That virgin pool of ecstasy, where I used to take refuge, was no more. It had gone to nothing in the face of the overpowering death throes.

Now I realised that I must be mindful of the sensations of body as they came whether pleasant or painful, for it was the only way to end suffering; it would not do for me to stray from the path. Like the animal in the burning forest I must break through the blazing path however fearsome it might be.

During the next session I doubled my efforts in breathing, getting over the crisis in the only way the meditation master taught me—by being mindful and striving harder. When the time came for the practice of mindfulness of the sensations of the body, my whole body seemed to be turned into a lump of lead. All my limbs had gone numb and deadened.

That moment I had strengthened the force of mindfulness so that I was aware of the action of my beating heart as it was. Soon there came a sensation of heaviness. The benumbed body grew heavy; but then this heaviness though it was terrifying was only a sensation. Because I could look upon the heart-beat without the clinging desire to wallow in its ecstasy, I could be aware of the sensation of mountainous heaviness without fear.

Then I reached a state wherein only two things remained of the being whom I called myself; namely, sensations and being aware of them, or being mindful of them. The power of mindfulness caught hold of the sensations in its grip so much so that the two forces hugged like two steel plates screwed together. I did not know how long I stayed like that. Suddenly the strength of mindfulness became so overpowering that it looked as if it would press down the sensations till they were completely rubbed out.

That moment I stayed like one on the threshold of Freedom tasting the first breath of the Great Joy that was to be. Just one step more and I would be free of all that was evil. Like a bird trying her wings for a long flight, I stood on the edge of Freedom. Waves of joy came over me.

The next moment, even before I knew what was happening, everything went black and I fell into depths of despair. I could not go on with the sitting. I threw myself down and wept as if my heart would break. My meditation master said a few comforting words and advised me to sleep on it. At that time U Sasana was away from the monastery so it was my other friend U Vinaya, who helped me over with the crisis. That night I was in great sorrow for something that I did not know. It was as if my mind had been unhinged for the time.

Two Great Forces at Work

The next morning I woke up refreshed in spite of the nightmare-like experience I had gone through the previous night. But that day was a dream-like experience, for I went through the routine of sittings like clock-work.

I had no difficulty in breathing. While I breathed smoothly, a vaporous mist enveloped me and a vision of myself as a tiny particle floating in an ethereal mist appeared and I watched fascinated. When I became conscious of the pit-a-pat of my heart, each heart-throb and the other that followed seemed to be in great conflict, as two great forces were coming against each other.

Of the two forces one was the desire to wallow in the cool serenity of the ecstasy instead of being mindful of the sensations of the body; the other force was the realisation that the pool of ecstasy however pleasant was not the Goal I was seeking; more than that the pool of ecstasy was not a safe place and I would be helpless when the pains of death overtook me.

Though realising the necessity to leave the pool of ecstasy and face the unpleasant sensations with mindfulness, the desire to wallow in the pool of ecstasy was strong. The two forces were at tug-of-war within me. This conflict went on for the remaining four days of my retreat. When the time came for me to go home I was steadfastly determined to walk the Path my meditation masters had laid down for me.

Only back at home I had time to contemplate over my experiences during the week's retreat and get everything into focus. I realized it was not an easy task to tame the mind. The crises which often threatened to interfere with the hard breathing session were the result of the mind straining itself to wander away from the point of the touch. When with great effort I succeeded in keeping the mind on the sensations of the body, only two things remained of my body, they were the sensations and being aware of them. This was an important step; for with that realisation I stood on the brink of freedom.

But why was I thrown back into depths of despair the next moment? Only when I looked back I realised that I had instinctively turned back. The reason was quite simple: I did not want to be free from what is Suffering; for the end of suffering meant the end of life. Life and suffering cannot be separated; if one wished to end suffering life must be ended too—that is, the unending cycle of rebirths must be ended. Even though one could accept that life meant suffering one could not accept the corollary that to end suffering, life must be ended. I realised that my clinging desire to life had made me turn back from the bound of freedom.

I realised that to end suffering I must end the craving for life. Only if one stopped craving one could end suffering. I knew I must follow my meditation master's instruction that I must be mindful of the unpleasant sensations of the body, its aches, pains, and agonies. Once again I saw that the road to Deliverance lay not in wallowing in the pool of ecstasy but in breaking through the blazing pathway of painful sensations. If I wanted to be free, I must be brave. This Path—the practice of mindfulness—I was convinced, was the Path I must travel.

On the Path
With the steadfast conviction that the practice of mindfulness would surely lead to Deliverance from Suffering, I went on with the practice. I went to the monastery once a week and there I sought the advice and guidance of my meditation masters.

Try as hard as I could, I kept on falling into the pool of ecstasy. The only comfort was that my mindfulness would not allow me to stay there long. I could practise mindfulness of the unpleasant sensations for a longer duration.

As I went on with my practice, in one of my sittings I found my mind firmly fixed on the bodily sensations. I tried to be mindful of the pains only, taking great care not to let my mind wander. Somehow or the other I found my mind had strayed. I was greatly exasperated, for I had been doing my best to be mindful. Still the mind strayed.

I understood then how important it was to keep my mind on the bodily sensations, strictly on the single point without the slightest deviation. It was like balancing a grain on the tip of a pin. The situation was so delicate that the slightest flutter of "oh" or "ah" would upset it.

The Threatening Crash

Apart from the weekly visits to the monastery I tried to practise at home. Even though I might not do as well as I did under supervision, it at least gave continuity. Living the life of a householder, being full of cares, I found a refuge in the practice even if I could but spare a few minutes out of the twenty-four hours of the day.

One day while I was practising at home I felt my body was dashing away at a terrific speed towards something but I did not know what. Like a runaway car crashing against a rocky hill I thought I would be smashed to pieces. A great fear seized me and I jerked myself away from that sensation. Once I was free from the clutches of the terrible sensation I realised I had missed a great experience. I knew I should have faced that terrible sensation without fear. With mindfulness as my only stay, I should abandon myself to whatever happened.

I told U Vinaya about the threatening crash, and he said, "Remember, in seeking Truth or Deliverance, you must be prepared to lay down your life. It is not easy to abandon yourself to the unknown. You are treading the Path the Buddha and His Disciples trod before you. You need courage to follow the Path. Without anyone telling you, you now know that you lack courage. You must practise mindfulness more rigorously until you are ready to receive the gift of Truth the Buddha had taught and thereby win Deliverance."

I knew I was very near achieving my goal but two things always came between me and my attainment. One was the nameless fear I had described and the other was the joy of expectancy. Knowing I was near my goal I could not restrain my joy of expectancy. One slight "Oh" or "Ah," then all was gone. When I succeeded in restraining the joyful feeling I could not overcome that nameless fear. It was always one or the other that came at the crucial moment.

An Unforgettable Experience

I knew then that this craving for self had made me afraid of breaking through the bounds of pain and suffering. When I asked my meditation master how I could overcome this nameless fear, that rose from clinging to my self, he told me to be more zealous in my practice of mindfulness. This practice of mindfulness is something one can never overdo and however much one might try it is always a little short of perfection.

One day, I went to a lecture by Martha Graham, who was at that time on a visit to Burma. I listened to the famous dancer's lecture with great interest. I tried to be mindful of the touch of my body on the chair I sat [on] even when I listened.

In course of her lecture Martha Graham mentioned a famous ballet dancer who did spectacular leaps. She told us how that dancer (I have forgotten the name) practised the leaps for hundreds of times (she did mention the number of times) for a great show, but he could not attain perfection. Even at the dress rehearsal he had not attained the required standard. [It was] only when the actual show took place that the dancer did his several hundredth leap and then and there he attained perfection. Martha Graham commented that it was the hundreds of leaps he had practised and missed that culminated in the final perfection on the stage.

I could leap with joy to hear that. All the times I had missed because I slunk away in fear or because my mind strayed away to joyous expectation— all these were not in vain. One day these forces would be mobilized so that the moment of perfection would be won.

One night I lay in a restful trance practising mindfulness of the bodily sensations. At first the sensations were not unpleasant as my body was throbbing softly. Later my whole body began to vibrate as if an electric shock was running through me. I no longer could be restful. I had to rally all my strength to be mindful of the sensations. The vibrations grew more and more violent. I went on being mindful unswervingly. My mindfulness was strong but the violence of the sensations seemed to match and challenge it. Mindfulness and sensations met in a death struggle in which fear caused by the thought, "What shall become of me?" had no place. When two things, namely the sensation and mindfulness existed, there was no place for I. The illusion of I was broken. As the sensations increased in violence the power of mindfulness matched its fearful intensity. I did not know how long this went on. Then suddenly like nerves bursting under a great strain there was a big explosion. The next thing I knew I was sitting cross-legs, my whole body wide open like the boundless sky, with nothing to hang on, nothing to cling to. It was an indescribable moment.

I faced the dawn of the day paying my respects down at the household shrine with the simple prayer,

> I take refuge in the Buddha
> I take refuge in His Law
> I take refuge in His Order of the Yellow Robe.

How many times all through my life had I uttered this prayer! But this time I meant every word of it. I knew I was crowned again with the Three Gems. There was nothing but peace in my heart.

Notes

Preface

1. *The Book of the Discipline*, vols. I–VI, trans. I. B. Horner (London: Luzac, 1938, 1940, 1942, 1951, 1952, 1966), vol. IV, p. 45 (*Mahāvagga* I.21).
2. *The Middle Length Sayings* (*Majjhima Nikāya*), vols. I–III, trans. I. B. Horner (London: Luzac, 1954, 1957, 1959), II, p. 106 (I.436). Hereafter noted in text as *MLS*; (I.436) above indicates Trenckner text numbers.

Chapter 1   *Gotama Buddha's Enlightemment*

1. Vishwanath P. Varma, *Early Buddhism and Its Origins* (Delhi: Munshiram Manoharlal, 1973), pp. 357–58.
2. Paul Younger, *Introduction to Indian Religious Thought* (Philadelphia: Westminister, 1972), p. 23.
3. S. Radhakrishnan and C. A. Moore, eds., *A Sourcebook in Indian Philosophy* (Princeton: Princeton University Press, 1967), pp. 37, 38.
4. Ibid., p. 72.
5. Ibid., p. 95.
6. In this context the Sunlun intensification of pain by a species of breath-stopping exercises, to be discussed later, may seem to revert to the ascetic pattern that was rejected by the Buddha, according to the Pāli Canon. Sunlun devotees, however, would contend that such mild measures as they use are still well within the Middle Way of Buddhism. They are only forcefully existentializing the enlightenment-producing awareness of the pain, emptiness, and impersonality of existence.
7. See E. J. Thomas, *The Life of Buddha*, 3d rev. ed. (London: Routledge & Kegan Paul, 1949), pp. 184, n.2; 229–30.
8. Bhadantācariya Buddhaghosa, *The Path of Purification* (*Visuddhimagga*), trans. Bhikkhu Nyāṇamoli, 2d ed. (Colombo: Semage, 1964), XXIII, 30. Hereafter noted in text as *PP*, chapter and section number as above.
9. *The Life of Buddha*, pp. 184–85.
10. Taking only the *Middle Length Sayings*, in which the references are more numerous than in any other canonical work, there are the following instances, in addition to those already quoted, that speak of the four jhānas: vol. I, pp. 27–29 (I.21–22); pp. 41–42 (I.33); pp. 117–19 (I.89–90); p. 151 (I.117); pp. 227–30 (I.181–84); pp. 300–303 (I.246–49); pp. 323–24 (I.270); pp. 330–33 (I.276–79); pp. 370–71 (I.308–9); vol. II, pp. 12–14 (I.347–48); pp. 19–20 (I.354); pp. 112–14 (I.441–42); pp. 200–201 (I.521–22); pp. 215–21 (II.15–21); p. 227 (II.28); pp. 392–93 (II.204). Two jhānas only: vol. III, pp. 12–13 (II.226); pp. 54–55 (III.4); p. 61 (III.11); pp. 63–64 (III.14); pp. 88–89 (III.36); pp. 137–38 (III.98); pp. 154–55 (III.111); pp. 182ff. (III.136). Some of these references are extensive, others merely mention the jhānas.
11. *MLS*, vol. I, p. 5 (I.3); pp. 348–49 (I.289). Vol. II, pp. 104–107 (I.435–37) up to no-thing plane only; pp. 213–14 (II.13) connected to other, non-jhānic series. Vol. III, pp. 40–42 (II.255–56); pp. 47–51 (II.263–65); pp. 142–43 (III.103); pp. 148–51 (III.105–108); pp. 290–92 (III.244–45); pp. 311–13 (III.260–61). None of these mentions cessation as the climax, though sometimes it is stated that Nibbāna may be achieved by means of them, as in III, 290–92 (III.244–45).
12. *MLS*, vol. I, pp. 51–54 (I.40–42); pp. 200–203 (I.158–60); pp. 218–19

(I.174–75); pp. 251–52 (I.203–204); pp. 258–61 (I.207–209). Vol. II, pp. 15–17 (I.350–52) up to no-thing plane only; and pp. 66–69 (I.398–400); pp. 77–80 (III.25–27); pp. 92–94 (III.42–45); pp. 268–71 (III.220–22). In all of these except I, 51–54 (I.40–42) and II, 15–17 (I.350–52), cessation is included as the climax of the attainments.

13. *Die Buddhistische Versenkung* (Munich: Reinhardt), pp. 47–51 particularly.

Chapter 2   *Lower Levels of Meditation*

1. It may have been Buddhaghosa's prime inspiration. His language is close to it in many places. His larger and more inclusive work has almost superseded *The Path of Freedom* throughout Theravāda Buddhism. The *Vimuttimagga*, attributed to Arahant Upatissa, was translated from a sixth-century Chinese version by N. R. M. Ehara Thera, as *The Path of Freedom* (Colombo: D. Roland Weerasuria, 1961).

2. *The Questions of King Milinda*, part I, II, trans. T. W. Rhys Davids (New York: Dover Publications reprint, 1963), vols. XXXV and XXXVI of *The Sacred Books of the East* (Oxford: Clarendon Press, 1890 and 1894), pt. I, pp.43–44.

3. *Psalms of the Early Buddhists*: II, *Psalms of the Brethren*, trans. Mrs. C. A. F. Rhys Davids (London: Oxford, 1937), p. 383 (stanzas 1150–51). In *The Path of Purification*, to be noted in detail later, this theme of body-repulsiveness as a meditation subject is extensively elaborated.

4. *The Book of the Discipline* vol. IV (*Mahāvagga*), p. 45 (I.21.2).

5. This *is* the case in general, as set forth in *The Questions of King Milinda*, but there are exceptions. In *The Book of the Kindred Sayings*, vol. I, pp. 149–53 [text i, 118; IV.3.3] Godhika is a monk who had "touched temporary emancipation" six times and fallen away each time. Upon achieving emancipation the seventh time he cut his throat. But according to the Buddha this was not wrong, since he did not kill himself because he desired another rebirth; having achieved final Nibbāna he was forever beyond Māra's (the Evil One's) reach. So too in *MLS*, III, pp. 315–19 (III.262–66) and *The Book of the Kindred Sayings*, IV, pp. 30–33 (text IV.55; XXV. II.4.87), a monk named Channa, who was in the last stages of a painful illness, committed suicide despite the exhortations and warnings of his fellow monks. But, as with Godhika, the Buddha says that Channa was blameless since he was emancipated from the desire for, or fear of, another birth.

6. See Guy R. Welbon, *The Buddhist Nirvana and Its Western Interpreters* (Chicago: University of Chicago Press, 1968).

7. In this connection see the graphic pictorial representations of the saṃsāric Wheel of Life in Tibetan Buddhism, in which existence is portrayed as a great wheel on whose rim are the twelve links (*nidāna*) that cause rebirth. Inside the wheel are delineations of existence in all forms (hells to heavens) and at the hub as the motive power of the wheel's revolution, are greed, hatred, and delusion in the form of cock, snake, and hog, respectively. Although this representation is distinctively Tibetan, its ideology is also Theravādin.

8. In general confirmation of this basically nonmetaphysical stance of the Buddha we may note another instance. When questioned by a certain Vacchagotta as to whether there is a self or not, the Buddha remained silent. He said in answer to a later question by Ānanda that to have affirmed or denied the self would have further confused Vacchagotta—a clear case of fitting truth to the hearer's capacity. *The Book of the Kindred Sayings*, IV, trans. F. L. Woodard (London: Luzac, 1965), pp. 281–82 (XLIV.x.10). Edward Conze, in *Buddhist Thought in Indian* (London: Allen and Unwin, 1962), speaks thus of the Buddha's discourse on not-self (*anattā*) in *The Book of the Kindred Sayings*, III, 59–60 (XXII.59.7), in which self is dis-identified with all body-mind components: "The formula is manifestly intended as a guide to meditation, and not as a basis for speculation" (p. 37).

9. *Psalms of the Sisters*, pp. xxxi–xxxii.

10. T. W. Rhys Davids in *Early Buddhism*, p. 73, quoted in Bhikshu Sangharakshita, *A Survey of Buddhism* (Bangalore: Indian Institute of World Culture, 1959), p. 74.

11. *The Path of Freedom* (see note 1), p. 90. Hereafter *PF* in textual notes.

12. On this general topic, see E. J. Thomas, *The History of Buddhist Thought* 2d ed., 1967 reprint (New York: Barnes and Noble, 1951), p. 26.

13. Practically speaking, this organization of the Saṅgha, almost the first organized, permanent group of holy mendicants in India living in houses, required a supportive organization of laymen. The general community might support a few wandering seekers, that is, the traditional Indian holy men, and perhaps a well-known guru and his disciples in some location. But an extensive brotherhood with many local groupings required a parish arrangement which was *steadily* supportive of the monastery in its midst. This of course led to a modification of the monkish way of life because the monk was obliged to teach the lay disciple to be as good a Buddhist as possible for a layman, in the hope of eventual enlightenment in some future life. And no doubt in thus opening the monastery to lay contact, more so than in Western-Christian monasteries, the intensity of meditational life was much diluted —as it is today in most monasteries. E. Lamotte states that the laymen were "included" in the Saṅgha originally as a kind of afterthought born of purely utilitarian motives on the part of the monks. (See *Histoire du Bouddhisme Indien* [Louvain: Institut Orientaliste, 1958], pp. 71ff.) In a sharply worded modern restatement of this position we read: "The Buddhist Sangha form an integral part of the religion itself, and are entitled to an equal adoration with the Buddha and the Dharma. The religion of Buddha consists of only three elements of Buddha, the Dharma and the Saṅgha and nothing more. By the laws of Buddha, the laity form no part of religion. The Saṅgha are the only living representatives of Buddhism on earth." Quoted in Heinz Bechert, *Buddhismus, Staat und Gesellschaft in den Ländern des Theravada Buddhismus* (Frankfort: Alfred Metzner Verlag, 1966), vol. I, p. 67.

14. In Theravāda this represents the stage of becoming a Stream-Enterer (*sotāpanna*) after which a person cannot be reborn in any less-than-human form and, at most, has only seven more possible rebirths before reaching Nibbāna. The Ledi Sayadaw equated this with the essential destruction of attachment to self within a person, though some further refinement remains necessary before full release in Nibbāna. See my "A Comparison of Theravada and Zen Buddhist Meditational Methods and Goals," *History of Religions*, IX, no. 4, 1970, pp. 304–15.

15. Nyanaponika Thera, *The Heart of Buddhist Meditation* (Colombo: Word of the Buddha Publishing Committee, 1953), p. 74. Italics added.

16. See my *In the Hope of Nibbāna* (LaSalle: Open Court, 1964), Chapter 3, for a fuller discussion.

17. For a more extensive discussion of the teacher-pupil relationship in Theravāda Buddhism see my "Role of the Meditation Master in Theravada Buddhism," *Newsletter Review* (Montreal: R. M. Bucke Memorial Society), IV, nos. 1 and 2, Spring, 1971, pp. 5–10.

18. "Insight" refers to vipassanā-type meditation.

19. See my *In the Hope of Nibbāna* (LaSalle: Open Court, 1964); H. Saddhatissa's *Buddhist Ethics* (London: Allen and Unwin, 1970); S. Tachibana's *The Ethics of Buddhism*, 3d ed. (Colombo: Bauddha Sahitya Sabha, 1961).

20. *Dialogues of the Buddha*, pt. I, trans. T. W. Rhys Davids (London: Luzac, 1956), pp. 79, 82 (Sutta II.42, 68), respectively.

21. A note on "consciousness-concomitant" defines it as "a collective term for feeling, perception, and formations," i.e., aspects of mentality that arise together with consciousness."

22. The closed-eye method of seated meditation predominates in many meditation centers in Southeast Asia today. I do not know whether this practice is an extension of the here-preliminary closing of the eyes (no "visible data"), or because kasina

and cemetery meditation is now less used, or is perhaps assumed to be especially suitable to vipassanā-type meditation.

Chapter 3   *Jhānic and Formless States*

1. Jhāna has been variously translated as musing, meditation, trance, and absorption. I prefer "trance" and "absorption" but will as a rule use the word jhāna itself.

2. Here "meditation" equals jhāna. The Pāli Canon generally recognizes only four jhānic stages, but the Theravāda tradition has divided stage two into two sub-stages in which "initial and sustained thought" are eliminated one at a time rather than together as in the canonical version. Here, however, this division will be ignored.

3. I have no data indicating whether the successive levels are easier to attain *after* one has crossed the attention barrier from access concentration into the jhānic level. The Japanese Zen experience with the breakthrough of the first kōan-solving and first satori suggests that this is the case. In any event the levels are clearly separable for the experiencer.

4. This confirms an earlier comment about the carryover of meditational skill and attainment states from one rebirth to another. Basic material on the kasina is found in *PP*, ch. IV, V, and *PF*, ch. VIII.

5. Nyanatiloka, *Buddhist Dictionary* (Colombo: Frewin and Co., 1956), p. 74.

6. See Archie I. Bahm, *Yoga: Union with the Ultimate* (New York: Unger, 1961), p. 114.

7. *PF*, p. 75, interestingly calls it a *maṇḍala*.

8. This ability to produce such an image, with or without the physical stimulation, though viewed in the West with suspicion and disbelief, is standard in the East. A young American working with Shingon ritual in Japan told me that with six months' practice "anyone" could learn to produce a round, moonlike disk before his sight and with further practice learn to produce specific forms within it. Significantly, Shingon is deeply impregnated with Indian-Buddhist ritual and practice, with strong yogic overtones.

9. L. S. Cousins, "Buddhist Jhāna: Its nature and attainment according to the Pāli sources," *Religion*, vol. III (Autumn 1973), p. 125. *Javana* is "swift-moving consciousness [of] the kind with which good or bad mental acts are normally performed" (ibid., p. 123).

10. *Buddhist Dictionary*, p. 107.

11. Hindrances to jhāna are sense desires in general (IV.81) and lust, ill-will, stiffness and torpor (of mind), agitation and worry, and uncertainty in particular (IV.86, 105). Applied and sustained thought are two of the factors of the jhānas, the others being happiness, bliss, and concentration (III.21).

12. It should be emphasized, however, that delightful and pure as these jhānic states are, they still differ from the vipassanic moments of fruition when Nibbāna is directly apprehended. That is, Nibbāna as object of consciousness is peerless and utterly transcendent; compared to it, jhānic states are fetters, even though pleasant ones.

13. This is different from the "initial thought and discursive thought," which are eliminated by the attainment of the second jhāna. Here there is no discursive, that is, discriminative, conceptual-object oriented thought, only the totally nonconceptual centering of awareness on a diffuse "object" such as boundless space.

14. Again, this process is similar to the yogic cultivation of a specific awareness of indistinctness as a conscious datum. Only the terminology differs. In the yogic pattern perhaps "indistinctness" is an absolutized somethingness; here space is an absolutized nothingness. But then is the psychological atmosphere in the two processes completely the same?

Chapter 4 *Jhānic-Related "Buddhist" Meditations*

1. Why this is the case I am not certain. Two reasons can be suggested. First, ordinarily there must be some object affinity between successive levels of meditational attainment. Thus one uses the *same* kasina, in progressively rarefied form, for attaining all four jhānas. To shift kasinas, or to shift to some other object, would make progress impossible. (Since body-foulness as object leads only to the first jhāna, it is of course necessary to begin with another object to go to higher jhānas.) Thus the earth, air, fire, water, and light kasinas have more affinity to a boundless space object for concentration than does loving-kindness or even body parts. Second, the four jhānic progressions are perhaps to be seen fundamentally as changes in the mental factors rather than the objects of meditation. Factors here signify the emotional-psychological accompaniments of the meditational process itself. Thus the factors of initial and sustained thought, rapture, and joy, respectively, are left behind at each stage, though the object of concentration may remain identical. But from the fourth jhāna onward the object itself is changed.

2. For a general ethical treatment of the abidings, see my *In the Hope of Nibbāna*, ch. 5, and Nyanaponika in "The Four Sublime States," *Light of the Dhamma* (Rangoon: Sāsana Council), VI, no. 2 (April 1959).

3. A Burmese monk for whom I had done a small favor, which he had not been immediately able to acknowledge, wrote: "I could not write; I did nevertheless think of you, visualize you, and send my thoughts of mettā for your well being."

4. Curiously, and to me somewhat obscurely, the "loss" of the object here spoken of is the death of the personal object of the attitude embodied in the abiding. When, unbeknownst to the meditator, his "object" had died, his meditation could not succeed. Apparently a nonexistent being, though seeming real, would not do (*PP*, IX.7).

5. With respect to extension there are three general types of practice that may be carried out to gain mastery of the given illimitable: "unspecified pervasion" of all types of beings (five in number) with the illimitable (or abiding); "specified pervasion" of seven sorts of beings, such as women, men, Noble Ones, deities, and so on; "directional pervasion," that is, of the eight compass points, zenith, and nadir (IX.49–51).

6. *Dialogues of the Buddha*, pt. III, p. 328 (ii:292).

7. *The Book of the Kindred Sayings*, V, 119–20 (text V.141; III.I.iii).

8. Vol. I, Sutta 10, "Discourse on the Applications of Mindfulness."

9. "Synovic fluid" means "oil of the joints."

10. The last sentence refers to the body as a whole.

11. Another phrasing of this subject reads: "In this manner, the Bhikkhu contemplates this body of his own, inspires the mental image of the constituent parts of the body." U Ba Khin, *The Noble Truths* (Rangoon: Thinbawa Press, 1967). (This is a different U Ba Khin from the Thray Sithu U Ba Khin mentioned in ch. VI.)

12. *The Noble Truths*, p. 50; italics added.

13. Materials in this section are based on *PP*, X.1–94 unless otherwise specified.

14. *Psalms of the Brethren*, p. 124 (151–52).

15. Such an instance is given in *Psalms of the Brethren* p. 190 (315–16). A monk, feeling lust rise within him as he meditated on a woman's body, fled from the charnel field, and returning to his cell, there gained arahantship.

16. It is also the prime favorite in today's vipassanā-type meditation centers in Burma and Thailand. It is esteemed because of its easy access for the beginner, and yet it carries him fastest and furthest toward the goal. I will return to this theme in the discussion of contemporary methods.

17. The almost identical passage is also found in the twenty-second suttanta of the *Dialogues of the Buddha*.

18. Ledi Sayadaw, *The Manuals of Buddhism* (Rangoon: Union of Burma Sāsana Council, 1965), p. 176.

19. *Dialogues of the Buddha*, pt. II, p. 329 (ii.292–93); italics added.

20. *The Heart of Buddhist Meditation*, p. 74; italics added.

21. This phrasing is based on Sutta 62, the *Middle Length Sayings*.

22. *The Heart of Buddhist Meditation*, p. 81; italics added.

23. This statement follows Sutta 10, the *Middle Length Sayings*. Ariyan truths are the truths regarding suffering and its conquest.

Chapter 5   *Vipassanā Meditation*

1. *Buddhist Dictionary*, p. 3; cf. the *Middle Length Sayings*, II, Sutta 73.

2. Why does Buddhaghosa emphasize the extreme difficulty of such attainments? Perhaps because he saw the Buddha Dhamma as decayed in its observance in his own "latter days." Or perhaps his vipassanā-geared Buddhist conscience needed some excuse for dealing at all with such this-worldly matters not directly conducive to Nibbāna seeking.

3. In *Dialogues of the Buddha* we read that the Buddha spoke to this effect: "It is because I perceive danger in the practice of mystic wonders, that I loathe, and abhor, and am ashamed thereof" (*Kevaddha Sutta*, I, p. 213). Again in *The Book of the Discipline* [vol. I, pp. 158–59 (IV.2)] it was an offense against the Order to display extraordinary powers before laymen; and [vol. V, pp. 149–52 (V.8.1–2)] to *falsely* claim such powers was to invite expulsion from the Order. It might be remarked, however, that the Buddha of the suttas never seems to have been worried by such scruples in his own or his leading disciples' cases!

4. See Maurice Collis's *Into Hidden Burma* (London: Faber and Faber, 1953), pp. 92, 174.

5. According to H. C. Warren in *Buddhism in Translations* (New York: Atheneum, 1963), p. 289, it is found in an Abhidhamma-based work, the *Abhidhammattha-Sāngha*. At least one canonical basis is the *Middle Length Sayings*, I, p. 348 (I.289).

6. The reader is reminded again of the earlier statement that "yogic" and "Buddhist" are used here in a structural-dynamic sense, rather than a completely accurate historical sense—though the formal school of Yoga may have contributed some doctrines to historical Buddhism as well as methods.

7. *Buddhist Dictionary*, p. 177.

8. Materials drawn from *Buddhist Dictionary*, p. 178.

9. Ibid., p. 180. Apparently quoted from *The Path of Purification*, but location of passage is not clearly indicated.

10. *The Book of the Gradual Sayings*, IV, trans. E. M. Hare (London: Luzac, 1955), p. 284 (4.421). Jhāna is here rendered "musing."

11. Note the earlier analogy in which the visceral, subconscious (mind-set type of) "knowledge" of impermanence and suffering remains an awareness within the meditator, even when consciousness is no longer explicitly focused on them.

12. *Buddhist Dictionary*, p. 18.

13. Ibid., pp. 18f. The ten progressively broken "fetters" are as follows: personality-belief, doubt, attachment to rule and ritual, sensuous craving, ill-will, craving for fine-material realm existence, craving for immaterial-realm existence, conceit, restlessness, ignorance. The First Path attainment destroys the first three; the Second weakens, and the Third totally destroys the next two; the Fourth utterly destroys the last five. The biases, or cankers (*āsavas*), or influxes, are: sensuous bias, bias for eternal existence, bias of views, and bias of ignorance. Their complete destruction is the accomplishment of the arahant. He is often defined as one who is canker-free.

14. This knowledge is irrevocable, for once Nibbāna is seen directly, the Stream-

Enterer can never revert to a lower-than-human rebirth and is irreversibly on the way to full Nibbāna attainment.

15. *Buddhist Dictionary*, p. 131.

16. *Compendium of Philosophy* (London: Luzac, 1963), p. 70.

17. "Personal Experiences of Candidates," (Rangoon: International Meditation Centre, n.d.) p. 15; second italics added.

18. U Nu, *What is Buddhism?* (University of Northern Rangoon: Buddha Sāsana Council Press, 1956), p. 27.

19. Quoted from the *Middle Length Sayings*, I, p. 357 (I.296).

Chapter 6   *Attainment of Cessation* (Nirodha-Samāpatti)

1. Some writers use the term "trance" rather than "attainment," and I incline to its use in view of the jhānic ancestry of cessation. However, Professor Harvey B. Aronson (University of Virginia) strongly objects to "trance" on the grounds that it implies *some* sort of mental activity, whereas cessation is specifically stated to be the absence of all such activity. Although not fully convinced—since trance states *are* cut off from all ordinary and perceptible mental activity—I shall nevertheless use "attainment" in place of "trance" in most instances to avoid dubious overtones. Often the shorter form of "cessation" or else "nirodha-samāpatti" will be substituted. (See *JAAR*, XLV/2 Supplement [June, 1977] for author's shorter but similar treatment of this same subject.)

2. *Aspects of Mahāyāna Buddhism and Its Relation to Hīnayāna* (London: Luzac, 1930), p. 167.

3. *Compendium of Philosophy*, p. 73.

4. Idem.

5. A person emerging from samādhi (jhāna) said in my hearing: "I can't *remember* anything, but now it's as if I had just wakened from a beautiful sleep, or been in a wonderful, dew-fresh rose garden."

6. P. 101. Cf. earlier quotation in which the three monks tell the Buddha that they can "remain for as long as we like" in this state.

7. The last part is quoted from the *Middle Length Sayings*, I, p. 365 (I.302). The 1954 edition of this work uses "aloofness" in place of Buddhaghosa's "seclusion" and interprets it (note) as "Nibbāna."

8. The anāgāmin (nonreturner) stage may seem to be less than the perfection of vipassanā. But so far as *human* existence is concerned, the anāgāmin is a virtual arahant. His freedom from saṃsāric fetters is so great that he will be born but once more, in some heavenly realm, and will not return to ordinary space-time existence.

9. Apparently there must be no psychic break between neither-perception-nor-nonperception and cessation, if the meditator is to reach cessation. Italics added.

10. With respect to this "visionary" jhānic light-effect:

How Visions Appear

When practising this method of concentration on the breath at the nose, after three, four, or five days, twelve kinds of visions may appear, and out of the twelve one will last from one to ten minutes. You cannot keep it longer. Return to concentration on the breath at the nose. Do not go after these visions or let your thinking be influenced by them. Do not expect them to come again. They are merely distractions.

Second Kind of Vision

If you continue with your practice you may see a second type of vision such as the following: a column of smoke, a cyclone or willy-nilly fire works, a necklace of pearls, a chain of diamonds or emeralds, the light of a star, or moon or planet, flashes of lightning, heaps of fluffy cotton, garlands of flowers falling, smoke rising, a spider's web, clouds drifting across the sky, a lotus flower, a wheel of a cart, a moon with halo, the sun's rays. Some have visions of forests, mountains, images, buildings, mansions, meditation huts, or other things to do with meditation such as the rosary, Buddhas or arahants—all these may be seen by the meditator, but the meditator should nonetheless go on meditating on the breath at the nose. These temporary visions are called Uggaha.

Third Kind of Vision

Out of all the foregoing visions one will have light and be the size of a small or big lime, six inches away from your eye. The vision will come and disappear. You try to fix it, and ultimately it will remain fixed and shining like a mirage. Fix it until it remains steady. This is called Vitakka, the first stage of the first jhāna. As you go on practising it may become brighter, like an electric light, the sun or moon, and you feel coolness. In Pāli this vision is called the Patibhaga. When you see this vision in a fixed manner you come to the second stage of the first jhāna. Then you see the vision again and the light gets brighter and a feeling of joy comes; this is the third stage of the first jhāna. After this the fourth and fifth stages of the first jhāna follow. At this stage the concentration is called Upacara Samādhi. As you go on fixing your mind the vision and yourself become one. Then the five stages of the first jhāna are complete and you are stiff and still. This stage is called Appana Samādhi.

After following the aforementioned practice for from three to five days, and having seen the visions with the lights, the meditator has attained sufficient mindfulness to proceed with the practice of Vipassanā meditation.

From Marie Byles, *Journey into Burmese Silence* (London: Allen and Unwin, 1962), pp. 203–4.

11. *The Buddhist Experience: Sources and Interpretations* (Belmont, Calif.: Dickensen, 1974), p. 206.

12. *Aspects of Mahāyāna Buddhism and Its Relation to Hīnayāna*, pp. 167–68. *Saññāvedayitanirodha* is the equivalent of nirodha-samāpatti.

13. Th. Stcherbatsky, *The Conception of Buddhist Nirvana* (Leningrad: Academy of Sciences of the USSR, 1927), pp. 3f. The difficulty involved in calling cessation an "experience" has already been noted as not insuperable.

14. U Ba Khin said in personal conversation that Hindus were always wanting to be filled with divine power, whereas Buddhism sought self-emptying.

15. *Aspects of Mahāyāna Buddhism and Its Relation to Hīnayāna*, p. 168.

Chapter 7   *Contemporary Theravāda Meditation in Burma*

1. My direct knowledge of meditational practice is limited to a few centers in or near Rangoon. This has been supplemented by discussions with some Westerners who have meditated at different places in Southeast Asia, and by numbers of books on the subject.

2. The Webu Sayadaw, "Sayadaw" meaning revered elder monk or teacher monk, living near Kyaukse in central Burma, was an example of the first type. He was reputed to be an arahant, and reported to be adept in jhānic meditation as well. Other meditation masters, such as the late Sunlun Sayadaw—founder of the Sunlun methodology of vipassanā—and the Ashin U Okkata, now living in Theingu monastery at Hnawgone near Hmawbi, are primarily vipassanā-only practicers and teachers.

3. *The Book of the Gradual Sayings*, IV, trans. E. M. Hare (London: Luzac, 1955), pp. 184–85 (IV.277). "Saddhamma" means true religion, good practice, that is, the teaching of the Buddha and its practice in its original purity and power.

4. For a discussion of some of these varieties see Étienne Lamotte's *Histoire du Bouddhisme Indien*, pp. 210–22.

5. *Dialogues of the Buddha*, pt. III, pp. 73–74 (iii.77).

6. The extreme rarity of birth as a human being is thus phrased in the scriptures: "Monks, it is like a man who might throw a yoke with one hole into the sea. An easterly wind might take it westwards, a westerly wind might take it eastwards, a northerly wind might take it southwards, a southerly wind might take it northwards. There might be a blind turtle there who came to the surface once in a hundred years. What do you think about this, monks? Could that blind turtle push his neck through that one hole in the yoke?"

"If at all, revered sir, then only once in a very long while."

"Sooner or later, monks, could the blind turtle push his neck through the one hole in the yoke; more difficult than that, do I say, monks, is human status once again for the fool who's gone to the Downfall" [*MLS*, III, pp. 214f. (III.169)]. "The Downfall" is rebirth in one of the four nether planes including animal, ghostly, and demonic existences, and the hells.

7. "Small" is interpolated here since this statement of the Ledi Sayadaw seems inconsistent with the usual view of Metteyya's coming in this *present* world age. But Indian cosmology recognizes lesser (*yugas*) and greater (*mahāyugas*) eons.

8. *The Manuals of Buddhism*, p. 170. All italics added, except Pāli words. It is interesting that the Ledi Sayadaw (1846–1923) considered the Buddha Dhamma to be "flourishing" in his day. He probably meant that it was as yet fully present in its potentiality for enlightenment.

9. Ibid., p. 173.

10. *The Heart of Buddhist Meditation*, pp. 8–9.

11. Ibid., pp. 27f.

12. Ibid., pp. 38f.

13. Marie Byles in *Journey into Burmese Silence*, p. 55, suggests that *one* of the earliest lay meditation centers was that of Saya Thet near Rangoon. Perhaps it was in existence some thirty years earlier than her own visit there in 1957, for the center had been founded by Saya Thet's parents.

14. It may be axiomatic that Burmese turn to more "vigorous" spirituality in times of stress. The current popularity of meditation in Burma was attributed by a Burmese friend of mine to the frustrations being suffered under current conditions in Burma.

15. Theoretically, this avenue for periods of meditation would seem to have been open to the Burmese laity for a long time. But on the whole it is probable in past centuries that such attempts by laypersons to be part-time monks would have been strongly discouraged by the "regulars."

16. An American friend (Joseph Johnston) meditating under a Burmese master in Thailand observed a Tibetan monk who "complained" that he had been used to "cutting off" his thoughts (the jhānic control method) and found it quite different to meditate in the midst of, indeed upon, the on-flowing of those thoughts themselves.

17. See my *A Thousand Lives Away* (Cambridge: Harvard University Press, 1964), pp. 233–34.

18. See my account of my own brief experience in meditation under U Ba Khin in the appendix of my *A Thousand Lives Away*.

19. These were the basic five—avoidance of killing, lying, stealing, sexual indulgence, and use of intoxicants—plus noneating of solid food after midday, avoidance of worldly music and entertainment, and no sleeping on high, luxurious beds.

20. See, for example, the method of Mahasi Sayadaw, described in the next section, and that of another Ledi Sayadaw teacher, U Thein, as described by Marie Byles in her book *Journey into Burmese Silence*, especially pp. 197–212 of the appendix.

21. This information is taken from "A Short Biography," pp. 34–35 of *The Progress of Insight*, by Mahasi Sayadaw (Kandy, Ceylon: Forest Hermitage, 1965). Quoted by kind permission of Mahasi Sayadaw. References in text are to page numbers therein.

22. This is the perfection of Stage Five of this method, the "Knowledge of Dissolution" in which the meditator becomes exclusively aware of the cessation of phenomena and of the observing consciousness itself (pp. 14–16). Cf. also a statement interpreting the Japanese Zen master, Dōgen, thus: "Therefore genuine nirvana is nothing but the realization of impermanence as impermanence." Masao Abe, in "Dōgen on Buddha Nature," *The Eastern Buddhist* (New Series) (Kyoto: Eastern Buddhist Society), IV, no.1, p. 53.

23. One may, when seated or doing anything whatsoever, mentally "travel" from one point of touch-awareness to another in turn, and then reverse the direction to avoid a merely mechanical repetition from which the attention has departed. It would go thus: rising, left thigh touching, left calf touching, left ankle touching, right thigh touching, right calf touching, right ankle touching. Falling, left thigh, and so on. (Rising and falling refer to the rising of phenomena into existence and their falling out of existence into oblivion.) The words are not said or even fully thought. There is just the flick of conscious attention on the touch sensation at each point. (Courtesy of Mr. Joseph Johnston, Nashville, Tennessee.)

24. Used by kind permission of Mahasi Sayadaw. This quotation, and some of the following ones—those without page references—are taken from a tape for beginning meditators, acquired in 1971.

25. Mr. Joseph Johnston (see n. 23), who meditated under a Mahasi Sayadaw-trained monk in Thailand, reports the following variation in seven or more stages. The purpose of the steady expansion of the number of elements observed is to provide subject matter for the increasingly subtle attentiveness and to keep the attention from flagging by presenting new materials:
1. "Stepping" (right foot), "stepping" (left foot).
2. "Lifting," "placing" (each foot in turn).
3. "Lifting," "moving," "placing."
4. "Raising" (heel), "lifting," "moving," "touching" (toe), "placing."
5. "Raising," "lifting," "moving," "touching" (toe), "placing."
6. "Raising," "lifting," "moving," "pointing" (toe), "touching," "placing."
7. To each of these stages of movement, in turn, may be added "intending to," that is, "intending to raise," and so on. Method used by Asaba Thera, at Wat Wiwekasom, Cholburi, Thailand.

26. Almost all Burmese meditation, as before noted, is done with closed eyes; walking meditation is done with downcast eyes, observing just enough to keep from stumbling.

27. The information given here and in the final description of the Sunlun method is taken from *The Yogi and Vipassana*, by Sunlun Shin Vinaya and U Win Pe (Rangoon: Sunlun Meditation Center, n.d.). Used by kind permission of U Win Pe. The Center is located at 505–8 Prome Road.

28. This statement has some interesting likenesses to the ancient Sautrantika (Buddhist) position that perception never grasps the instantaneously occurring reality of the "world" because its true reality has ceased to be, by the time perception actually seizes it. [Historically this led to the Yogācāra (idealistic) view that there *is* no world out there to be perceived.] The author of this passage, U Win Pe, is a very articulate and well-read layman. Perhaps this interpretation of Sunlun is reflective of his knowledge of Buddhist philosophy.

29. At the Ashin U Okkata Sayadaw's meditation center in Theingu Monastery near Hmawbi, Burma, in which a Sunlun-derivative method is used, I saw and heard (1971) a meditation group of fifty or more persons breathing in time to a loud, buzz-sawlike, tape-recorded "breathing" rhythm.

30. Our source, p. 21, maintains that even Stream-Enterers and Once-Returners can participate in the world as laymen. But Non-Returners (anāgāmins) and arahants must perforce leave the lay life for the monkhood.

Selected and Annotated Bibliography

Relevant Pāli Scriptures.   Though all of the canonical texts presuppose the meditative discipline and make passing references to it, those chosen here contain specific and sometimes extended statements. Except where noted these volumes are published by Luzac (London) for the Pāli Text Society. Dates indicate most recent printings or editions.

The Book of the Gradual Sayings (Anguttara-Nikāya). Vols. I, II, V translated by F. L. Woodard, 1970, 1963, 1972, respectively. Vols. III, IV translated by E. M. Hare, 1952, 1965, respectively. Scattered references to various meditative states.
The Book of the Kindred Sayings (Saṃyutta-Nikāya). Vol. I translated by Mrs. Rhys Davids, 1950. Vols. II-V translated by F. L. Woodard, 1952, 1955, 1956, 1965, respectively. Scattered references to meditative states.
Dialogues of the Buddha (Dīgha-Nikāya). Translated by T. W. Rhys Davids and C. A. F. Rhys Davids. Pt. I, 1956; II, 1959; III, 1971. Short occasional statements about meditative powers and states.
The Expositor (Atthasālinī) or *Buddhaghosa's Commentary on the Dhammasangani.* Translated by Pe Maung Tin and C. A. F. Rhys Davids. Vols. I, II, 1958. A general discussion of the "risings of consciousness" with special attention given to the jhānas in pt. V, vol. I.
The Middle Length Sayings (Majjhima-Nikāya). Translated by I. B. Horner. Vols. I–III, 1954, 1957, 1959, respectively. These volumes contain the largest number of references to meditative states and techniques. Vol. I contains the most extensive account of Gotama's own enlightenment.
Points of Controversy (Kathā-Vattu). Translated by S. Z. Aung and C. A. F. Rhys Davids, 1960. A few discussions of jhānic consciousness.
Psalms of the Early Buddhists; The Sisters (Therīgāthā), 1932; *The Brethren (Theragāthā),* 1937. Translated by Mrs. Rhys Davids (new translations by K. R. Norman, 1971, 1969). These volumes contain stylized yet seemingly genuine firsthand accounts of enlightenment experiences in the early Buddhist community.

Works of near-canonical status, dealing directly with meditation.
Compendium of Philosophy (Abhidhammatha-Sangha). Translated by Shwe Zan Aung and Mrs. Rhys Davids. London: Luzac (Pāli Text Society), 1963. Discussion of jhānic states and *nirodha-samāpatti,* both in text and introduction.
Manual of a Mystic. Translated by F. L. Woodard, 1970. London: Oxford (Pāli Text Society), 1916. An eighteenth-century (?) Ceylonese document; seemingly a meditational manual used in Ceylon at that time, giving detailed instructions and descriptions, particularly of the mantric elements. In general follows the model of *The Path of Purification.*
The Path of Freedom (Vimuttimagga) by Arahant Upatissa. Translated by N. R. M. Ehara Thera. Colombo: D. Roland Weerasuria, 1961. Model and predecessor for Buddhaghosa's work, adding valuable sidelights.
The Path of Purification (Vissudhimagga) by Bhadantācariya Buddhaghosa. Translated by Bhikkhu Nyāṇomoli. Colombo: A. Semage, second edition, 1964. (Paperback reprinting now available, Shambhala Press.) The classic meditation manual of the Theravāda establishment for 1500 years.
Questions of King Milinda. Translated by T. W. Rhys Davids. Two parts. New York: Dover, 1963. Scattered references to various aspects of meditation.

Other words dealing wholly or partly with Theravāda meditation.

Ba Khin, U. *The Noble Truths.* Rangoon: Thinbawa Press, 1967. A contemporary, scholastic-traditional exposition of Buddhist doctrine with some references to meditation.

Ba Khin (Thray Sithu), U. *Personal Experiences of Candidates.* Rangoon: International Meditation Centre, n.d. A pamphlet containing selected experiences in the words of several meditators under U Ba Khin and his evaluation of some of them.

——. *The Real Values of True Buddhist Meditation.* Rangoon: Vipassanā Association, 1962. A pamphlet showing the practical values of meditation; their consonance with U Ba Khin's active career in the business world.

Buddhadasa, Bhikkhu. *Ānāpānasati (Mindfulness of Breathing).* Translated by Nāgasena Bhikkhu. Bangkok: Sublime Life Mission, n.d. A traditionalist Theravāda exposition of meditation up to the fourth-jhāna level that is not over burdened with technical phraseology. Based on the *Middle Length Sayings* sutta on breath mindfulness (I.X).

Byles, Marie. *Journey into Burmese Silence.* London: George Allen and Unwin, 1962. An Australian's account of her meditational experiences in Burma. An appendix contains the exposition of a Ledi Sayadaw-derived mode of meditation.

Coleman, John E. *The Quiet Mind.* New York: Harper and Row, 1971. The author's account of his spiritual quest in Asia. Some chapters on meditation at International Meditation Centre in Rangoon and in Thailand. Popular.

Conze, Edward. *Buddhist Meditation.* London: Allen and Unwin, 1956. A scholar's exegetical account of Theravāda-style meditation from scriptural and traditional sources. Little interpretation.

Cousins, L. S. "Buddhist Jhāna: Its Nature and Attainment according to the Pāli Sources." *Religion* vol. III, (Autumn, 1973): 115–31. A clear, technical discussion of the subject.

Dhiravamsa, V. R. See Sobhana Dhammasudi.

Dutt, Nalinaksha. *Aspects of Mahāyāna Buddhism and Its Relation to Hīnayāna.* London: Luzac, 1930. Extended discussion of Theravāda-type meditation, techniques, and stages in chapter on Nirvāna.

Goldstein, Joseph. *Experience of Insight: A Natural Unfolding.* Santa Cruz, Calif.: Unity Press, 1976. A personal, somewhat Western-modernized version of Southeast Asian vipassanā meditation.

Govinda, Lama Anagarika. *The Psychological Attitude of Early Buddhist Philosophy.* London: Rider, 1961. Numerous references showing how meditation both strengthens and expresses the Buddhist philosophy.

Hamilton-Merritt, Jane. *A Meditator's Diary.* New York: Harper and Row, 1976. A popular but good report of a meditative stint in Thailand that gives an authentic account of life and meditation in Thai monasteries.

Humphreys, Christmas. *Concentration and Meditation.* London: John M. Watkins, 1959. A generalized exposition (Western-modern) of Buddhist meditation, with several sections on Theravāda.

Johansson, Rune. *The Psychology of Nirvana.* London: Allen and Unwin, 1969. An attempt to relate the psychological experience of Nibbānic attainment to Western mental health concepts.

Khin Myo Chit, Daw. "A Buddhist Pilgrim's Progress." *The Guardian Magazine* (January, February, 1963): 13–16 and 13–19, respectively. A contemporary experience with Sunlun-type meditation in Burma.

King, Winston L. "A Comparison of Theravada and Zen Meditational Methods Goals." *History of Religions,* IX, no. 4, 1970, pp. 304–15.

——. "The Role of the Meditation Master in Theravada Buddhism." *Newsletter Review* of R. M. Bucke Memorial Society, IV, nos. 1 and 2, Spring, 1971: pp. 5–10.

————. *A Thousand Lives Away*. Cambridge: Harvard, 1965. One chapter on meditation; appendix relates experience at International Meditation Centre, Rangoon.

Kornfield, Jack. *Living Buddhist Masters*. Santa Cruz, Calif.: Unity Press, 1976. A discussion of several contemporary Southeast Asian meditation masters and their methods by one who has worked under some of them.

Ledi Sayadaw. *The Manuals of Buddhism*. Rangoon: Buddha Sāsana Council, 1965. Numerous passing references to meditation (particularly the sotāpanna stage, pp. 160–69) by eminent early twentieth-century Burmese monk-scholar.

————. *The Requisites of Enlightenment*. Kandy: Buddhist Publication Society, ca. 1971. A discussion of the development of attitudes and practices conducive to enlightenment, though not precisely a technical manual.

Magness, T. "Life and Teaching of the Ven. (Abbot) Chao Khun Mongkol-Thepmuni." Bangkok, n.d. A pamphlet containing a chapter dealing with a Thai variant on vipassanā.

————. *The Dhammakaya*. Bangkok, n.d. A booklet devoted to T. Magness' method of meditation learned from the abbot mentioned above. Considerable emphasis on body location of meditational effects and upon seeing and internalizing the sphere of light.

Mahasi Sayadaw. *The Progress of Insight*. Kandy: Forest Hermitage, 1956. A meditation-description manual by a contemporary Burmese meditation teacher whose method is widely used in Southeast Asia. Orthodox Theravāda tradition.

Ñānamoli, Thera. *Mindfulness of Breathing (Ānāpānasati)*. Kandy: Buddhist Publication Society, second edition, 1964. An organized collection of texts from the Pāli Canon and commentaries.

Nu, U. *What Is Buddhism?* Rangoon: Sāsana Council Press, 1956. Printed lecture dealing with meditation and meditational stages in latter part.

Nyanaponika Thera. *The Heart of Buddhist Meditation*. London: Rider, third edition, 1962. Excellent discussion by a former Westerner of basic Theravāda meditation patterns. Analysis and relevant Pāli texts. This is an expanded version of the 1953 edition quoted in the text.

————. *The Power of Mindfulness*. San Francisco: Unity Press, 1972. This is a compact, simplified, and updated discussion of the "bare mindfulness" presented in his more extensive and earlier *The Heart of Buddhist Meditation*.

Nyanatiloka. *Buddhist Dictionary*. Colombo: Frewin and Co., third revised edition, 1972. A useful, reliable set of definitions of Buddhist terms and doctrines. That used in text, the 1st. 1956 edition. See note 5, ch. 3.

Paravahera, Vajirananna. *Buddhist Meditation in Theory and Practice*. Colombo: Gunasena, 1962. One of the best and most extensive of the solidly orthodox-traditional expositions, by a Western-educated Singhalese.

Pe Maung Tin. *Buddhist Devotion and Meditation*. London: S.P.C.K., 1964. A small-scale exposition by a Burmese Christian, though in Buddhist terms and without evaluations. From traditional materials. He refers appreciatively to Nyanatiloka's *Path to Deliverance*, Colombo, 1952, unknown to me.

Saddhatissa, H. *The Buddha's Way*. London: Allen and Unwin, 1971. A clear, erudite exposition of meditation in nontechnical terms.

Sobhana Dhammasudi. *Insight Meditation*. London: Committee for the Advancement of Buddhism, second edition, 1968. *Beneficial Factors for Meditation*. Hindhead (England): Vipassanā Foundation, second edition, 1970. *The Real Way to Awakening*, author's copyright, 1971. Under lay name, V. R. Dhiravamsa. *A New Approach to Buddhism*, author's copyright, 1972.

Sunna Bhikkhu (Jack Kornfield). *A Brief Guide to Meditation Temples of Thailand*. Bangkok, 1972. A listing of sixteen temples that admit foreigners for meditation, with a few pertinent features of each one described.

Than Daing, U. *Cittānupassanā and Vedanānupassanā*. Rangoon: Society for the Propagation of Vipassanā, 1970. Exposition of the method of a contemporary Burmese meditation teacher, based on meditation on mind and feeling. Heavy with traditional terms.

Thomas, E. J. *Life of the Buddha.* London: Routledge and Kegan Paul, 1960. Contains a discussion of Gotama's enlightenment.

————. *History of Buddhist Thought.* New York: Barnes and Noble, 1967 printing. A chapter on yoga and early Buddhism, containing analysis of the jhānic progression.

University of Northern Rangoon. *What is Buddhism?* Rangoon: Sāsana Council Press, 1956. A pamphlet portraying meditation as the heart of Buddhism.

Walters, John. *Mind Unshaken.* London: Rider, 1961. A British journalist's version of Buddhist meditation from his own experience as a believer. Geared to the "modern world" and to easy understanding.

Win Pe, U and Sunlun Shin Vinaya. *The Yogi and Vipassana.* Rangoon: Sunlun Meditation Center, n.d. The best and almost only authentic exposition of the Sunlun method.

Index